A JUNIOR MANUAL
OF
FRENCH COMPOSITION

A JUNIOR MANUAL

OF

FRENCH COMPOSITION

BY

R. L. GRÆME RITCHIE, M.A., D.Litt.

*Docteur de l'Université de Paris: Lauréat de l'Académie
Française:* Professor of French in the
University of Birmingham

AND

JAMES M. MOORE, M.A.

CAMBRIDGE

AT THE UNIVERSITY PRESS

1955

CAMBRIDGE
UNIVERSITY PRESS

University Printing House, Cambridge CB2 8BS, United Kingdom

Cambridge University Press is part of the University of Cambridge.

It furthers the University's mission by disseminating knowledge in the pursuit of
education, learning and research at the highest international levels of excellence.

www.cambridge.org
Information on this title: www.cambridge.org/9781316601730

First edition 1926
Reprinted 1927
Second edition 1928
Reprinted 1931, 1940, 1941, 1949, 1955
First paperback edition 2015

A catalogue record for this publication is available from the British Library

ISBN 978-1-316-60173-0 Paperback

PREFACE

EVER since our *Manual of French Composition* appeared in 1914, teachers have asked us for an easier book, introductory to it and leading from the very beginnings up to the standard of the School Certificate Examinations. What has delayed us is the extreme difficulty of making 'easy' anything that relates to French Composition.

The problem confronting us from the outset was two-fold: Where could we find English simple enough to afford boys and girls in the lower classes in schools a reasonable chance of turning it into correct French? And how could we reduce to a minimum the very considerable mass of grammatical and linguistic information which Composition presupposes? It would assuredly have demanded little effort to translate passages of easy French into easier English, offer them as material for elementary Composition and preface them with extensive remarks on French Grammar, Syntax and Idiom. But that would not have been helpful either to teachers or to examination candidates. Retranslation is a useful enough exercise, up to a certain point. But it is one which beginners can perfectly well practise for themselves, and it is not Composition. In English which has been translated from French the form remains essentially French, and the difficulties are not those which arise in the passages of genuine English set in the School Certificate Examinations. All parts of Grammar, Syntax and Idiom do not directly affect Composition. Of those parts which do, some, but only some, can be taught within the time available. We have therefore had to solve our twofold problem by other methods.

Confining ourselves in the main to passages of

original English, we have simplified them by omissions and adaptations which do not alter their essentially English character. Experience having shown us that the greatest number of easy constructions and ordinary words are provided in Fairy Tales, Anecdotes and Stories intended primarily for young people, we have drawn largely upon these, adding to them such passages from standard or contemporary authors as could, by being shorn of difficult phrases, technical vocabulary and certain literary graces, be brought within the powers of beginners in French Composition. Since one never can tell what a passage will produce until it has been actually tried and a 'fair copy' written, we have selected from the very large number of pieces set in Examinations in which we have taken part those which proved the most interesting and the most instructive.

This varied material, nearly all of which has stood the test of actual experience, we have graded in four Sections. Sections I and II contain no passages beyond the standard of Matriculation and First School Certificate; Sections III and IV lead up to that of the University Entrance, Scottish Leaving Certificate, etc., and the various Higher School Certificate Examinations. We have added notes—but sparingly, to avoid two dangers. When notes are withheld, the very necessary hints in the Introduction are apt to be ignored. Very numerous notes, on the other hand, lead to dull and mechanical work, and the continual reference they impose on the learner soon degenerates from mental training to physical exercise in turning over the pages. All the passages in Sections I and II, but only alternate passages in Sections III and IV, are therefore provided with a strictly limited number of references, by page and paragraph, to essential matters discussed in the

Introduction. The nature of these matters is indicated in each case, so that the learner need not set off in quest of information which he already possesses.

The grammatical and linguistic Introduction we have reduced to practicable dimensions, thus: We assume that those who use this book have already been through a French Course and have learned those elements of Grammar and Vocabulary without which it is premature to begin Composition. Our Introduction is neither a concise French Grammar nor a miniature French Dictionary, but a memorandum of those rules and facts which as teachers and examiners we have found to be the most important in elementary French Composition. In particular we have made a determined effort to deal once for all with the difficulties of Gender and Tense and the construction after Verbs.

We have resolutely brushed aside all extraneous matter. At the Junior stage the prime essential is that the French used should be sound and correct. Style will come in due course, and its main element will always be correctness. Our ambition here is not to discuss the minutiæ of French style, but to halve the number of grave errors in French made annually in the School Certificate Examinations. That number, in the aggregate, runs into astronomical figures. Composition books vary, Examiners come and go, but the errors remain. Yet the fantastic total is made up by the same errors recurring over and over again. When classified, they are seen to be extraordinarily persistent, but surprisingly limited. In fact they are all enumerated and discussed in our short Introduction. Whoever masters it will not indeed have learned French, for that is the work of a lifetime, but at least he will send in papers which will not become one mass of blue pencil marks, and he will have placed his future studies in French upon a firm basis. Sound knowledge of a language and success in examinations coincide more closely than some critics would have us believe.

After thus treating the subject from its negative, or realist, side, we show in four Model Lessons how to construct a piece of correct French prose. These Model Lessons form an integral part of this book, and discussion of the points raised in them is not always repeated elsewhere.

In short, we have dealt honestly—and, we hope, clearly—with the long-standing and difficult problem of French Composition at the School Certificate stage.

Our thanks are due to Miss E. M. Churley for help in revising the proofs and drawing up the Vocabulary; to Mr C. A. Dawson for reading the proofs; and to the following publishers for permission to use short passages from copyright works issued by them: Messrs H. R. Allenson, Ltd., for extract No. 39; Messrs William Blackwood and Sons for No. 71; J. M. Dent and Sons, Ltd., for Nos. 36, 37 and 100; Geo. G. Harrap and Co., Ltd., for Nos. 2 and 61; Jarrolds, Publishers, London, Ltd., for Nos. 40 and 96; Macmillan and Co., Ltd., for Nos. 66 and 67; Seeley, Service and Co., Ltd., and Messrs G. P. Putnam's Sons, New York, for Nos. 3 and 81; John F. Shaw and Co., Ltd., for Nos. 62 and 63; Frederick Warne and Co., Ltd., and Messrs Charles Scribner's Sons, New York, for Nos. 30, 64 and 65. The extract on page 124 is reproduced by kind permission of the Controller of H.M. Stationery Office.

R. L. G. R.
J. M. M.

April 1926

CONTENTS

PASSAGES FOR TRANSLATION

INTRODUCTION

§ 1. HOW TO WRITE FRENCH CORRECTLY

Two pieces of advice may be fitly offered at the beginning of this 'Junior Manual.' One belongs to the
moral sphere and concerns the reader's attitude to the
study of French. The other is of a practical character,
showing the way in which he can best use this book.

It is impossible to read large numbers of French
papers in the School Certificate Examinations without
feeling that many of the candidates have not taken
their French studies very seriously. The nature, even
more than the number, of the mistakes they make in
French Composition suggests that they look upon gross
errors as trifling accidents which may befall anyone
and are unavoidable by any known method. It is
certainly difficult to translate even very simple English
into correct French. But it is not impossible. No great
change is required in the Syntax or in the Order of
Words. Observe the rules of French Grammar, and
most of the difficulties disappear. To write a piece of
French prose free from at least elementary grammatical errors is a task well within the powers of
British boys and girls and one which many of them
successfully perform. But it demands time and con-
centrated effort, and it presupposes a frame of mind in
which an error of gender or tense appears in its true
light. In Mathematics an elementary mistake ruins the
whole calculation, yet it is no more blameworthy than
a wrong gender or a wrong tense. To know a rule, and
not apply it, is just as silly in a French Examination as

it would be in a game. The most helpful question which a prospective candidate can ask himself is not, 'Shall I pass?' but, 'Shall I *deserve* to pass?' If, as may be hoped, future generations of British boys and girls come to write French more correctly than their predecessors, it will not be by a change of method, but by a change of heart.

As regards the way in which this book should be used, we suggest that the Introduction be first read without the sections in small type, then read in full and gradually mastered. The better it is known, the less difficulty will be found with the Passages for Translation. The examples should be committed to memory. In themselves they best teach the rules which they illustrate, many of them illustrate other rules at the same time, and most are stock phrases, sure to be useful in writing French. It is easier and more practical to learn concrete instances than abstract rules, and a repertory of ready-made expressions is the first requisite in all language-study. The Model Lessons can be taken as the reader proceeds through the book. In writing the Passages for Translation, there will be further opportunity of revising the Introduction until the facts stated therein become familiar. When that stage has been reached, the reader will have gone a long way in the art of writing correct French.

§ 2. ON ACQUIRING THE NECESSARY STOCK OF WORDS

The real difficulty in French Composition is not so much to find suitable French words as to use French words correctly in the sentence. When a candidate coming out of the Examination Room is asked by a

friend how he fared, he will often say, 'I have done
very badly. I could not for the life of me think of the
French for so-and-so.' He may in fact have done very
badly, but not for that reason. By not knowing a word
here and there, he will only have forfeited a mark here
and there, and the total loss cannot have been very
heavy. Nor will he have sunk very low in the esteem
of the Examiners, who realize that a word quite common in French may not happen to have occurred in the
particular French books which the candidate has read.
Words really uncommon are known to none of his
competitors and cannot therefore affect his place in the
order of merit.

Errors in grammar and syntax are much more deadly.
They will not be confined to any part of the passage for
translation, but will occur throughout and make up a
formidable total to be deducted from the available
marks. They will excite little commiseration. They
show that the candidate has not a proper grip of the
elements and they warrant the darkest suspicions as to
the soundness of his attainments in French. Insufficient
vocabulary is thus a lesser evil than slovenly grammar
and faulty syntax.

Yet words are the material with which Composition
builds. Without them, it is impossible to construct a
sentence and display one's knowledge of grammar and
syntax. The first step towards French composition
must therefore be to acquire the necessary stock of
words and phrases. These can only be learned gradually, as the student extends his reading in French and
as he proceeds through this book. Meantime, and
indeed at all times, he must do the best he can with
the words he does know. It is extremely dangerous
to coin words; 'ascendre,' 'exemplifier,' 'exertions,'

'vivide,' and the like do not, unhappily, exist in French, and the Examination Room is not a safe place from which to advocate their adoption by the French Academy.

There are two methods of learning words, and both must be applied. The first, and the better, is by the context, in the course of general reading. The context will often show not only what a word means, but also what manner of word it is, how it is used, what associations it carries with it. When the meaning has been verified in the Dictionary, a word so learned will be of the greatest value for general purposes. It will be of the greatest value also for composition purposes, but only on condition that it is learned complete, i.e. together with its gender, spelling and accents, if any. To know a word without its gender and spelling is to run the risk of making a grammatical error. Reading of a good prose Anthology is the best means of increasing one's vocabulary, because the frequent change of author and the variety of subject-matter provide the richest material. But the word-lore acquired in reading is apt to be vague. To be of real service in composition, it must be verified in the Dictionary and a watchful eye kept on gender and spelling. Composition itself is a valuable aid. If after writing an exercise one commits to memory all the words and phrases in the 'fair copy,' one very quickly builds up a large vocabulary useful not only in writing French, but in reading and speaking it.

The second method supplements the first. It is to take the bull by the horns, so to speak, and 'learn off' lists of words likely to be required in writing French, together with their English meaning, their spelling and gender. This method may be followed in any of the well-known 'Vocabularies for Repetition' and 'Phrase-Books.' It is possible to use these unintelligently and get little benefit from the exercise. But it is also possible to apply one's mind to the task, reflect upon what one learns and associate it with what one already knows, and thus acquire a useful nucleus of words known thoroughly and completely and ready for instant use. It is an effort of memory, but it is not to be despised for that reason. Memory plays as great a part as judgment in the initial stages of all language-study.

§ 3. AIDS TO MEMORY

In applying both methods, we must not neglect certain aids to memory which save time and trouble. When we learn a foreign language we are dealing with facts in very large numbers. It is clearly desirable that these facts should not be kept separate, but linked together. Words fall naturally into groups and it is best to learn them in these groups.

The first is more than a group, it is a family, i.e. those words which are derived from a common source. You know a friend better when you make acquaintance with the other members of his family. His father and mother, his brothers and sisters, throw some light on his character and general outlook. In character, as well as in features, there may be a family likeness. So it is with words. It may not be absolutely necessary, but it is always useful, to know where a word comes from. It is not essential to know that *créer* = 'to create' comes from the Latin verb *creare*, but it is quite worth while, when we learn *créer*, to make the acquaintance of the other members of the family, viz. *le créateur*, 'the creator,' *la créature*, 'the creature,' *la création*, 'creation.' When we learn *une rose* we naturally associate it with its Latin ancestor *rosa* for gender, or its English relative 'rose' for meaning, and it is convenient to learn at the same time its derivatives, such as *le rosier*, 'the rose-bush,' *la roseraie*, 'the rose-garden,' the diminutive *rosette*, and the adjective *rose*, 'pink.' Having made the acquaintance of that family, we may find it well to bear in mind that it has no connection with the family next door, despite the similarity of name, *la rosée*, 'the dew' (Latin *ros*), *arroser*, 'to water,' *un arrosoir*, 'a watering-can.'

Another basis of grouping is meaning, not derivation. When we learn that 'a shop' is *une boutique*, it is convenient to learn that there is another word for 'shop,' *un magasin*. They do not have quite the same meaning; no two words ever have. *Une boutique* is a small (retail) shop, and we had best learn it with a suitable adjective attached to remind us both of its meaning and its gender: *une petite boutique*. *Un magasin* is a large (wholesale) shop or store, e.g. 'les Grands Magasins du Louvre.' To associate such words is the best way both of remembering them and of realizing the difference in their usage.

Words also may be learned with their opposites. They are often of similar formation and the chances are that both will be required in the same passage. In a passage describing, shall we say, a sloping meadow the author, having told us what was to be seen 'at the top,' *en haut*, will probably tell us also what was to be seen 'at the foot,' *en bas*. If he has been speaking about '*up* the river,' *en amont*, he may, before he has finished, say something about '*down* the river,' *en aval*. And since the memory tends to link together as many ideas as possible, it will be all the easier to remember these expressions when we reflect that *amont* comes from Latin *ad montem* and means 'in the direction of the *mountain*,' while *aval*, coming from Latin *ad vallem*, means 'in the direction of the *valley*.'

In learning words with their opposites, derivation is thus often a useful aid. This is especially so with regard to prefixes. *Un rang* is 'rank' or 'order'; ar*ranger* is 'to put things in some order,' dé*ranger* is the opposite, 'to disarrange,' 'to disturb'; *un bouton* is 'a button,' *boutonner* is 'to button,' dé*boutonner*, 'to unbutton'; *une barque* is 'a boat,' em*barquer*, 'to put aboard,' dé*barquer*, 'to put ashore.' We must employ any means we can devise to fix new words in our memory.

§ 4. NAMES OF COUNTRIES AND TOWNS AND THEIR INHABITANTS

There is one particular class of words which must be learned by a special means, the names of countries and their inhabitants. They are very important. They are sure to be wanted frequently in examinations, particularly for historical prose, and it looks bad not to know at least the more common ones. Yet candidates are remarkably ignorant of all that concerns names of countries and towns. They know of course, though they do not always remember, that a definite article is required before the name of a country, e.g. England = *l'*Angleterre (except in apostrophe: 'Douce France! France, mère des arts!'), and are woefully apt to extend this usage to names of towns and say '*la* Rome,' '*le* Paris,' etc., which is ridiculous. (The article is required only when the name is qualified: ancient Rome, *la* Rome *antique*; *le* Paris *de Louis XV*.) But they seldom know the French names. Since geography, like charity, begins at home, it is not too much to expect everyone to know, besides *l'Angleterre* (f.) and *anglais*: *la Grande-Bretagne*, and *britannique* [with one *t* and two *n*'s]; *l'Écosse* (f.), *écossais*; *l'Irlande* (f.), *irlandais* [both without an *e*]; *le pays de Galles* [*le pays de* is necessary, except of course in the title, *le Prince de Galles*] and *gallois* [which must not be confused with *gaulois* = 'Gaulish']. The names of at least the chief European countries and their inhabitants should also be learned, and learned exactly, i.e. with the proper gender and spelling. *L'Allemagne* = 'Germany' is to be distinguished from *l'Allemande* = 'the German lady' as carefully as *la Belgique* = 'Belgium' from *la Belge* = 'the Belgian lady.' The French names of a few important towns are also useful acquisitions; such are: Antwerp, *Anvers*; Brussels, *Bruxelles*; The Hague, *La Haye*; Edinburgh, *Édimbourg*; Warsaw, *Varsovie*.

The final *s*, so common in French, must not be forgotten: Londre*s* = London, Versaille*s*, Douvre*s* = Dover, and Gêne*s* = Genoa. On the other hand, an *s* must not be tacked on to *Lyon* and *Marseille*, which have none.

The names of the inhabitants of a country or a town generally end either in *-ois* or in *-ais*. Each must be learned separately. Thus franç*ais*, portug*ais*, marseill*ais*, lyonn*ais*; but gall*ois*, suéd*ois*, lill*ois*, bruxell*ois*.

N.B. 1. The *adjective* is spelled with a small letter, the *noun* with a capital: une armée *f*rançaise, but un *F*rançais.

2. With feminine names of countries, both 'in' and 'to' are regularly expressed by *en*: Il est établi *en* France depuis dix ans; il est allé *en* Amérique. When the name is qualified, *dans* is substituted for *en*: Il y a beaucoup

de mines *dans* la France du Nord; il est allé *dans* l'Amérique du Sud. The reason for this is that *en* is generally vague and *dans* precise. When the name is masculine, *au* (*aux*) is used, not *en*: Il a un frère *aux* États-Unis, un autre *au* Japon; il va souvent *au* Pérou; similarly: Il y a des mines de charbon *au* pays de Galles. Exceptionally, 'in India' is *aux Indes*, although *Inde* is a feminine noun.

3. With names of even large towns 'in' is *à*: *à* Londres, *à* Paris.

§ 5. SPELLING

For composition purposes it is useless to learn a word without at the same time learning the exact spelling. Those which we find most frequently misspelled are as follows, the letter or letters requiring special attention being shown in italics:

acc*u*eil	éc*u*eil	négligence
a*d*resser	en*n*emi	n*ei*ge
a*g*randir	exa*g*érer	préten*t*ion
agr*é*able	ex*e*mple	publi*c*, fem.
ba*t*aille	fati*g*ant	publi*q*ue
ca*n*on	gre*c*, fem.	rec*u*eil
caractère	gre*cq*ue	réfle*x*ion
cons*c*iencieux	lan*g*age	responsa*b*le
correspond*a*nce	ma*r*iage	re*ss*embler
correspond*a*nt	ma*r*ier	vi*ei*llard

[N.B. la v*ie*ille = 'the old woman' is to be distinguished from la v*ei*lle = 'the eve.']

How are we to remember the above spellings? Not altogether by reasoning. That would help us, as regards the *u* which is inserted in *accueil, écueil, recueil*, to show that the *c* is hard. The pronunciation will

keep us right with *neige, veille, vieillard, vieille.*
Reasoning would help us also in the case of *grecque,*
feminine of *grec* = Greek; if there were no *c*, the *e*
would require an accent as in *un chèque.* To carry
such reasoning further, however, would be dangerous.
Thus in *fatiguer* the stem is *fatigu-* and all parts of the
verb take the *u*, but *fatigant* does not. The only thing
to be done is to have a good look at the spellings above
and fix one's attention on the dubious letter. Spellings
are best learned by the eye. There are, however, some
facts to which it is useful to direct attention now:

1. Such general rules as that final *n* is doubled in
composition, e.g. the *n* in millio*n* becomes *nn* in
millio*nn*aire: so also cano*nn*ier, priso*nn*ier, raiso*n-
n*able, etc.

2. The spelling of such common forms as: *quelque
chose*, always written in two words, though *quelquefois* is
written in one; *plus tôt* = 'sooner,' but *plutôt* = 'rather';
leurs and *plusieurs*, feminine plurals, but taking no *e*:
leurs femmes, plusieurs choses.

3. The practice of elision: The *i* of *si* is elided only
before *il* (*ils*), the *e* of *presque* and *quelque* only in
presqu'île (f.) = a 'peninsula' and *quelqu'un*; *e* must
not be elided before an *h* aspirate. Note particularly
le onze mars, *le haut, le huitième, le héros* [but
l'héroïne].

4. The verbal endings, *-ais, -ait, -aient.*
Confusion of these forms, which are all pronounced
alike, is often more a slip than an error, and is not uncommon in France. But it is very dangerous in this
country, because what may really be a mistake in
spelling looks like a grave error in grammar—as grave
as the use of 'je porta' for *je portai*, which is a potent
factor in the reduction of marks, whether ignorance or
inadvertence be the cause.

§ 6. ACCENTS

Correct accentuation is not one of the main items in good composition, but it has its value in distinguishing careful work from slipshod. The accents which we can least afford to neglect are those showing the difference between words which would otherwise be confused, e.g. *ou* = either, *où* = where; *la* = her, *là* = there; *ça* = that, *çà* = here, as in *çà et là*; *le pécheur* = the sinner, *le pêcheur* = the fisherman; *les côtes* (f.) = 'the coasts,' also 'the ribs,' *les côtés* (m.) = the sides; *une tache* = a stain, *une tâche* = a task.

Despite the persistent efforts of examination candidates to bestow a circumflex accent on *bateau, couteau, jeune, déjeuner, j'eusse*, these words do not yet possess one. On the other hand, *bâtiment, bâtir, château, connaît, coûter, eût* (Subjunctive), and *gâteau* have, and the fact that the accent on *extrême* and *suprême* is a circumflex is often forgotten.

§ 7. FRENCH SYNONYMS

In building up a vocabulary it is important to observe the distinctions made between many words which have in a general way the same sense, but differ in usage. These so-called Synonyms are never quite synonymous and seldom interchangeable. The following list includes the most common of those words which must on no account, even in elementary composition, be confused with each other:

TO ADVANCE:

avancer denotes simply the action of advancing; s'*avancer* adds to that some *further idea*, as of dignity, difficulty: Musique en tête, le régiment s'*avance*. In descriptive passages therefore s'*avancer* is much more likely to be required.

A G E :

The general word is *âge* (m.): deux enfants du même *âge*. An historical period is *un siècle* or *une époque*: le *siècle* de Louis XIV; une *époque* reculée.

T O A P P E A R :

paraître is the general word; *apparaître* is usually said of something unexpected or rather remarkable.

A P P E A R A N C E :

This word often = *aspect* (m.); *apparition* (f.), said of someone coming into sight; *apparence* (f.), external appearance: Selon toute *apparence*, c'est l'*aspect* sombre de leur maître, bien plus que son *apparition* inattendue, qui a fait taire les élèves.

B A L L :

une balle = a bullet (also a tennis ball); *un boulet* = a cannon-ball. [N.B. *un obus* = a shell.]

B E L L :

une cloche = a big bell; *une clochette* = a small bell, the 'bell' of a flower; *une sonnette* = a door-bell; *un timbre* = a bicycle-bell.

B O A T :

un bateau, the general word; *une barque* = a fishing-boat; *un canot* = a small (rowing) boat.

B O N E :

un os, of an animal (or human being); *une arête*, a fish-bone.

B O O T :

une botte = top-boot; *une bottine* = a light boot; *un soulier*, properly 'a shoe,' but also 'strong boot.'

B O Y :

garçon is never used alone as = 'boy,' except when contrasted with *fille*, expressed or understood: une école de garçons. When accompanied by an adjective, it translates 'boy': un petit garçon. Otherwise 'boy' is e.g. *un gamin,* 'an urchin'; *un écolier* = a boy attending school; *un élève* = a boy *in* school; *un enfant,* e.g. un enfant de chœur = a choir-boy; *un jeune homme* = a 'lad': 'Message-boy wanted' = On demande jeune homme pour faire des commissions.

TO BREAK:

briser is the general and literary term, often metaphorical; *casser* indicates a sharp fracture, to 'snap'; *rompre* suggests that it is not a 'clean' break, often to 'burst through.' The usage of each of the three words is well shown in Ostervald's version of the Bible (Ecclesiastes xii): Avant que la corde d'argent se *rompe,* que le vase d'or se *brise,* que la cruche se *casse* sur la fontaine.

TO BRING:

apporter = to *carry* to; *amener,* to *lead* to: *apportez* votre musique, *amenez* votre ami.

CITY:

une ville; *une cité* is a purely literary word.

CLIFF:

un rocher generally; *une falaise,* by the sea only: les *rochers* des Montagnes Rocheuses; but les *falaises* blanches de Douvres.

TO CLIMB:

monter; *grimper* = to clamber; *faire l'ascension de.*

CLOCK:

une horloge, a clock usually in a steeple; *une pendule,* a clock on a mantelpiece, or hanging on a wall.

CLOUD:

un nuage; *une nuée* = a cloud ready to break, often figuratively: une *nuée* de traits obscurcit le ciel.

COAT:

habit (m.), the general word, now usually = dress-coat; *veste* (f.), *veston* (m.) = jacket; *pardessus* (m.) = overcoat; *redingote* (f.) = frock-coat.

TO CONQUER:

conquérir = acquire by conquest; *vaincre* = to defeat: Guillaume, duc de Normandie, ayant *vaincu* Harold, *conquit* l'Angleterre.

COUNTRY:

la campagne, opposed to the town; *un pays* = a district or nation; *la patrie* = one's native land.

TO CRY:

pleurer = to weep; *s'écrier* = to exclaim; *crier* = to call out: 'Faites donner la Garde!' *cria*-t-il.

END:

la fin = the conclusion; *le bout* = the point, tip; *le but* = the aim: 'He is coming to the *end* of his long task' = Il arrive à la *fin* de sa longue tâche; 'the finger-*tips*' = les *bouts* des doigts; 'to gain one's *end*' = parvenir à son *but*.

FAULT:

une faute = a mistake; *un défaut* = a defect, failing.

GENTLEMAN:

gentilhomme = a man of gentle birth, a nobleman; *monsieur* (any well-dressed man); often = *un homme bien élevé*, or *un gentleman*.

GIRL:

fille is used alone only when contrasted with *garçon*: une école de filles. In all other cases, it means 'girl' only when qualified, e.g. une petite fille, une jolie fille, etc. In nine cases out of ten, 'girl' = *jeune fille*; 'young lady' = *demoiselle, jeune personne*.

TO KNOW:

connaître = 'to be acquainted with'; it is not commonly followed by a *que*-clause; *savoir* = to be aware of: il *connaît* Paris, mais il ne *sait* pas le français; je ne *sais* pas s'il me *connaît*.

LANGUAGE:

le langage = choice of words, diction: 'Je vis de bonne soupe et non de beau *langage*' (Chrysale, in *Les Femmes Savantes*); *la langue* = the 'tongue' of a nation: l'étude des *langues* vivantes.

LINE:

une ligne of prose, *un vers* of verse: quelques *lignes* plus loin, nous lisons....Citons un *vers* célèbre....

TO LOOK:

avoir l'air, of outward appearance; *sembler*, of appearance to the mind's eye: 'He *looks* a very serious-minded young man' = Il *a l'air* d'un jeune homme très sérieux; 'It *looks* likely that...' = Il *semble* probable que....

TO MARRY:

épouser quelqu'un, or *se marier* (avec quelqu'un): 'She does not want to *marry*. Besides, nobody would dream of *marrying* her' = Elle ne veut pas *se marier*. D'ailleurs, personne ne songerait à l'*épouser*. When 'marry' is said of the parents or the clergyman it is *marier*: 'Mr and Mrs X are in no hurry to *marry* their daughter' = M. et Mme X ne sont pas pressés de *marier* leur fille.

NEW:

neuf = brand-new, unused; *nouveau* = newly come, newly published, etc.: un *sou* neuf; notre *nouveau* professeur.

NIGHT:

la nuit = the time when people sleep; *le soir* = any time between mid-day and bed-time: La *nuit*, tous les chats sont gris; Venez souper chez nous demain *soir*.

NUMBER:

le nombre (cardinal); *le numéro* (ordinal): Les maisons de cette rue sont au *nombre* de quarante. Nous habitons le *numéro* 17.

OLD:

vieux, the general word; *ancien* = 'former' or 'going back for generations'; *antique* = old-world; *âgé,* of the time of life: *âgé* de quatre ans = four years old.

PAIN:

la peine = effort, trouble, mental pain; *la douleur* = grief, physical pain.

TO PERCEIVE:

apercevoir, with the eye; *s'apercevoir,* with the mind's eye: je l'*aperçus* qui s'en allait; je m'*aperçus* de mon erreur.

POINT:

un point (mathematical), often a 'speck'; *une pointe* = the sharp end of something: Il était sur le *point* de danser, sur la *pointe* des pieds.

TO RETURN:

rentrer = to come *home*; *retourner* = to go back; *revenir* = to come back: 'Il va au fond de l'eau, il *revient,* il *retourne,* il *revient* encore' (Sévigné).

RIVER:

un fleuve = a river which you *sail* across; *une rivière* = one which you *ford.*

ROOM:

une pièce, the general word; *une chambre* = a bedroom; *une salle* = a reception room; *une classe* = a classroom; un appartement de cinq *pièces* = a five-roomed flat.

SOUND:

le son = musical sound; *le bruit* = any sound; *la rumeur* = confused sound: le *son* des clairons; le *bruit* de la foule; la *rumeur* de l'Océan.

STORM:

un orage = a thunder-storm; *une tempête* = a wind-storm.

TO SUCCEED:

succéder (+ à) = to come after; *remplacer* = to take the place of; *réussir* (+ à) = to be successful: George V ayant *succédé à* Édouard VII, ce ministre ne *réussit* pas *à* se maintenir au pouvoir et fut *remplacé* par M. X.

TIME:

le temps, the general term; *une époque* = a period; *une heure,* with reference to the clock; *un moment* = a point of time; *une fois,* la prochaine fois: A une triste *époque* de l'histoire. Vous m'avez dit de venir à l'*heure* que je voudrais. Oui, mais je suis occupé pour le *moment.* Venez à un autre *moment.* La prochaine *fois,* j'aurai plus de *temps* à vous donner.

TO WONDER:

s'étonner = to be surprised; *se demander* = to ask oneself: Je *m'étonne* qu'il ne soit pas venu. Je *me demande* s'il aura manqué son train.

WORDS:

des mots (m.), words, words, words! *des paroles* (f.) = words meaning something: La *parole* est un assemblage de *mots.*

§ 8. FRENCH AND ENGLISH HOMONYMS

One of the reasons why so many people think they know French when they do not, is that a very large number of words occur both in French and in English and are fondly imagined to have the same meaning in both languages. The following cases are only some among many in which English proves a treacherous guide to the meaning of the French. (The *homonym* is given in *italics,* the USUAL FRENCH TRANSLATION in SMALL CAPITALS.)

| ADVICE | *avis* (m.) = opinion | CONSEIL (m.) |
| ASSIST | *assister à* = to be present at | AIDER |

AUDIENCE	*audience* (f.) (of a King)	ASSISTANCE (f.), AUDITOIRE (m.)
CHANGE	*change* (m.) = foreign exchange	CHANGEMENT (m.), (of money) MONNAIE (f.)
DEMAND	*demander* = to ask	EXIGER
DRESS	*dresser* = to train	HABILLER, VÊTIR
EDUCATION	*éducation* (f.) = upbringing, breeding	INSTRUCTION (f.)
FIGURE	*figure* (f.) = face	LA TAILLE, (numbers) LE CHIFFRE
LABOURER	*laboureur* (m.) = ploughman, peasant	TERRASSIER
LARGE	*large* = wide, broad	GRAND, GROS
MONEY	*monnaie* (f.) = change	L'ARGENT (m.)
OPPORTUNITY	*opportunité* (f.) = opportuneness	UNE OCCASION
PARENTS	*parents* usually = relatives though sometimes = father and mother	PÈRE ET MÈRE
PLACE	*place* (f.) = square	ENDROIT (m.)
PRETEND	*prétendre* = to claim	FAIRE SEMBLANT DE
PREVENT	*prévenir* = to warn	EMPÊCHER
REALIZE	*réaliser* = to convert into reality: Ses rêves se sont *réalisés* = His dreams have come true	SE RENDRE COMPTE DE
RESPECTABLE	*respectable* = worthy of respect	CONVENABLE
REST	*rester* = to remain	(SE) REPOSER
SUPPORT	*supporter* = to put up with	APPUYER
TRAIN	*traîner* = to drag	DRESSER
TROUBLE	*troubler* = to unsettle, disturb	ENNUYER, DÉRANGER

§ 9. PHRASES

Sentences are built up with phrases more often than with isolated words. These phrases we cannot as a rule invent for ourselves. Most of them are stock expressions, which have been handed down from father to son. We either know them or we do not. If we do not, we can hardly guess them, for nobody could tell what conventional form of words has been adopted in the course of ages. If we do know them, we must know them very precisely. The slightest alteration in the order of the words, or the substitution of one word for another which seems equally suitable, makes a phrase un-French or incorrect. Phrases must therefore be 'learned off' as they stand, complete and word-perfect, if they are to be of any use for Composition.

The best way to acquire a good stock is to note useful phrases when reading. One like *quoi qu'il en soit* = 'be that as it may' can never come amiss. It is sure to be required somewhere, if not in Set Composition, then in Unprepared Translation or in Free Composition. To fill a small note-book with such obviously serviceable phrases and gradually commit them to memory is to take a very wise precaution. If you do not know the set phrase which the English seems to call for, you must make the best of a bad job, i.e. simplify the English and express it in the French words which you do know.

§ 10. ON AVOIDING DIFFICULTIES

The last remark applies equally well to difficult constructions. An examination is not a suitable opportunity for making hazardous experiments. Unless the candidate is quite sure of a construction, it is prudent to simplify the English and render the sense in a less ambitious manner. To exercise a little worldly wisdom may be as useful in examinations as in later life.

It is of course an excellent rule never to shirk difficulties, but grapple with them boldly and, by opposing, end them. But it is sometimes well to pause first and inquire whether the difficulty we are about to attack is not of our own making. Here is a heroic phrase which we might well be tempted to turn heroically into French: 'England expects that every man will do his duty.' We well know that 'expects' is a little difficult; *s'attendre* is a Reflexive Verb and, other things being equal, we should have preferred a verb which was not Reflexive; the construction after *s'attendre* is *à ce que* and the Subjunctive; this mood we would fain have avoided had it been possible. But undaunted by these dangers, we attack boldly and, more fortunate than some of our comrades, we escape grammatical error and arrive triumphantly at 'L'Angleterre s'attend à ce que chacun fasse son devoir.'

But the hard-won triumph is short-lived. The phrase seems heavy and unconvincing. One feels in one's heart that a French Nelson would put it better; *s'attend* + *à* + *ce* + *que* + Subjunctive might give the signallers some trouble. Is there no simpler verb? Would not *compter* do? It is true that it is not Reflexive, takes only the Indicative and presents no greater obstacle than the spelling, with *p*. But nevertheless it is the right word and gives a shorter, neater, more telling sentence: 'L'Angleterre compte que chacun fera son devoir.' For tackling so successfully the difficulties of *s'attendre à ce que* + Subjunctive we deserve less credit than we had thought. It was magnificent, but it was not war, because the risks we took were quite unnecessary. There are already quite enough difficulties for us in French; we need not create any more.

An awkward, perhaps a dangerous, Subjunctive may not be required at all. Thus, 'He did not think he was wrong' could of course be translated 'Il ne croyait pas qu'il eût tort,' but would be much more simply, and therefore much better, rendered by 'Il ne croyait pas

avoir tort.' Similarly, 'I do not think I shall be able
to go' = 'Je ne crois pas pouvoir y aller.' The difficulties that loom in 'I had not gone far before I
noticed,' etc., are easily met by a skilful use of the
Infinitive and inversion: '*Avant d'avoir* fait beaucoup
de chemin, je remarquai,' etc. 'I was the only person
who knew her feelings' could, if the worst came to
the worst, be translated literally, with an Imperfect
Subjunctive in the Relative Clause, but it is both safer
and neater to say 'Je fus le seul *à connaître* ses senti-
ments.' 'He was the first who perceived that they
were wrong' would be quite correctly rendered as 'Il
fut le premier *à* s'apercevoir de *leur erreur*.'

To those about to use *jusqu'à ce que* or *à moins que…
ne* our advice is: Don't—until you have made sure
that there is no other way. It is often best to omit
'till'; put a semi-colon and begin a new clause, or else
begin a new sentence, with *Alors* or *Enfin*. We are
very much fonder of our neat little 'till' than the
French are of their cumbrous *jusqu'à ce que*. When a
French writer can do without it, he does. The normal
French equivalent is often *ne…que*: 'I will not leave
till the dance is over' = 'Je *ne* m'en irai *qu*'à la fin du
bal'; 'I did not know it *till* afterwards' = 'Je *ne* l'ai su
qu'après.'

The same convenient turn enables us to avoid *à
moins que…ne*.

'We cannot give you good marks *unless* you do good
exercises' = 'Nous *ne* pouvons vous donner de bons
points *que si* vous nous faites de bonnes copies.'

It is a great mistake to think that French always
uses the same part of speech as English. An English
Adjective may be best rendered by a French Adverb:
'*nice* and warm' = *bien* chaud. An English Verb

may well be translated by a French Noun. Do not begin seeking for a verb which may not exist, until you have exhausted the possibilities of Nouns: 'when day dawned,' is simply *au point du jour*. For 'as soon as he arrived' the best equivalent is *dès son arrivée*; 'after he had gone' is merely *après son départ*; 'when the battle was over' = *après la bataille*.

In short, French Composition means translating English into French, not capping each English word with a French word.

GRAMMATICAL HINTS

The following observations, arranged according to the order in which they occur in English grammar, are not of course exhaustive. But we are confident that they deal with the main difficulties likely to be found in translating comparatively simple English into French.

§ 11. THE INDEFINITE ARTICLE

'A' is not to be translated:

(*a*) Before a second Noun in apposition: 'It was at Megara, *a* suburb of Carthage' = C'était à Mégara, faubourg de Carthage;

(*b*) After *il* (*elle*) *est*, with names of trades, professions and nationality: 'He is by trade *a* carpenter' = Il est menuisier de son état; 'She is *a* hospital nurse' = Elle est infirmière; 'She is by birth *a* Frenchwoman' = Elle est Française de naissance.

On the other hand, *un* is necessary after *c'est*: 'He is a doctor' = C'est *un* médecin, and French requires the

Indefinite Article in phrases like 'Of considerable size' = D'*une* grandeur considérable.

Two idioms concerning 'a' should be noted here: 'These workmen make four pounds *a* week' = Ces ouvriers gagnent quatre livres *par* semaine; 'These oranges are sold at two shillings *a* dozen' = Ces oranges se vendent deux shillings *la* douzaine.

§ 12. THE DEFINITE ARTICLE

'The' before a second Noun in apposition is not usually to be translated: 'The ill-fated Prince, *the* last scion of that ancient line' = Ce prince infortuné, dernier rejeton de cette ancienne lignée.

On the other hand, French requires the Definite Article, though English does not, with

(*a*) *Titles*: Le roi George V, *le* maréchal Foch, *le* professeur X;

(*b*) *Proper Names qualified by an Adjective*: 'Little Red Riding Hood' = *Le* petit Chaperon rouge; 'ancient Rome' = *la* Rome antique;

(*c*) *Abstract Nouns*: *le* vice, *la* vertu;

(*d*) *Nouns meaning parts of the body*: 'The ass has long ears' = L'âne a *les* oreilles longues;

Nouns used in a general sense: 'Iron is often found near coal' = *Le* fer se trouve souvent près de *la* houille; 'Are boys as clever as girls?' = *Les* garçons sont-ils aussi intelligents que *les* filles? 'Fine feathers make fine birds' = *Les* belles plumes font *les* beaux oiseaux.

'The' is not to be rendered in: 'at *the* same time' = *en même temps*; 'on *the* other hand' = *d'autre part*; although it is rendered in: de *l'*autre côté = 'on the other side.'

§ 13. THE PARTITIVE ARTICLE

The Partitive Article is simply the Preposition *de* used with or without the Definite Article: 'On the ground there are dead leaves, dry moss and lichen' = Par terre il y a des feuilles mortes, de la mousse sèche, du lichen [pronounced li-kène].

Partitive *de* does not take the Definite Article before an Adjective: *de* grands hommes; or in a negative sentence: je n'ai pas *de* crayon. In some cases the Adjective and Noun are considered to form a single idea and the phrase is treated as a Noun, thus: On voyait là *des* jeunes filles et *de* vieux guerriers.

A sharp distinction must be drawn between *de* partitive, i.e. when represented in English by 'some' or 'any,' expressed or implied, and *de* prepositional, i.e. when represented in English by 'of,' 'with,' 'by,' etc. Thus, 'leaves' are *des* feuilles, but 'a heap of leaves' is un tas *de* feuilles; so *des* chênes, but un bois *de* chênes.

Note, however, 'most people' = la plupart *des* gens. 'Many people' = *bien des* gens, but *beaucoup de* gens.

'Of the' is of course *des*. If we say '*Les* garçons sont plus intelligents que *les* filles,' then we must say, 'L'intelligence *des* garçons est supérieure à celle *des* filles.'

§ 14. GENDER

Gender is perhaps for English people the chief and the permanent difficulty of French. To the French mind, Gender is something almost innate and accepted as natural from earliest childhood, while to the English mind it is something artificial, to be learned by conscious effort. In writing French, both in Free and in Set Composition, the total loss of marks under this head is colossal. Errors in gender utterly mar sentences otherwise correct. When they occur at all, they occur with alarming frequency and bring innumerable other errors in their train. Before we can hope to write French correctly, we must first make up our minds to learn genders. To make up one's mind is indeed half the battle. Many beginners think that gender does not matter, and others perhaps reflect that there is one chance in two of being right by guess-work. The next thing is to learn by itself the gender of each Noun in very common use, and associate it in one's mind with an Adjective recalling the gender. Thus, it may not be easy to remember the gender of *voix, choix, art, empire*. Learn it therefore in a phrase: *à haute voix, au choix, les beaux-arts, un grand empire*. Meantime, you can proceed with the task of learning the general rules from the following lists.

It is obvious that in conversation one has not time to reflect whether a word does or does not occur in such and such list, but in writing there is more time for reflection. It will be found that by long practice the gender of a word will come instinctively to the mind. All the important cases are included in the following lists, treating the matter from the double point of view of meaning and termination. These lists will not take very long to learn. Whoever masters them and applies his information, will have solved the problem of French gender in English examinations.

1. By Meaning

MASCULINE:

(*a*) Names of males, except e.g. 'a new recruit' = une nouvelle RECRUE; 'a vigilant sentinel' = une vigilante SENTINELLE; 'persons unknown' = des PERSONNES inconnues.

(*b*) Names of seasons, months and days: les longs ÉTÉS chauds; JANVIER dernier; DIMANCHE prochain.

(*c*) Points of the compass, etc., e.g. la Mer du NORD; le Chemin de Fer du MIDI.

(*d*) Trees and shrubs: *arbre* itself, e.g. des ARBRES fruitiers = fruit-trees; de grands HÊTRES = tall beeches. [Except: la VIGNE australienne = the Australian vine; la haute BRUYÈRE = the tall heather; la RONCE = the briar; la PERCE-NEIGE = the snowdrop; une longue ÉPINE = a long thorn.]

(*e*) Decimal weights and measures: Ce fromage se vend 15 francs le KILOGRAMME (or le KILO).

(*f*) Compound words formed of a Verb and a Noun governed by it, e.g. un beau PORTEMONNAIE = a handsome purse; un grand PORTEFEUILLE = a big portfolio.

FEMININE:

(*a*) Names of females.

(*b*) Abstract Nouns: e.g. une grande PARESSE; la première VERTU; la haute SAGESSE. [Except: le VICE grossier.]

(*c*) Names of countries, provinces, *ending in e mute*, e.g. la Nouvelle ÉCOSSE = Nova Scotia. Of those which do *not* end in *e* mute and are therefore masculine, the chief are: au CANADA, le petit DANEMARK, le vieux JAPON, l'opulent PÉROU, le riant PORTUGAL.

2. BY TERMINATION

MASCULINE:

The termination -AGE (Latin -*aticum*), e.g. le vill-age, le feuill-age, le plum-age, notwithstanding the fact that these are derived from feminine words.

Before we apply this rule we must be sure that -*age* really is a termination (as e.g. in le *cour-age*, where *cour* is an older form of *cœur*). In the following five words -*age* is not a termination, viz. *cage, image, page, plage, rage* [coming from Latin feminines: *cavea, imago, pagina, plaga, rabies*]; these words are feminine. N.B. also *la nage* = swimming.

-EAU: au CHÂTEAU-Gaillard, le PLATEAU central, as opposed to two cases where *eau* is not a termination, viz. l'EAU fraîche and la PEAU blanche.

-ÈGE: un CORTÈGE imposant.

-ÈME: un long POÈME; son THÈME favori; un PROBLÈME important; le SYSTÈME métrique.

-ISME: le Génie du CHRISTIANISME.

-MENT: Tous mes COMPLIMENTS!

FEMININE:

-AISON: pour une bonne RAISON; la morte-SAISON; une belle FRONDAISON.

-ENCE: La PRUDENCE est la mère de la sûreté; Il a commis une grosse IMPRUDENCE. [Except *silence* which is masculine, because it comes from a Latin neuter and not because, as a schoolboy once said, girls cannot keep it.]

-EUR: Abstract Nouns in *-eur*: par les grandes CHALEURS; de bonne HUMEUR. [Except: L'HONNEUR est sauf; à son grand DÉSHONNEUR; un dur LABEUR; l'HEUR = 'luck,' and therefore BONHEUR and MALHEUR.]

-ION: INFORMATION exacte; une grande NATION. [UNE EXCEPTION importante est *million*: un million de francs.]

-TÉ: Abstract Nouns in *-té*: une grande QUALITÉ; une VÉRITÉ courante; LIBERTÉ, ÉGALITÉ, FRATERNITÉ.

The above rules are well worth learning. If you *never* make a mistake in the gender of nouns ending e.g. in *-ion*, *-eur*, *-age*, you *cannot* make so very many others, because these Nouns account in themselves for a not inconsiderable part of the whole French vocabulary. But if you wish not only to pass an Examination but to learn French, it will be necessary to know the genders not of selected words, but of all. The following are the complete lists and are given for reference only:

MASCULINE TERMINATIONS

-AGE (Lat. *-aticum*): *la feuille*, leaf, *le feuillage*, foliage; *la langue*, tongue, *le langage*, language; *la plume*, feather, *le plumage*, plumage; *la ville*, town, *le village*, village. (Except: *la cage*, cage; *une image*, image, picture; *la nage*, swimming; *la page*, page (of book); *la rage*, hydrophobia, rage.) N.B. *âge* is masc., e.g. *un grand âge* (Old Fr. a-age).

-EAU (Lat. *-ellum*): *le bateau*, boat; *le château*, castle. (Except: *l'eau*, e.g. *l'eau fraîche*, cold water; *la peau*, skin.)

-EUR (Lat. *-orem*) denoting an agent, Masculine: *un acteur*, actor; *un chasseur*, hunter, sportsman.

-ENT and **-MENT**: *un accident*, accident; *le torrent*, torrent; *un instrument*, instrument; *le sacrement*, sacrament. (Except: *la jument*, mare.)

-EL, -ET and **-ER**: *un appel*, call; *le jouet*, toy; *un autel*, altar; *le projet*, plan; *le foyer*, hearth, fire-side; *le rocher*, rock.

-ÈS: *un accès*, access, way of approach; *le succès*, success.

-ÈGE: *le collège*, school (secondary); *le cortège*, procession.

-ÊME, -ÈME: *le baptême*, baptism; *le problème*, problem.

-EU: *le feu*, fire.

-IER: *le grenier*, granary; *le papier*, paper; *un officier*, officer; *le sentier*, path.

-ICE: *un exercice*, exercise; *le sacrifice*, sacrifice; *le service*, service, e.g. *au service du roi*. (Except: *la police*, the police; *la malice*, ill-will.)

-IGE: *le prodige*, prodigy; *le vestige*, trace.

-AL: *le journal*, newspaper; *le signal*, signal.

-AIL: *le gouvernail*, helm; *le travail*, work.

-EIL: *un appareil*, apparatus, camera; *le soleil*, sun.

-AUME: *le chaume*, stubble, thatch; *le royaume*, kingdom.

-ISME: *le catéchisme*, catechism; *l'héroïsme*, heroism.

-ASME: *un grand enthousiasme*, great enthusiasm.

-ACLE: *un obstacle*, an obstacle; *le spectacle*, spectacle, play.

-É (not Abstract Nouns in **-TÉ, -ITÉ**): *le congé*, holiday; *le marché*, market; *le gué*, ford; *le thé*, tea; *bon gré, mal gré*, willingly or unwillingly; *le comté*, county.

-I: *un emploi*, employment; *un appui*, a support; *un ennui mortel*, deadly boredom; *le cri*, cry, shout; *le parti*, party, side; *le souci*, care. (Except: *la fourmi*, ant; *la foi*, faith; *la loi*, law; *à la merci de*, at the mercy of; *paroi*, inside wall.)

-OIR: *le miroir*, the mirror; *le mouchoir*, handkerchief; *le savoir*, knowledge.

-OIRE: *le laboratoire*, laboratory; *le purgatoire*, purgatory; *le territoire*, territory. (Except: *une armoire*, a cupboard; *une histoire*, a history, story; *la victoire*, victory.)

-ON: *le bâton*, stick; *le gazon*, turf; *le rayon*, ray; *le salon*, drawing-room. (Except: *la boisson*, drink; *la façon*, manner, way; *la comparaison,* comparison; *la chanson,* song; *la liaison,* liaison; *la livraison,* delivery; *la maison,* house; *la prison,* prison; *la raison,* reason; *la rançon,* ransom; *la saison,* season; *la toison,* fleece; *la trahison,* treason.)

-OT: *le sabot,* wooden shoe.

-OU: *le chou,* cabbage; *le sou,* halfpenny; *le trou,* hole.

-OUR: *un grand amour,* a great love; *le labour,* ploughing, tilling; *le tour,* turn, trick. (Except: *la cour,* court, yard; *la tour,* tower.)

-TÈRE: *le caractère,* character; *le ministère,* ministry.

Most nouns ending in a consonant are Masculine, e.g.:

le bois, wood	*le miel,* honey
le bruit, sound, noise	*le sac,* sack
le but, end, aim	*le sel,* salt
le cœur, heart	*le sol,* soil, ground
le cor, horn	*le temps,* time
le corps, body	*les beaux-arts,* the fine arts
le lac, lake	

Some common nouns which end in a consonant are Feminine:

la chair, flesh. *L'esprit est prompt et la chair est faible.*
la clef, key. *J'ai perdu une petite clef.*
la dent, tooth. *Il mangeait à belles dents.*
la dot, dowry. *Elle a une belle dot.*
la faim, hunger. *Il a grande faim.*
la fin, end. *Il resta jusqu'à la fin.*
la fleur, flower. *J'aime les fleurs blanches.*
la fois, time. *Une fois pour toutes, je vous en avertis.*
la forêt, forest. *Nous traversions une épaisse forêt.*
la main, hand. *Il s'avançait, l'épée à la main.*
la mer, sea. *La mer Méditerranée.*
les mœurs, customs, manners. *Ce peuple a des mœurs bien différentes des nôtres.*
la mort, death. *Je suis votre ami à la vie et à la mort.*
la nuit, night. *Par une belle nuit d'hiver.*
la paix, peace. *La paix la plus profonde régnait partout.*
la part, part, share. *La part du lion.*
la plupart, majority, greater part. *La plupart des hommes le croient.*
la soif, thirst. *J'ai une soif brûlante.*

FEMININE TERMINATIONS

-ION (Lat. *-ionem*): *une action,* action; *la nation,* nation. (Except: *un million, un bastion.*)

-ENCE (Lat. *-entia*): *une imprudence,* an act of imprudence; *la pénitence,* penitence. (Except: *le silence* (Lat. *silentium*), silence.)

-EUR (Lat. *-orem*): Abstract Nouns such as *la chaleur,* heat; *la peur,* fear. (Except: *l'honneur,* honour; *le labeur,* toil; *le bonheur,* happiness; *le malheur,* misfortune.)

-ANCE: *une grande importance,* great importance; *la vengeance,* vengeance; *une alliance,* alliance; *la confiance,* confidence.

-ELLE (Lat. *-ellam*): *la ficelle,* string; *une hirondelle,* swallow.

-ETTE: *la lunette,* telescope; *la sonnette,* small bell. (Except: *le squelette,* skeleton.)

-ÉE: *une année,* year; *une armée,* army; *une bouchée,* mouthful; *une poignée,* handful; *une pensée,* thought; *la rentrée,* return. (Except a few Greek words: *le lycée,* lyceum, secondary school; *le mausolée,* mausoleum; *le musée,* museum.)

-ESSE: *la jeunesse,* youth; *la politesse,* politeness; *la sagesse,* wisdom; *la tristesse,* sadness.

-ILLE: *la famille,* family; *la faucille,* sickle.

-AILLE: *la limaille,* filings; *la volaille,* poultry.

-TUDE: *une habitude,* habit; *la multitude,* multitude; *une grande inquiétude,* great anxiety; *la lassitude,* weariness.

-UE: *la vue,* sight; *une avenue,* avenue.

-TÉ (abstract), -ITÉ, -ITIÉ: *la majesté,* majesty; *la sûreté,* safety; *la qualité,* quality; *la vanité,* vanity; *une amitié,* friendship; *la pitié,* pity.

-INE: *la famine,* famine; *la ruine,* ruin.

-ISE: *la franchise,* frankness; *la sottise,* foolishness.

-UNE: *la fortune,* fortune; *la rancune,* ill-will.

-URE: *la créature,* creature; *la peinture,* painting; *la morsure,* bite; *la nature,* nature.

-ULE: *la formule,* formula; *une virgule,* comma.

-IÈRE: *la manière,* manner; *la sucrière,* sugar-bowl; *la matière,* matter; *la théière,* teapot.

-IE: *une grande envie,* great envy, longing; *la jalousie,* jealousy; *la folie,* folly; *la sortie,* way out, going out. (Except: *le génie,* genius; *un incendie,* a fire.)

§ 15. COMMON ERRORS IN GENDER

The gender of the following words, for some rather mysterious reason, is so very commonly mistaken that it seems advisable to repeat them here, in the hope that the correct gender will be remembered by the prominence they are given and by the phrases in which they appear:

Il s'est adonné à la BOISSON = He took to drink; de la même
FAÇON = in the same way; Ce sera une bonne LEÇON pour vous
= It will be a good lesson to you; Dans tout troupeau il y a
des BREBIS galeuses = There are black sheep in every flock; la
basse-COUR = the poultry-yard; une belle DOT = a good dowry;
une FOIS pour toutes = once for all; dans la FORÊT = in the
woods; Une LOI, une FOI, un roi = One law, one faith, one
King (the motto of *La Ligue*); à la MAIN droite = on the right
hand; les anciens de la TRIBU = the elders of the tribe; le
chemin de la VERTU = the path of virtue; à VOIX basse = in
a whisper.

§ 16. MASCULINE NOUNS IN *E* MUTE

It is very dangerous indeed to assume, as so many
do, that *e* mute is necessarily a feminine termination.
Most Nouns ending in *e* mute *are* feminine, but
exceptions are so numerous that the rule does not
help us very much, and many of these exceptions are
everyday words certain to figure largely in passages for
translation. The best we can do, we have done. We
have gone through the whole of the Dictionary and
noted in the subjoined lists the most common masculine words in *e* mute. The first is a 'first aid' list of
absolutely essential words, which had best be learned
in a phrase or with an Adjective attached, showing the
gender. The second list is to be learned at leisure, the
third is for reference only:

I. VERY COMMON WORDS

le blâme, blame: Tout le blâme en tombe sur lui = He
gets all the blame.

le caractère, character, disposition: Il a bon caractère
= He is good-natured.

le charme, charm, spell: Le charme est rompu = The
spell is broken.

le commerce, trade: le commerce étranger = foreign
trade.

le compte, account: Je lui ferai son compte = I shall settle with him.

le conte, story, tale: J'aime les vieux contes de fées = I like the old fairy tales.

le crime, crime: C'est un crime honteux = It is a shameful crime.

le doute, doubt: Il n'y a aucun doute = There is no doubt.

l'échange, exchange: Il a fait un échange avantageux= He has made a profitable exchange.

un empire, empire: l'empire romain = the Roman Empire.

un espace, space: un grand espace = a great space.

le fleuve, river: un fleuve profond = a deep river.

le groupe, group: un petit groupe de matelots = a little group of sailors.

le livre, book: Ce livre français m'a beaucoup intéressé = This French book interested me very much.

le ménage, housekeeping, etc: Ils font bon ménage = They get on well together.

le mensonge, lie, falsehood: Quel impudent mensonge! = What a shameless falsehood!

le mille, mile: un mille anglais = an English mile.

le monde, world: Tout le monde le voit = Everybody sees it.

le murmure, murmur: un doux murmure = a gentle murmur.

le nombre, number: le plus grand nombre = the greater number.

un ordre, order: Ils se sont retirés en bon ordre = They retired in good order.

le parapluie, umbrella: J'ai perdu mon parapluie neuf = I have lost my new umbrella.

le peuple, people, nation: le peuple français = the French nation.

le règne, reign: le règne glorieux de Louis XIV = the glorious reign of Louis XIV.

le style, style: un style merveilleux = a wonderful style.

II. Less Common Words

un abîme, abyss
un acte, act
un ange, angel
un article, article
un asile, asylum, shelter
un astre, star
le beurre, butter
le cadre, frame
le calme, calm
le centre, centre
le cercle, circle
le chapitre, chapter
le contraste, contrast
le costume, costume
le crépuscule, twilight
le domaine, estate
un épisode, episode
le fiacre, cab
le genre, kind
le gouffre, gulf
le guide, guide, guide-book
un insecte, insect
un intervalle, interval
le légume, vegetable
le lièvre, hare
le linge, linen (wearing)
le luxe, luxury
le manque, want (of)
le mérite, merit
le miracle, miracle
le modèle, model
le monstre, monster
le mystère, mystery
le peigne, comb
le piège, snare
le poème, poem

le prétexte, pretext
le principe, principle
le privilège, privilege
le pupitre, desk
le refuge, refuge
le régime, regime
le remède, remedy
le reproche, reproach
le rêve, dream
le rire, laughter
le risque, risk
le rôle, rôle, part
le rythme, rhythm
le sable, sand
le sabre, sabre
le salaire, wages
le sexe, sex
le siècle, century
le siège, seat
le signe, sign
le songe, dream
le sourire, smile
le sucre, sugar
le temple, temple
le timbre, stamp
le titre, title
le tonnerre, thunder
le triomphe, triumph
le trône, throne
le trouble, trouble
un uniforme, uniform
le vase, vase
le verre, glass
le vice, vice
le voile, veil
le vote, vote

III. Other Words

un adverbe, adverb
un aigle, eagle
un angle, angle
un antidote, antidote
un antre, cavern, den
un augure, augury

le bronze, bronze
le câble, cable
le carrosse, carriage
le casque, helmet
le catalogue, catalogue
le châle, shawl

le chiffre, figure (number)
le cloître, cloister
le coche, coach
le code, code
le coffre, coffer
le contrôle, control
le coude, elbow
le couvercle, lid
le crâne, skull
le cratère, crater
le culte, cult
le cygne, swan
le déluge, flood
le dialogue, dialogue
le diplôme, diploma
le disque, disk
le divorce, divorce
le dogme, dogma
le dôme, dome
le domicile, dwelling
un elfe, elf
un éloge, eulogy
un estuaire, estuary
l'évangile, gospel
le faîte, summit
le fantôme, phantom
le feutre, felt
les gages (plur.), wages
le geste, gesture
le gîte, lair
le glaive, sword
le globe, globe
le golfe, gulf
le grade, step
l'hémisphère, hemisphere
un homonyme, homonym
un hymne, hymn
un idiome, idiom, language
un interstice, chink
le jeûne, fast
le labyrinthe, labyrinth
le liège, cork
le lustre, lustre
le marbre, marble
le massacre, massacre

le mélange, mixture
le mémoire, memorandum, memoir
le merle, blackbird
le meuble, piece of furniture
le microscope, microscope
le muscle, muscle
le mythe, myth
le navire, ship
le négoce, business
un ongle, nail
un opéra, opera
un orbe, orb, orbit
un orchestre, orchestra
un organe, organ (not musical instrument)
le pampre, vine shoot
le paradoxe, paradox
le paragraphe, paragraph
le parterre, flower-bed
le participe, participle
le phénomène, phenomenon
le plâtre, plaster
le poêle, stove
le pôle, pole
le porche, porch
le pouce, thumb
le précepte, precept
le proverbe, proverb
le registre, register
le scandale, scandal
le scrupule, scruple
le semestre, half-year
le suffrage, vote
le symbole, symbol
le symptôme, symptom
le synonyme, synonym
le terme, term
le tertre, mound
le texte, text
le tube, tube
le tumulte, tumult
le type, type
le verbe, verb

§ 17. WORDS SPELLED ALIKE BUT OF DIFFERENT GENDER

le GUIDE, guide: un GUIDE prudent = a prudent guide.

la GUIDE, rein: lâcher la GUIDE = to loose the rein.

le LIVRE, book.

la LIVRE, pound: CE LIVRE m'a coûté *une livre* sterling = This book cost me a pound.

le POSTE, situation: Il brigue un POSTE de secrétaire = He is a candidate for a post as secretary.

la POSTE, the post-office: J'ai mis cette lettre à la POSTE hier = I posted that letter yesterday.

le SOMME, sleep, nap: faire un SOMME = to take a nap.

la SOMME, sum: une forte SOMME = a large sum.

le TOUR, trick: Il m'a joué un mauvais TOUR = He played me a nasty trick.

le TOUR, turn, walk: faire un TOUR = to go for a walk.

la TOUR, tower: la vieille TOUR de Londres = the old Tower of London.

le VAPEUR: un VAPEUR anglais en détresse = an English steamer in difficulties.

la VAPEUR, steam: une machine mue par la VAPEUR = a steam-driven machine.

le VOILE, veil: un VOILE épais = a thick veil.

la VOILE, sail: des VOILES blanches à l'horizon = white sails on the horizon.

§ 18. WORDS SOMEWHAT SIMILAR IN APPEARANCE BUT OF DIFFERENT GENDER

le CAPITAL: l'impôt sur le CAPITAL = a capital levy.

la CAPITALE: Paris est la plus belle CAPITALE du monde = Paris is the most beautiful capital in the world.

le LIEU, place.

la LIEUE, league: une LIEUE plus loin = a league further on.

le MORT, the dead man.
(*la* MORTE, the dead woman.)
la MORT, death: Il a fait une belle MORT = He died
  like a Christian.
le PARTI, legal party: Les PARTIS sont d'accord = The
  parties are agreed.
la PARTIE, the part: division en quatre PARTIES = division into four parts.
la PART, the share: la PART du lion = the lion's share.
le SORT, fate: par une étrange ironie du SORT = by a
  strange irony of fate.
la SORTE, manner: une SORTE de guerre = a sort of
  a war.

§ 19. THE ADJECTIVE: AGREEMENT

Everyone knows of course that the Adjective agrees
with its Noun, but everyone does not remember the
fact at the critical moment, especially when several
words intervene, e.g. Les *personnes* que vous men-
tionnez étaient *absentes*. Carelessness, not ignorance,
is the worst enemy here.

N.B. 1. Remember that before a vowel the forms
bel, nouvel, vieil are required: un *bel* homme, le *Nouvel*
An, un *vieil* aristocrate.

2. An Adjective must be feminine when placed
before *gens*, masculine when placed after: e.g. les
vieilles gens, but des gens *occupés*.

§ 20. THE ADJECTIVE: POSITION

This is a matter which is determined by use and
wont and by considerations of harmony. The be-
ginner can only observe the usage of good French
authors and hope that before long his ear will tell him
where the Adjective ought to come. At the same time
some general principles should be kept in mind:

1. An Adjective expressing an idea contained in the Noun usually precedes: une *noire* trahison; an Adjective adding a new idea to the Noun usually follows: un cheval *noir*. Consequently Adjectives of form, colour and nationality usually follow.

2. Short Adjectives generally precede; certain Adjectives regularly do so, of which the most important are: *beau, bon, cher, grand, gros, haut, jeune, joli, long, mauvais, meilleur, moindre, petit, pire, vieux, vilain.*

N.B. 'The *first three* pages' = *Les* trois premières *pages.*

§ 21. NUMERALS

1. The chief point to note is the use and abuse of *s*; *cent* takes an *s* when not followed by another number: trois *cents* hommes, but trois *cent* cinquante hommes. If we want a Noun for 'hundred,' we use *centaine*: 'about a hundred soldiers' = environ *une centaine* de soldats; des *centaines* de francs. *Mille* (= 'a thousand') never takes *s*. It is an indeclinable Adjective, and when we require a Noun we must use *millier*: un *millier* de soldats. Being a Noun, *millier* takes the usual *s* of the plural: trois *milliers* de soldats.

Quelque takes an *s*, but not when it means 'approximately': J'ai gagné *quelques* milliers de francs, but J'ai gagné *quelque* trois mille francs. The reason is that *quelques* is an Adjective, but *quelque* an Adverb here.

2. Remember that *un* in *vingt et un, quatre-vingt-un,* and *cent un* naturally agrees with the Noun in gender and not in number, e.g. vingt et *une* années.

3. Remember that 'than' with numerals is *de*, in such a case as: 'There are *more than* five hundred pupils at my school' = Il y a plus *de* cinq cents élèves à mon école; il y en a cinq cent trois.

In the preceding sentence 'than' has prepositional
force: whereas in 'A horse can draw more than three
donkeys' = Un cheval peut traîner *plus que* trois ânes,
the sentence can be completed by 'can draw,' i.e. 'than'
is a conjunction.

§ 22. DATES

1. Do not give the year in words. Figures are
sufficient in Prose Composition.

2. In giving the day of the month use the ordinal for
'first,' but in all other cases the cardinal number: le
premier février, le deux mars. The names of days and
months usually begin with a small letter, e.g. le lundi
quatre août.

§ 23. THE PERSONAL PRONOUN

1. French being more explicit than English, the
Pronoun is considered more necessary and is more
freely repeated: 'I eat, drink and sleep' = Je mange,
je bois, *je* dors. 'I replied' is usually 'Je *lui* ai répondu,'
and the parenthetical 'he said' is often '*lui* (leur) dit-il.'
There is a tendency to associate *le* with the Verb. Thus
le is commonly used to complete the sense of *être*:
Pierre est plus grand que ne *l*'est Paul; Êtes-vous
content?—Je *le* suis; 'As I always do' = Comme je *le*
fais toujours. When Inversion of the usual order occurs
and the object is placed first, the Personal Pronoun
must always be supplied: Pierre, je *le* connais, mais qui
est Paul? 'That I do not know' = Cela, je *l*'ignore. It
must also be given twice when emphasized: 'Say
nothing about it to *him*' = Ne *lui* en dites rien *à lui*;
Vous aussi, *vous* vous trompez.

2. This peculiarity of French is very marked in the case of *en* and *y*.

When we ask someone 'Have you any brothers?' and are answered 'Yes, I have three,' it is sufficiently clear to us that 'three brothers' are meant. Not so in French. The answer is 'J'*en* ai trois,' where *en* makes the reference quite explicit. Similarly, *en* is added when some Noun is vaguely understood as completing the sense. 'There are many who do not believe it' = Il y *en* a beaucoup qui ne le croient pas [i.e. beaucoup *de gens*]. As with *en*, so with *y*: Avez-vous été à la poste?—Non, j'*y* vais.

3. In dealing with 'you,' it must always be borne in mind that *tu* and *toi* may be required. Since in France near relatives occasionally do address each other as 'vous' (when they are formal people), it is safer in an examination to avail oneself of that fact, whenever possible, than to venture on the less well-known forms of the second person singular. But there are cases in which *tu* and *toi* are unavoidable, e.g. in talking to the cat one would hardly say 'vous.' Once adopted, *tutoiement* must of course be used consistently throughout the passage.

§ 24. THE PERSONAL PRONOUN: USE OF THE ACCENTED FORM

In translating 'he,' 'they,' etc., which look so easy, it is nearly always forgotten that, whenever any stress is laid on them, they must be rendered by the accented forms, *lui, eux*, etc. The rule is absolute, though often broken by English people writing French. The reason is that we can pause on 'he,' 'they,' etc., but the French cannot pause on 'il,' 'ils,' etc. To the question

'Who is there?' we can reply 'I!' the French cannot reply 'Je!' This difference between French and English must be borne in mind in three important cases:

1. No doubt in an extreme case, where the stress is very marked and the English Pronouns are printed in italics, few candidates miss the point. Thus '*I* am going away, *he* is staying on' is clearly '*Moi*, je pars, *lui* reste.' 'I am speaking to *you*' = C'est à *vous* que je parle. But vigilance is always necessary. Whenever the subject changes abruptly, French requires the accented form. Thus, 'She continued on her way; he turned slowly home.' 'She' and 'he' are contrasted and in French this would be explicitly shown: Elle continuait sur son chemin, *lui* s'en retournait lentement. The best test is to read the sentence over to oneself, and note if one naturally pauses after the pronoun. If so, its French equivalent will be the accented form. Many French authors in fact show this by putting a comma after the pronoun: Moi, je pars; lui, reste.

2. For exactly the same reason, we say quite naturally 'to encourage him and his friends,' but the French cannot say 'pour *l'*encourager et ses amis.' The *l'* is too inconspicuous; it does not attract enough attention for the meaning to be quite clear. French therefore expresses the phrase thus: pour l'encourager, *lui* et ses amis, i.e. it uses the unaccented Pronoun in the ordinary way and then repeats it, in the accented form, to show the connection of 'et ses amis' with what went before.

Further examples may not come amiss: 'He was there with his wife.' This will often be simply 'Il était venu avec sa femme.' If, however, there is something in the preceding or the following sentence which makes us naturally stress the English Pronoun, the French will be *lui*: Elle était venue avec son mari, *lui* était venu avec sa mère; or *Lui* est là, sa femme n'est pas venue. Similarly 'He and his daughter were there' = *Lui* et sa fille étaient là.

3. There is a difference, as regards the force of the Pronoun, between 'He gave it to me' and 'He came up to me.' The first 'to me' is the ordinary Dative Case = 'me,' and the French is of course 'Il *me* le donna.' The second 'me' is not an indirect object at all, but an extension of 'came,' showing where 'he' came to, and the French for it is often 'Il vint *à moi*.'

This use of *à* and the accented form is customary with Verbs of motion. It is general also with reflexive Verbs: 'I entrust myself to him' = Je me confie *à lui*, and in such a sentence as 'He wanted to introduce me to her' = Il voulait me présenter *à elle*, where two unaccented Pronouns would make an awkward effect.

Here is a single illustration of the above three points: 'When the Germans entered the room, my friend's wife did not budge. He bowed stiffly. I rose, and went to them. They moved forward, and shook hands with me, but not with my companions' = Quand les Allemands entrèrent dans la salle, la femme de mon ami ne bougea pas. *Lui* s'inclina froidement. *Moi, je* me levai, j'*allai à eux*; *eux* s'avancèrent, et *me* donnèrent la main *à moi*, non pas à mes compagnons.

§ 25. ORDER OF THE PERSONAL PRONOUNS

When several object Pronouns come before the Verb the first and second persons take precedence over the third: Elle *me l'*a donné; Nous *vous le* donnons. When there are two Pronouns in the third person the direct object takes precedence over the indirect: Je *le leur* ai dit.

With the Imperative used affirmatively the order is not fixed: Donnez-*le-moi*; Racontez-*nous-le*; Rends-*nous-les* (V. Hugo).

§ 26. 'HE IS,' 'IT IS,' *IL EST, C'EST*

1. The Infinitive with *de* defines or explains a Noun *or* Pronoun, e.g. in 'le désir de plaire,' *de plaire* explains what *le désir* is. In '*Il* est facile *de dire* cela' the *il* is merely a grammatical subject, used for convenience, the real subject being *de dire cela. Ce* for this *il*, e.g. *C*'est facile de faire cela, is merely conversational, and to be avoided in literary style.

On the other hand, in 'C'est facile à dire' the *à dire* goes with *facile*, defining and restricting its meaning; somewhat as in *maison à louer*.

2. For 'he is,' followed by a Noun, use *il est* when the Noun is not qualified, *c'est* when it is, e.g. *il* est *médecin*; *c*'est *un* médecin de mes amis. Hence *ce* is universal in phrases like '*Ce* n'est pas ma faute.'

When 'it' is very general in its meaning, it is safe to use *ce*, e.g. J'aurais voulu le faire, mais *c*'était impossible.

3. In expressions of time like 'Quelle heure *est-il?* il est* midi' (trois heures, sept heures et demie, huit heures moins le quart, etc.), the use of *il* is not easy to account for. It must be accepted as a fact.

4. 'That is' = *c'est là* (or *voilà*): *C'est là* le problème.

§ 27. THE DEMONSTRATIVE PRONOUN: 'THIS,' 'THAT'

Never use CELUI (celle, ceux, celles) unless with

(*a*) a Relative Clause: '*Anyone who* thought that would be quite wrong' = *Celui qui* croirait cela aurait bien tort.

(*b*) *de*: 'Have you repaired my bicycle and my brother's?' = Avez-vous réparé ma bicyclette et *celle de* mon frère?

(*c*) *-ci, -là*: 'Take *this one*, leave *that one*' = Prenez *celui-ci*, laissez *celui-là*.

'This is *the one* I like best' = C'est *celui-ci* que j'aime le mieux.

CE, CECI, CELA are neuter forms. They never take the place of a Noun previously used:

'These houses are not for sale. *That* on the left is ours' = Ces maisons ne sont pas à vendre. *Celle* qui est à gauche est la nôtre.

N.B. 'The one who (which)': be careful to use *celui qui* and not the monstrosity 'l'un qui.'

§ 28. THE RELATIVE PRONOUN

1. The objective case of *qui* Relative, when dependent on a Verb, is *que*. Before a vowel *que* becomes *qu'*; *qui* does not change. Unlike English, French never omits the Relative Pronoun: 'A book I know and like very much' is in no circumstances anything else than 'Un livre *que* je connais et *que* j'aime beaucoup.'

The objective case of *qui* Relative, when dependent on a preposition, is *qui, when a person is referred to*. Otherwise *lequel* is used: L'homme *à qui* j'ai parlé; but: 'You have habits which you must give up' = Vous avez des habitudes *auxquelles* il faut renoncer.

2. It is one thing to know that the Relative agrees with its Antecedent in gender, number and person. It is unfortunately quite another to apply that information at the critical moment: 'It was I who *told* you' = C'est moi qui vous l'*ai* dit; 'It is we who, in spite of all our critics have said, *saved* the situation' = Ce sont nous qui, malgré tout ce qu'en ont dit nos critiques, *avons sauvé* la situation.

3. The Relative must always come immediately after its Antecedent: '*He* would be very rash *who* would do that' = *Celui qui* ferait cela serait bien imprudent.

4. When 'which' means 'a thing which' it is *ce qui*: Il se peut qu'il se soit trompé, *ce qui* lui arrive souvent.

§ 29. *DONT, LEQUEL*

Dont = de + Relative. L'homme *dont* je parle = L'homme *de qui* je parle. It follows that *dont* (not *que*) must be used with all Verbs construed with *de*: 'the money I *inherited*' = l'argent *dont* j'ai hérité; 'the good health he *enjoyed*' = la bonne santé *dont* il jouissait. The position of *dont* is a fixed one—first in its clause: '*Dont* est un mot *dont* la position dans la phrase est invariable.' When the first place is required for some other word, then we must substitute for *dont* DUQUEL (de laquelle, desquels, desquelles), e.g. when a prepositional phrase necessarily stands at the head of the relative clause: 'Scientists, among whom we may count Mr X, have said' = Des savants, au nombre *desquels* on peut compter M. X, ont dit.

Lequel, besides taking the place of *qui* Personal, is used to avoid ambiguity, e.g. where there are two Antecedents with either of which *qui*, if used, might be taken to go: Il y a une *édition* de ce *livre laquelle* ne se vend pas.

§ 30. 'IN' (AT, TO) 'WHICH' = *OÙ*

The Relative Adverb *où* is often the neatest translation of 'IN,' etc. + 'WHICH,' e.g. 'the times *in which* we live' = l'époque *où* nous sommes; 'the district I am going to' = le pays *où* je vais. The Relative, so often omitted in English, must be accounted for in a corresponding French phrase, e.g. 'everywhere I go' = partout *où* je vais; 'the next time I see him' = la prochaine fois *que* je le verrai. Similarly, even though there is no definite Antecedent in English, one is required in French. Thus 'where' is often *là où*: '*Where* you see my white plume' = *Là où* vous verrez mon panache blanc.

§ 31. 'WHO?' 'WHAT?' INTERROGATIVE

1. Great care must be taken not to confuse *qui* Interrogative with *qui* Relative. *Qui* Interrogative is generally used of persons and its objective case is also *qui*: '*Whom* have you seen?' = *Qui* avez-vous vu? The distinction, too often neglected, is shown in the phrase *Qui est-ce qui*...? In the objective case the first *qui* does not change, being an Interrogative, but the second *qui* does, being a Relative Pronoun, e.g. *Qui* est-ce QUE vous avez vu?

2. WHAT? (Pronoun) is *Que?* (accented form *Quoi?*): 'What do you think of it?' = *Qu*'en pensez-vous? 'What are you speaking about?' = De quoi parlez-vous?

It must not be overlooked that while 'What did he say?' = *Qu*'a-t-il dit? and *Qu*'est-ce qu'il a dit? 'Tell me what he said' = Dites-moi CE QU'il a dit.

3. WHAT? (Adjective) is *quel*: '*What* books have you

brought?' = *Quels* livres avez-vous apportés? '*What* is your address?' = *Quelle* est votre adresse?

N.B. Used in exclamations, *quel* takes no Article: 'What a fine book!' = *Quel* beau livre!

§ 32. INDEFINITE PRONOUNS: 'EACH,' 'SOME,' 'OTHERS'

1. EACH, SOME. When 'each' is an Adjective it is *chaque*; when a Pronoun, it is *chacun*: '*Each* article is guaranteed and *each* is carefully made' = *Chaque* article est garanti, et *chacun* est soigneusement fait.

The rule for *quelque* and *quelqu'un(e)* is identical: *Quelques* articles sont mal faits; *Quelques-uns* de vos articles sont mal faits.

2. OTHERS. Two cases are to be differentiated:

(*a*) When it means '(*all*) *the* others' it is *les autres*: 'He never thinks of others' (i.e. of other people) = Il ne songe jamais *aux autres*.

(*b*) When it means '*some* others' it is *d'autres*: 'Some have gone, *others* remain' = Quelques-uns sont partis, *d'autres* sont restés.

Since *autres* is of adjectival origin, the partitive used with it is *de*, and not *des*. *Des autres*, wrongly used for the second case, is a very common error. It is often rather a silly one, because *des autres* means 'of the others' = *de* + *les autres*, and is not likely to occur at the beginning of a sentence. The form *autrui* is confined to more or less Biblical phrases like le bien *d'autrui* = 'the good of others'; les biens *d'autrui* = 'other men's goods.'

3. ONE ANOTHER, EACH OTHER. The most important point is to remember to use the Reflexive form with *l'un l'autre*: 'They love one another' = Ils *s*'aiment

l'un l'autre; 'They succeed one another' = Ils *se* succèdent les uns aux autres.

The Reflexive is in fact the essential element and *l'un l'autre* can often be dispensed with: 'They never speak to each other' = Ils ne *se* parlent jamais.

4. 'Another' = 'a *further* one' is *encore un*; = 'a *different* one' it is *un autre*, e.g. Donnez-moi *encore une* tasse, j'ai grand'soif; but, Donnez-moi *une autre* tasse, celle-ci n'est pas propre.

5. ELSE in 'someone else,' 'no one else,' is not *autre* but *d'autre*: quelqu'un *d'autre*, personne *d'autre*.

§ 33. *ON*

1. *On* is always nominative and always singular. For the dative and accusative say *vous*. 'Common sense would tell *one* that...' = Le sens commun *vous* dirait que...; 'What surprises *one* is that...' = Ce qui *vous* étonne, c'est que.... For 'one's' use *son*, for 'oneself' *soi* or *soi-même*. 'One must love *one's* neighbour as *oneself*' = Il faut aimer *son* prochain comme *soi-même*.

This peculiarity of *on* is shared with *chacun*: 'Everyone for *himself* and God for all!' = Chacun pour *soi* et Dieu pour tous!

2. French tends to avoid the Passive, which is considered cumbrous, by using *on* with the Active Voice: 'It *is said*' = *On* dit. This form must not, however, be abused. Another rule is not to use *on* for 'they,' if you know who 'they' are and have no special reason for feigning ignorance. When 'they' clearly refers to some preceding Noun, it is *ils*, not *on*.

§ 34. 'ANY,' 'ANYTHING'

ANY

For 'any' use *aucun* with the greatest caution. It is seldom right. The following various translations of 'any' should be kept constantly in mind:

1. Used POSITIVELY: 'Have you *any* ink?' = Avez-vous *de l'*encre? '*Any* thinking man' = *Tout* homme qui pense; 'Open your book at *any* page you like' = Ouvrez votre livre à *n'importe quelle* page; 'I am busy just now, but come at *any* other time, *any* day you like' = Je suis occupé en ce moment, mais venez à *n'importe quel* autre moment, le jour *que vous voudrez*; '*Any* line being given' = Une ligne *quelconque* étant donnée.

2. Used NEGATIVELY: 'No, I haven't *any*' = Non, je n'*en* ai pas; 'I do not know *any* of his poems' = Je ne connais *aucun* de ses poèmes.

ANYTHING

1. Used POSITIVELY: 'Do you know *anything* about him?' = Savez-vous *quelque chose* sur son compte?

2. Used NEGATIVELY: 'I do not know *anything* finer than his last poem' = Je ne connais *rien* de plus beau que son dernier poème.

It will be noticed that an Adjective used with *quelque chose* or *rien* is introduced by *de*. The reason is that *chose* is—and *rien* formerly was—a Noun: Latin *causam* and *rem*.

§ 35. THE POSSESSIVE PRONOUN:
'HIS,' 'HER,' etc.

1. Since *son*, etc. stands for 'her' as well as for 'his,' special measures must sometimes be taken to avoid ambiguity: '*his* sister, not *her* brother' = sa sœur *à lui*, non pas son frère *à elle*. When the gender or number of the Noun changes, the Possessive Adjective must be repeated in French: 'his brother and sisters' = *son* frère et *ses* sœurs.

2. Whereas English uses the Possessive Adjective of parts of the body, French often prefers the Definite Article: 'I raised *my* eyes' = Je levai *les* yeux; 'I have washed *my* face' = Je *me* suis lavé *la* figure; 'I was holding a book in *my* hand' = Je tenais un livre à *la* main; 'The courtiers kiss his hand' = Les courtisans *lui* baisent *la* main.

3. Unless there is some unusual need for emphasis, it is unnecessary to translate 'own' by *propre*: 'in our own country' = dans *notre* pays. This means that *propre* is a stronger word than 'own.'

4. The Possessive Pronoun, standing for Possessive Adjective + Noun, is *le mien*, etc.: 'I will take mine [= my + books], you will keep your own' = Je reprendrai *les miens*, vous garderez *les vôtres*. N.B. 'a friend of mine' = *un de mes amis*.

THE VERB

§ 36. IRREGULAR VERBS

It is idle to attempt to write French without a thorough knowledge of the conjugation of Verbs. The Irregular Verbs are the most important. They occur the most frequently and their forms are the most fruitful source of error. The Irregular Verbs are as it were the multiplication table of French, and had best be learned as such, i.e. by an effort of memory, until their use becomes second nature. They should be learnt by heart from the School Grammar, beginning with the most essential, such as *vouloir, pouvoir, savoir*.

A few common errors are: 'savant' for SACHANT; 'je vus, il vut' for JE VIS = 'I saw,' and IL VIT = 'he saw'; 'je lis' (present) for JE LUS = 'I read' (past); 'il écrit' (present) for IL ÉCRIVIT = 'he wrote.'

N.B. *bâti* = 'built,' but *battu* = 'beaten': Rome ne fut pas *bâtie* en un jour; Notre équipe de football n'a jamais été *battue*.

Other points which require particular attention are the following:

I. Past Historic

The *first person singular* of the PAST HISTORIC has three terminations: *-ai, -is, -us*.

1. Verbs with the Infinitive in *-er* take *-ai*;

2. Regular Verbs with the Infinitive in *-ir* and *-re*, together with many Irregular Verbs, take *-is*;

3. A certain number of Irregular Verbs take *-us* (see the subjoined list).

N.B. Two Verbs, *tenir* and *venir*, have a peculiar form, *tins* and *vins*.

List of Irregular Verbs with the Past Historic in -us:

AVOIR, eus; BOIRE, bus; CONNAÎTRE, connus; COURIR, courus; CROIRE, crus; CROÎTRE, crûs; DEVOIR, dus; ÊTRE, fus; FALLOIR, il fallut; LIRE, lus; MOURIR, mourus; MOUVOIR, mus; PARAÎTRE, parus; PLAIRE, plus; PLEUVOIR, il plut; POURVOIR, pourvus; POUVOIR, pus; RECEVOIR, reçus; RÉSOUDRE, résolus; SAVOIR, sus; TAIRE, tus; VALOIR, valus; VIVRE, vécus; VOULOIR, voulus.

II. The Future

The *first person singular* of the FUTURE is formed from the Present Infinitive by adding *ai* (dropping final *e* mute if it exists). The following are Futures of exceptional formation:

ALLER, irai; AVOIR, aurai; COURIR, courrai; CUEILLIR, cueillerai; DEVOIR, devrai; ENVOYER, enverrai; ÊTRE, serai; FAIRE, ferai; FALLOIR, il faudra; MOURIR, mourrai; POUVOIR, pourrai; RECEVOIR, recevrai; SAVOIR, saurai; TENIR, tiendrai; VALOIR, vaudrai; VENIR, viendrai; VOIR, verrai; VOULOIR, voudrai.

III. The Present Subjunctive

The *first person singular* of the PRESENT SUBJUNCTIVE is regularly formed from the Present Participle by changing *-ant* into *-e*. The following are Present Subjunctives of exceptional formation:

ALLER, aille; AVOIR, aie; BOIRE, boive; DEVOIR, doive; ÊTRE, sois; FAIRE, fasse; FALLOIR, il faille; MOURIR, meure; MOUVOIR, meuve; POUVOIR, puisse; PRENDRE, prenne; RECEVOIR, reçoive; TENIR, tienne; VALOIR, vaille; VENIR, vienne; VOULOIR, veuille.

§ 37. THE PRESENT PARTICIPLE

1. Two forms ending in *-ant* must be distinguished:

(*a*) The true Present Participle: 'Some ladies sat there in arm-chairs, talk*ing*, knitt*ing* or doz*ing*' = Quelques dames étaient là, assises dans des fauteuils, caus*ant*, tricot*ant* ou sommeill*ant*.

(*b*) The adjectival use. The word was originally a Present Participle, but has become an Adjective: 'She was all trembling (a-tremble) with fear and cold' = Elle était toute trembl*ante* de peur et de froid.

The difference both in syntax and in meaning is well illustrated in this sentence:

(i) J'ai vu des sauvages *errants* [= nomadic savages] dans les bois.

(ii) J'ai vu des sauvages *errant* [= savages wandering] dans les bois.

In doubtful cases an easy test is to see whether the participial form in *-ing* (*-ant*) can be expanded into a relative clause. If it can, it is the true participle and does not agree; otherwise it is the adjective, and agrees. For example in (ii) above *errant = qui erraient*.

2. The Present Participle is much less commonly used in French than in English. Frequently it is replaced by a relative clause, e.g. 'I saw a woman *reading* at the window' = J'ai aperçu une femme *qui lisait* à la fenêtre; or by an Infinitive, e.g. 'I saw him *coming*' = Je l'ai vu *venir*.

It is turned by *à* + Infinitive after Verbs like *rester*: 'He remained there *musing*' = Il restait là *à songer*.

§ 38. THE GERUND IN '-ING'

1. After Prepositions this is as a general rule to be translated by the Infinitive: 'without losing time' = sans perdre de temps; 'before going' = avant d'y aller; 'after reading the letter' = après avoir lu la lettre.

[N.B. With APRÈS, *avoir* is necessary; see Model Lesson II, p. 127.]

2. *Par* with the Infinitive occurs only after Verbs of beginning and finishing, such as *commencer* and *finir*: Il *finit par faire* des aveux complets = He eventually made a full confession. Only one Preposition, *en*, can be used with the form in *-ant*: 'He made his fortune *by working* hard' = Il a fait fortune

en travaill*ant* dur; and then only when the phrase refers to the subject of the sentence.

§ 39. THE PAST PARTICIPLE

1. The English Past Participle is rendered by an Active Infinitive, when *faire* is used: 'He makes himself *feared*' = Il se fait *craindre*.

2. The rules for the agreement of the Past Participle have been much simplified by the Academy in recent years and the following are the main points to bear in mind:

(*a*) With AVOIR: the Past Participle agrees with a direct object which *precedes* it: J'ai *perdu* mes clefs. Voilà les clefs *que* vous aviez *égarées*. But with *en* partitive the Past Participle is invariable: J'ai acheté des pommes et j'*en* ai mang*é*.

(*b*) With ÊTRE: the Past Participle agrees with the subject: Ma mère est *sortie*, mais mes sœurs sont *restées*.

(*c*) With REFLEXIVE VERBS: the Past Participle agrees with a direct, but not an indirect, object which precedes it: Sans s'être *parlé*, sans même s'être *regardés*, ils se sont *séparés*.

§ 40. THE SUBJUNCTIVE

The following are the chief uses:

1. In Independent Sentences:

(*a*) To give a command in the third person: 'Let them be brought in' = *Qu'on* les *fasse* entrer.

(*b*) To express a wish: 'May you be right' = *Puissiez*-vous avoir raison, Monsieur!; 'Would to God I had listened to his words!' = Plût à Dieu que j'*eusse* écouté sa voix!

2. In Noun-Clauses introduced by *que*, depending on verbs expressing:

(*a*) Wish, will, desire: 'Do you wish me to go away?' = Voulez-vous que je m'en *aille*?

(*b*) Command, or prohibition: 'The judge ordered the witness to be called' = Le juge donna l'ordre qu'on *appelât* le témoin; Je défends qu'on *sorte* d'ici.

(*c*) Doubt, denial, uncertainty: 'I doubt whether he will come' = Je doute qu'il *vienne*; 'He denies that his brother went out yesterday night' = Il nie que son frère *soit* sorti hier soir; 'It is possible you are wrong' = Il est possible que vous *ayez* tort.

(*d*) Mental emotion, such as fear, joy, etc.: 'I am glad you are here' = Je suis heureux que vous *soyez* ici.

3. In Relative Clauses depending on a negative: 'There is no one who understands these things' = Il n'y a personne qui *comprenne* ces choses-là; or on an indefinite antecedent: 'I want a pencil which will go into my waistcoat pocket' = Il me faut un crayon qui *tienne* dans la poche de mon gilet (i.e. of such a sort as to go).

4. In clauses dependent on a Superlative (and also on *seul*, which has the force of a Superlative): 'It is the finest book one can read' = C'est le plus beau livre qu'on *puisse* lire; 'You are the only person I have said that to' = Vous êtes le seul à qui j'*aie* dit cela.

The Indicative, however, is used if the Relative Clause refers not so much to the Superlative as to the Noun: 'Je regardais les amandiers, les PREMIERS *arbres* dont le vent de septembre *enlevât* les feuilles...et les grands chênes où se posaient les *premiers* CORBEAUX que l'hiver *amenait* régulièrement dans le pays'(Fromentin).

In the first case the emphasis is on *premiers*, in the second case it is on *corbeaux*.

5. In Adverbial Clauses introduced by the conjunctions:

bien que and *quoique*: 'Although he is rich, he is not happy' = Bien qu'il *soit* riche, il n'est pas heureux;

afin que, pour que, sans que: Un quart d'heure passa sans que personne *ouvrît* la bouche;

jusqu'à ce que: Ils restèrent jusqu'à ce que la nuit *fût* avancée. Despite all the grammars may say, the Subjunctive has now become universal in the best writers after *jusqu'à ce que*;

avant que: 'He disappeared before his friend could come to a decision' = Il disparut avant que son ami ne *pût* prendre une décision. [The *ne* is optional.]

soit que: 'Whether he does it or does not' = Soit qu'il le *fasse*, soit (*or* ou) qu'il ne le *fasse* pas.

The following take not only the Subjunctive but also *ne*:

à moins que: 'He will come unless he is ill' = Il viendra, à moins qu'il *ne soit* malade;

de peur (crainte) que: 'They warmed his boots, lest they might be damp' = On chauffa ses chaussures de peur qu'elles *ne fussent* mouillées.

N.B. 6. Many Impersonal Verbs and expressions come under the above headings and therefore, when not followed by the Infinitive, take the Subjunctive: e.g. *Il est nécessaire, il faut, il vaut mieux que* can be classed under heading (2). On the other hand, it is quite wrong to think that because a Verb or an expression is Impersonal, it necessarily takes the Subjunctive. Thus *il est clair, il est évident*, etc. naturally take the Indicative.

7. Some conjunctions are followed by the Indicative

or the Subjunctive according to the meaning of the subordinate clause, notably:

de manière (façon, sorte) que:

(*a*) Il travaillait d'une manière telle que son père en *était* satisfait.

(*b*) Travaillez de façon que votre père *soit* satisfait.

Sentence (*a*) gives the actual result, sentence (*b*) the result *aimed* at. It is not always the same thing.

§ 41. 'CAN (COULD),' 'MAY,' 'MUST,' 'SHOULD,' 'WILL,' 'WOULD'

C A N (modal):

1. *Pouvoir* is said of physical ability, *savoir* of knowledge and skill: Je ne *peux* pas nager [e.g. there is not enough depth]; Je ne *sais* pas nager [I have never learned].

2. The future sense, when implied in English, must be expressed in French: 'I cannot tell you till to-morrow' = Je ne *pourrai* vous le dire que demain.

C O U L D:

Three cases must be distinguished:

1. 'could' = 'was able to,' is *pouvais*: 'I was so ill, I could not read' = J'étais si malade que je ne *pouvais* pas lire.

2. 'could' = 'would be able' is *pourrais*: 'I could come to-morrow' = Je *pourrais* venir demain.

When it is difficult to decide between *il pouvait* and *il pourrait*, it is generally helpful to go back to the direct (present) form of the expression. For example, 'He said he *could* not come': What were his exact words? They were 'I cannot come,' i.e. either Je ne *peux* pas venir or Je ne *pourrai* pas venir, according to the circumstances. Of *Je peux* the reported form is *il pouvait*; of *Je pourrai* the reported form is *il pourrait*.

3. For 'could see (find, etc.)' the Verb alone is often sufficient in French: 'I *cannot find* my spectacles' = Je *ne trouve pas* mes lunettes.

COULD HAVE:

'I *could have* done it, but I did not want to' = J'*aurais pu* le faire, mais je ne voulais pas.

MAY:

'You *may* go out' = Vous *pouvez* sortir; 'It *may* rain to-morrow' = Il *pourra* pleuvoir demain, or Il *se peut* qu'il *pleuve* demain.

Sometimes 'may' is merely the sign of the Subjunctive and is not to be translated.

MUST:

Distinguish:

1. 'must' denoting probability: 'That *must* be true' = Cela *doit* être vrai; 'You *must* have made a mistake' = Vous *avez dû* vous tromper.

2. 'must' denoting compulsion: 'I *must* go this evening' = Je *dois* partir ce soir; also Il *faut* que je *parte* ce soir.

In such cases 'must' is often equivalent to a future and is to be translated as such: 'I *must* find an easier job' = Il me *faudra* trouver un emploi moins fatigant.

SHOULD:

'You *should* pay attention' = Vous *devriez* faire attention.

SHOULD HAVE:

'You *should have* paid attention' = Vous *auriez dû* faire attention.

WILL:

'Will' often denotes not the English Future, but 'to be willing': 'If you *will* excuse me' = Si vous *voulez* bien m'excuser. N.B. 'I wonder if they *will* come'= Je me demande s'ils *viendront*.

In no other circumstances can 'will' after 'if' be

rendered by a French Future. The practical rule is: Never use *si* with the Future, or with the Future in the Past, unless *si* can be translated by 'whether.'

When expressing the Immediate Future, 'will' is often to be rendered by *aller*: 'Do not trouble, I *will* fetch it for you' = Ne vous dérangez pas, je *vais* vous le *chercher*.

WOULD:

Distinguish three uses of 'would':

1. In a supposition: 'He *would* not do that if he were prudent' = Il ne *ferait* pas cela s'il était prudent.

2. = 'were willing': 'If you *would* excuse him, he would be grateful to you' = Si vous *vouliez* bien l'excuser, il vous serait très reconnaissant.

3. = 'used to': 'He *would* often stay' = Il *restait* souvent.

NOTES ON TENSES

§ 42. ENGLISH SIMPLE PAST

An English Past will be rendered by various French tenses, according to circumstances:

(1) By the HISTORIC PRESENT, when great vivacity and dramatic effect are desired: 'On *cherche* Vatel pour distribuer la marée [= the fresh fish], on *va* à sa chambre, on *heurte*, on *enfonce* la porte, on le *trouve* noyé dans son sang' (Mme de Sévigné).

(2) By the PERFECT, when the tone is conversational: J'*ai été* au théâtre hier soir.

(3) By the IMPERFECT, when we describe:

(*a*) An action that was taking place, or a state of matters which existed, when something else happened: Il *faisait* noir quand j'entrai dans le salon.

(*b*) A state of affairs existing in Past Time (Descriptive Imperfect; see examples, p. 60).

(*c*) An action taking place regularly or repeatedly in Past Time (Imperfect of Repetition): Charlemagne *fondait* des écoles.

(4) By the PAST HISTORIC in the ordinary narrative style, when we give *successive* events, each making a step forward in the story: La porte *s'ouvrit* brusquement et Anna *parut*; Il *prit* la lettre, il la *jeta* au feu; Quand on *s'aperçut* de son départ, on *s'étonna*.

At the present day this tense is not employed in ordinary conversation. As its name implies, it is used in historical narrative style.

Its use may be illustrated by a diagram, thus:

P   T   N   F

The straight line represents Time. *P* is for 'the Past,' *T* for 'To-day,' *N* for 'Now' or the present moment, *F* for 'the Future.' The section *PN* thus represents Past Time, the section *NF* represents Future Time.

The Past Historic is not used of any event occurring within the period *TN*. It is used only of an action which took place in a period regarded as completely past. That action may have taken a long time in the doing, but it is treated as a single complete fact in Past Time.

The essential difference between the Imperfect and the Past Historic in any passage is this:

The Imperfects are *descriptive*, filling up the framework of the narrative and denoting a state or action that was true before the action of the Verb in the Past Historic began. They do not carry forward the action. The Past Historics give the real beginning of the story and the successive events in it.

This will appear quite clearly from any historical passage, such as the following (Thierry, *Conquéte de l'Angleterre*):

L'armée se *trouva* bientôt en vue du camp saxon, au nord-ouest de Hastings. Les prêtres et les moines qui l'*accompagnaient* se *détachèrent* et *montèrent* sur une hauteur voisine, pour prier et regarder le combat. Un Normand, appelé Taillefer, *poussa* son cheval en avant du front de bataille, et *entonna* le chant, fameux dans toute la Gaule, de Charlemagne et de Roland. En chantant, il *jouait* de son épée, la *lançait* en l'air avec force, et la *recevait* dans sa main droite; les Normands *répétaient* ses refrains ou *criaient*: 'Dieu aide! Dieu aide!'

A portée de trait, les archers *commencèrent* à lancer leurs flèches; mais la plupart des coups *furent* amortis par le haut parapet des redoutes saxonnes. Les fantassins armés de lances et la cavalerie s'*avancèrent* jusqu'aux portes des retranchements et *tentèrent* de les forcer.

The verbs *se trouva* (here = arrived), *se détachèrent, montèrent, poussa, entonna, commencèrent, furent, s'avancèrent, tentèrent,* all carry forward the action. The Imperfect *accompagnaient* describes the monks and *lançait*, etc. describe what happened during Taillefer's song. *En chantant = pendant qu'il chantait.*

The best way to familiarize oneself with the use of Past Historic and Imperfect is to read attentively passages such as the above and consider *why* the tense changes. It is also helpful to practise exercises of the following type:

Write out the following passage replacing each Infinitive by the proper Mood, Tense, and Person of the same Verb:

Je me *lever* de mon fauteuil. J'*ouvrir* la fenêtre, et je me *mettre* à respirer l'air embaumé de la nuit. Une odeur de forêt *venir* à moi, par-dessus les murs, un peu mélangée d'une faible odeur de poudre; cela me *rappeler* ce volcan sur lequel *vivre* et *dormir* trois mille hommes dans une sécurité parfaite. J'*apercevoir* sur la grande muraille du fort une lueur projetée par la lampe de mon jeune voisin; son ombre *passer* et *repasser* sur la muraille, et je *voir* à ses épaulettes qu'il n'*avoir* pas même *songer* à se coucher. Il *être* minuit. Je *sortir* brusquement de ma chambre et j'*entrer* chez lui. Il ne *être* nullement étonné de me voir et *dire* tout de suite que s'il *être* encore debout, c'*être* pour finir une lecture de Xénophon qui l'*intéresser* fort.

(5) By the PLUPERFECT. This should be used much more generally by students. It is very often the normal equivalent of the English Past: 'I did not hear you ring' = Je ne vous *avais* pas entendu sonner; 'I *told* you yesterday that...' = Je vous *avais* dit hier que.... The force of *avais* is 'Something has happened since then which proves the truth of my remark.'

§ 43. REFLEXIVE VERBS

Reflexive Verbs are so called because the Subject acts upon itself (Latin *re* = 'back' and *flectere* = 'to bend'). Some Reflexive Verbs show that *part* of the Subject acts upon the other part, e.g. 'Ils *s*'épient' = They watch *each other* closely. In French, when the meaning is reflexive, the form also is reflexive. In English, as a rule, it is not. This fundamental difference between French and English must be borne in mind in Composition:

1. We must be on the look-out for hidden Reflexives: 'She dresses badly' = Elle *s*'habille mal; 'The hall *filled* quickly' = La salle *s'est* vite *remplie*; 'I hasten to add' = Je *me* hâte d'ajouter; 'I repent

of it' = Je *m*'en repens; 'They often meet at a friend's house' = Ils *se* rencontrent souvent chez un ami; 'We will endeavour to satisfy you' = Nous *nous* efforcerons de vous satisfaire.

2. Reflexive Verbs are often the proper equivalent of an English Passive: 'That *is* not *done*' = Cela ne *se fait* pas; 'Our articles *are sold* everywhere' = Nos articles *se vendent* partout; 'It is a book which *is* easily *read*' = C'est un livre qui *se lit* facilement.

3. Never forget that all Reflexive Verbs require *être* in their compound tenses: 'I got up late this morning' = Je me *suis* levé tard ce matin; 'after seeing each other' = après *s'être* vus.

4. Usually the Reflexive Pronoun is the Direct Object and therefore in the Accusative. The participle then agrees with it: *elles se sont levées*. Sometimes the Reflexive Pronoun is the Indirect Object and therefore in the Dative. The Participle then does *not* agree with it: *elles se sont parlé.*

§ 44. THE CONSTRUCTION AFTER CERTAIN VERBS

A I M E R: 'This boy *is fond of* reading books of adventure' = Cet enfant *aime à* lire les livres d'aventures.

A I M E R   M I E U X: 'I *prefer* you not to stay' = J'*aime mieux* que vous ne *restiez* pas.

    'I *would rather* die than do so bad a thing' = J'*aimerais mieux mourir* que de faire une si mauvaise action.

A L L E R: 'I'll *come and see* you often, father' = J'*irai* vous *voir* souvent, mon père.

    'My sister *is going* to give us a song' = Ma sœur *va chanter* une romance.

A P E R C E V O I R: 'He *saw* his mother *going home*' = Il *aperçut* sa mère *qui rentrait*.

'I *noticed* the mistake' = Je *me suis aperçu de* l'erreur.

'He *noticed* it was getting late' = Il *s'aperçut* qu'il se faisait tard.

N.B. The difference in meaning is that *apercevoir* means to see with the eye, *s'apercevoir* to see with the mind.

A P P R E N D R E: 'To *learn* to obey is to learn to command' = *Apprendre à* obéir, c'est apprendre à commander.

'His mother *taught him to* read' = Sa mère *lui apprit à* lire.

A P P R O C H E R: (1) '*Bring* the lamp *nearer*' = *Approchez* la lampe.

(2) 'We are *getting nearer* the town' = Nous *approchons de* la ville.

'The heron *drew nearer the* water's edge' = Le héron *s'approchait du* bord de l'eau.

N.B. The distinction in (2) is that *approcher* states the simple fact, *s'approcher* implies intention.

A S S I S T E R: 'To *help* the poor' = *Assister* les pauvres.

'Were you *at* the prize-giving?' = Avez-vous *assisté à* la distribution des prix?

A T T E N D R E: (1) '*Let us wait for* the end' = *Attendons* la fin.

'*Wait till* I come' = *Attendez que* je vienne.

N.B. Avoid 'jusqu'à ce que' after *attendre*: it is not only very clumsy, it is incorrect.

(2) 'I scarcely *expected* to see you' = Je ne *m'attendais* guère *à* vous voir.

'I do not *expect* he will come' = Je ne *m'attends* pas *à ce qu*'il *vienne*.

N.B. In translating 'to expect' it is often simpler, and less dangerous (see § 10), to use COMPTER (which see, below).

B A T T R E: 'We have completely *beaten* them' = Nous les avons complètement *battus*.

'These soldiers *have fought* bravely' = Ces soldats *se sont* bien *battus*.

N.B. For 'to fight' (intransitive) there are two translations: *combattre* and *se battre*, e.g. Nous avons *combattu* avec l'épée.

C A C H E R: 'You must not *hide* the truth *from* your father' = Il ne faut pas *cacher* la vérité *à* votre père.

C H A N G E R: 'That sentence will have to be *altered* a little' = Il faudra *changer* un peu cette phrase-là.

'I have no time to *change* my clothes' = Je n'ai pas le temps de *changer d*'habits.

'The water had been *changed into* wine' = L'eau avait été *changée en* vin.

C H E R C H E R: '*Let us look for* a reason' = *Cherchons* une raison.

'Go *for* the doctor' = Allez *chercher* le médecin.

'He did not *try* either *to* defend or to excuse himself' = Il ne *chercha* ni *à* se défendre ni à s'excuser.

C O M M E N C E R: 'The rain *began* to fall' = L'eau *commençait à* tomber.

'A bell *began* to toll' = Une cloche *commença de* tinter.

N.B. The construction with *à* has become the commoner in present-day French—except in cases where it would make an unpleasant hiatus, e.g. 'Quand le village commence*a de* s'endormir,' where 'commencer*a à*' would be unpleasant to pronounce.

C O M P T E R: 'I *expected* to see you' = Je *comptais* vous voir.

N.B. This is much easier and less likely to cause error than 'Je m'attendais à vous voir'; see also § 10.

C O N N A Î T R E: 'He *is a judge of* music, I am not' = Il *se connaît en* musique, moi, je ne *m'y connais* pas.

N.B. Je ne *lui connaissais* pas ce défaut = 'I did not *know he had* that fault.'

CONSEILLER: 'He has *given* his brother good *counsel*' = Il a bien *conseillé* son frère.

'He always *advises* prudence' = Il *conseille* toujours la prudence.

'This country *recommends* peace *to* its allies' = Ce pays *conseille* la paix *à* ses alliés.

'I *advised her* not to stay' = Je *lui* ai *conseillé de* ne pas y rester.

CONSISTER: 'The cottage *consisted of* only one dark narrow room' = La chaumière ne *consistait* qu'*en* une salle étroite et obscure.

'His defence *consists in* denying the facts' = Sa défense *consiste à* nier les faits.

N.B. The above shows that a Noun requires *en*, an Infinitive *à*.

CONTINUER: 'He *goes on working* though he is already very rich' = Il *continue à* travailler, bien qu'il soit déjà très riche.

'The darkness *deepens*' = La nuit *continue de descendre.*

N.B. The distinction is that *continuer à* denotes a regular practice, repeated action, *continuer de* refers to a single instance.

CRAINDRE: 'She is *afraid of* thunder' = Elle *craint* le tonnerre.

'I should be *afraid of making* a mistake' = Je *craindrais de* me tromper.

'He was *afraid* of being laughed at' = Il *craignait* qu'on ne se *moquât* de lui.

'I am *afraid* he *will* come' = Je *crains* qu'il *ne vienne.*

'I am *afraid* he *will not* come' = Je *crains* qu'il *ne vienne pas.*

'I am *not afraid* he *will* come' = Je *ne crains pas* qu'il *vienne.*

'I am *not afraid* of his *not* coming' = Je *ne crains pas* qu'il *ne vienne pas.*

CROIRE: 'Liars are never *believed*' = On ne *croit* jamais les menteurs.

'Do you *believe* that tale?' = *Croyez*-vous cette histoire-là?

'I *think* I *ought* to tell you' = Je *crois devoir* vous le dire.

'I *think* we *should have* to leave' = Je *crois* que nous *serions* obligés de partir.

'I *do not think* we *can* do it' = Je *ne crois pas* que nous *puissions* le faire.

'Do you *believe in* ghosts?—No, I do not' = *Croyez*-vous *aux* revenants?—Non, je n'*y* crois pas.

'I *believe* (or *trust*) in God' = Je *crois en* Dieu.

DÉCIDER: 'We have *decided to* start forthwith' = Nous avons *décidé de* partir sur-le-champ.

'That telegram *determined* me *to* start' = Cette dépêche m'a *décidé à* partir.

'At length I *decided to* tackle him' = Enfin je *me suis décidé à* l'aborder.

'We *are* quite *decided to* stay on' = Nous *sommes* bien *décidés à* rester.

N.B. The Active means nothing more than to 'decide,' the Reflexive means to come to a decision after some hesitation or with some reluctance.

DÉFENDRE: 'His mother *has forbidden him to* eat anything between meals' = Sa mère *lui a défendu de* rien manger entre les repas.

'I *said* that no one *must come* for me' = J'*ai défendu* qu'on *vînt* me chercher.

DEMANDER: 'He *asks for* an answer' = Il *demande* une réponse.

'The stranger *asked to* see my father' = L'inconnu *a demandé à* voir mon père.

'*Ask* his brother to lend him some money' = *Demande à* son frère de lui prêter un peu d'argent.

DÉPÊCHER: 'Let us *hurry up*' = *Dépêchons-nous*.
'*Hurry up and* get ready' = *Dépêche-toi de*
t'apprêter.

DÉSIRER: 'I *wish to see* him; bring him to me' = Je
désire le *voir*; amenez-le-moi.
'It *is to be desired* that he *will* succeed' = Il
est à désirer qu'il *réussisse*.

DEVENIR: '*What will become of us?*' = *Que de-*
viendrons-nous?
'I am going to see *what has become of her*' = Je
vais voir *ce qu'elle est devenue*.

DEVOIR: (1) 'I *must write* two letters this afternoon' = Je *dois écrire* deux lettres cette après-
midi.
(2) 'I *ought* to write to him' = Je *devrais* lui
écrire.
N.B. Cases (1) and (2) are by no means the same;
(1) = 'I have to,' 'I am to'; (2) = 'I ought to do it,
but perhaps I may not.'
(3) 'We *have had* to read this book' [and also
'We *must have* read this book'] = Nous *avons dû*
lire ce livre.
(4) 'We *ought to have* come home sooner' = Nous
aurions dû rentrer plus tôt.
(5) 'He *was* to be here' = Il *devait* être ici.

DIRE: 'At what time *did you ask them to call* for you?—
I *asked* the driver to come round at seven' = A
quelle heure *as-tu dit qu'on vienne* te chercher?—
J'*ai dit au* chauffeur de venir à sept heures.
N.B. *Dire* is a Transitive Verb. We must therefore
never say 'dire de' when we mean 'to speak about,'
but use *parler*.

DOUTER = 'to doubt': (1) 'We *doubt it*' = Nous *en*
doutons.
(2) 'I *doubted if* he *was fond* of flowers' = Je
*doutais qu'*il *aimât* les fleurs.
'She cannot *doubt* that I *know* about it' = Elle
ne peut *douter* que je *n'*en *sois* instruit.

N.B. The rule illustrated in (2) is (*a*) that *douter* requires the Subjunctive, (*b*) that, when negative, it requires *ne* in the subordinate clause.

(3) S E D O U T E R = 'suspect' comes under the general rule that Verbs of thinking, etc. (see § 40, 2) take the Subjunctive *when negative*.

'He *had been* long *suspecting* he *would have* to go' = Il *se doutait* depuis longtemps qu'il *devrait* partir.

'He *did not suspect* they *had* proofs against him' = Il *ne se doutait pas* [= Il ne croyait pas] qu'on *eût* des preuves contre lui.

É C H A P P E R: 'He *had* a miraculous *escape from* death' = Il *a échappé à* la mort par miracle.

'His secret *had escaped him*' = Son secret *lui avait échappé*.

N.B. *De* is also used after *échapper*, but with a difference, thus: 'The bird *escaped* the snare' [i.e. never got into it] = L'oiseau *échappa au* piège.

'The bird [was snared but] *escaped from* the snare' = L'oiseau *échappa* (also often *s'échappa*) *du* piège. Thus *échapper de* means distinctly to 'escape *out of*.'

N.B. *S'échapper* implies, as compared with *échapper*, a notion of effort.

É C O U T E R: 'Let us *listen to* the sound of the waves' = *Écoutons le* bruit des vagues.

N.B. Écouter *aux* portes = 'to listen *at* doors,' i.e. be an eaves-dropper.

E M P Ê C H E R: 'He *prevented me from coming* near the table' = Il *m'empêcha de m'approcher* de la table.

'You cannot prevent my being my father's son' = Vous *n'empêchez pas* que je *ne sois* le fils de mon père.

E M P R U N T E R: 'I *will borrow* the sum *from* one of my friends' = J'*emprunterai* cette somme *à* un de mes amis.

ENTENDRE: (1) 'Did you *hear* the church bell?'
= Avez-vous *entendu* la cloche de l'église?

(2) 'We have *heard of it*' = Nous *en* avons
entendu parler.

'We have *heard that* he is very ill' = Nous avons
*entendu dire qu'*il est très malade.

(ɔ) '*We get on* very well together' = *Nous nous
entendons* bien ensemble. See also under FAIRE.

ENTRER: 'We *entered* the wood' = Nous *sommes
entrés dans* le bois.

'He *entered* the school at fourteen' = Il *est
entré au* collège à quatorze ans.

N.B. *Entrer* is Intransitive and therefore cannot
possibly govern a direct object: it is regularly used
with *dans* or *à*.

ESPÉRER: 'I *hope to get home* next Monday'
= J'*espère rentrer* chez nous lundi prochain.

N.B. *Espérer de* + Infinitive is antiquated, except
in Belgium.

'I *hope* he *will* soon *come*' = J'*espère* qu'il
viendra bientôt.

'The doctor *has no hope* that he *will recover*' = Le
médecin *n'espère pas* qu'il *guérisse*.

N.B. *Espérer* is a Verb of thinking, not of mental
emotion, and therefore takes the same construction as
croire.

ESSAYER: 'Many swimmers *have tried to* swim the
Channel' = Bien des nageurs *ont essayé de* traverser la Manche.

FAIRE: 'They *made him leave*' = On *l'a fait partir*.
'They *made him tell the truth*' = On *lui a fait
dire la vérité*.

N.B. In the first case the direct object of *fait* is *le*,
in the second case it is *dire la vérité*.

The rule is that when the Infinitive depending on
faire [also on *entendre, laisser, voir*] has a direct object,

a Noun or Pronoun governed by these Verbs is put in the Dative.

'I have heard connoisseurs *say* that this picture is his master-piece' = J'ai entendu *dire* à des connaisseurs que ce tableau est son chef-d'œuvre.

'He was afraid of *seeing* him *make* a fool of himself' = Il craignait de LUI *voir faire* quelque sottise.

FALLOIR: 'I *require* a hundred francs; yes, I *require* them' = Il *me faut* cent francs; oui, il me *les* faut.

'I *shall have* to learn French' = Il *faudra* que j'apprenne le français.

'We should *require* first to learn French' = Il *faudrait* d'abord apprendre le français.

FINIR: 'When you have *finished speaking* (done speaking)' = Quand vous *aurez fini de* parler.

'He *eventually consented*' = Il a *fini par* y *consentir.*

FORCER: 'I *forced* him *to* sit down again' = Je le *forçai à* se rasseoir.

'The enemy *was forced to* surrender' = L'ennemi *fut forcé de* se rendre.

N.B. *A* with Active, *de* with Reflexive and Passive.

GARDER: 'He *took good care not to speak about it* to his friends' = Il *se garda bien d'en parler* à ses amis.

GOÛTER: 'At that time the country *enjoyed* profound peace' = A cette époque le pays *goûtait* une paix profonde.

'*Taste* this soup; it is excellent' = *Goûtez de* cette soupe; elle est excellente.

HÂTER: 'They *were* all *in a hurry to* get away' = Ils *se hâtaient* tous *de* s'en aller.

HÉRITER: 'I have *inherited* a small fortune' = J'ai *hérité d'*une petite fortune.

IMPORTER: 'It *matters* little *whether* it *is* you or he' = Peu *importe que* ce *soit* vous ou lui.

I N V I T E R: 'I scarcely care to *invite him to come* and see us' = J'ose à peine *l'inviter à venir* nous voir.

J O U E R: 'I used to leave off *playing the piano* to listen to them' = Je cessais de *jouer du piano* pour les écouter.

'For some years past tennis *has been played* more than golf' = Depuis quelques années *on joue* plus *au* tennis qu'*au* golf.

J O U I R: 'He *enjoys* perfect health' = Il *jouit d*'une parfaite santé.

L A I S S E R: (1) 'They *have been allowed to leave*' = On *les a laissés partir*.

(2) 'They *have let themselves be caught*' = Ils *se sont laissé prendre*.

N.B. In (1) *laissé* agrees with *les* because the Infinitive has an active meaning; in (2) *laissé* does not agree because *prendre* is Passive = 'to be caught.' See also under F A I R E.

M A N Q U E R: 'We have *missed* the train' = Nous avons *manqué* le train.

'We *are short of* money'=Nous *manquons d*'argent.
'He has *broken* his word' = Il a *manqué à* sa parole.
'The view will not *fail to* please you' = La vue ne *manquera* pas *de* vous plaire.

M A R I E R: 'She *married* an officer' = Elle *s'est mariée avec* (also *à*) un officier.

N.B. More commonly *épouser* translates 'to marry.'

M Ê L E R: (1) 'Oil does not *mix with* water' = L'huile ne *se mêle* pas *avec* l'eau.

'*Mind* your own business' = *Mêlez-vous de* ce qui vous regarde.

(2) 'They *mingled* with the crowd' = Ils *se sont mêlés à* la foule.

M E T T R E: 'How long do you *take to get* to school?' = Combien de temps *mettez-vous à venir* à l'école?

'She *began to* sing' = Elle *s'est mise à* chanter.

N I E R : 'He *denied having* ever visited this place' = Il *nia avoir* jamais visité cet endroit.

'Nobody *denies* that he *is* a wonderful poet' = Personne ne *nie* qu'il *ne soit* un poète merveilleux.

O B É I R : 'We must obey our parents' = Il faut *obéir à* nos parents.

O B L I G E R : 'His business *obliges him to* go away' = Ses affaires *l'obligent à* partir.

'I laugh at everything, for fear of *having to* weep' = Je ris de tout, de peur d'*être obligé d*'en pleurer.

Cp. FORCER; the construction is similar.

O F F R I R : (1) 'I *offer him* three thousand francs *for it*' = Je *lui en offre* trois mille francs.

(2) 'He *offered to* sell me his estate' = Il m'a *offert de* me vendre sa propriété.

O R D O N N E R : 'He *was ordered* out' = On *lui ordonna de* sortir. Cp. DÉFENDRE.

O S E R : 'I *venture to say*' = J'*ose dire*.

Ô T E R : 'The robbers *have taken* his purse *from him*' = Les voleurs *lui ont ôté* sa bourse.

O U B L I E R : 'Do not *forget to* answer me' = N'*oubliez* pas *de* me répondre.

P A R D O N N E R : 'I *pardon him* his suspicions' = Je *lui pardonne* ses soupçons.

'*Forgive me for having disturbed* you' = *Pardonnez-moi de* vous *avoir dérangé*.

'Thy sins *are forgiven thee*' = Tes péchés *te sont pardonnés*.

P A S S E R : 'I *passed* his house this morning' = J'ai *passé devant* sa maison ce matin.

'Several years *have passed*' = Plusieurs années *se sont passées*.

N.B. 'To pass' = 'overtake' = *dépasser*.

P E N S E R: 'He *is* always *thinking of* the happiness of others' = Il *pense* toujours *au* bonheur des autres.

'Well, what do you *think of* him?' = Eh bien, que *pensez*-vous *de* lui?

For other constructions, see under CROIRE.

P E R M E T T R E: 'His employment *allows him to live* as he likes' = Son emploi *lui permet de vivre* à sa guise.

'*Allow me to tell* you what I think of it' = *Permettez-moi de* vous *dire* (or *Permettez que je* vous *dise*) ce que j'en pense.

Cp. DÉFENDRE. Beware of using the Passive *personally*: 'If I *am allowed* to say so' = S'il *m'est permis* de le dire.

P E R S U A D E R: 'We *have persuaded them to* give up their idea' = Nous *leur avons persuadé d'*y renoncer.

'Are you sure?—I *am convinced of it*' = En êtes-vous sûr?—J'*en suis persuadé*.

P L A I N D R E: 'I am *sorry for you*' = Je *vous plains*.

'She *complained of having been* kept waiting' = Elle *s'est plainte qu'*on *l'ait* fait attendre.

P L A I R E: 'Everyone *likes* him' = Il *plaît à* tout le monde.

'He *is fond of* reading' = Il *se plaît* à lire.

N.B. 'We are *pleased* to see you' = Nous sommes *contents* de vous voir.

P R E N D R E: 'His father *took* the money *out of* his hands' = Son père *lui prit* l'argent *des* mains.

'He took some papers out of the drawer (from the table)' = Il *prit* des papiers *dans* le tiroir (*sur* la table).

P R É T E N D R E: 'He *claims* to be a connoisseur' = Il *prétend* se connaître aux arts.

N.B. Not = 'to pretend,' which is usually *faire semblant de.*

P R I E R: '*Ask him to come* and speak to me' = *Priez-le de venir* me parler.

P R O M E T T R E: 'I *promise to* do what I can' = Je vous *promets de* faire ce que je pourrai.

S E   R A P P E L E R: (1) 'She *remembered* the grammatical rule' = Elle *s'est rappelé* la règle de grammaire.

(2) 'I do *remember seeing you*' = Je *me rappelle vous avoir vu.*

N.B. No Preposition is used in (2).

R É F L É C H I R: 'I have *thought of* what you said to me' = J'ai *réfléchi à* (or *sur*) ce que vous m'avez dit.

'*Think of (over) it*' = *Réfléchissez-y.*

R E F U S E R: 'He *refused to* come' = Il *refusa de* venir.

R E G R E T T E R: 'We *are sorry to* inform you that...' = Nous *regrettons de* vous informer que....

S E   R É J O U I R: 'The enemy *gloated over* our misfortunes' = Les ennemis *se sont réjouis de* nos malheurs.

N.B. *Se réjouir* = 'to rejoice at,' not 'to enjoy.'

R E M E R C I E R: 'I *thank you for* all your kindness' [lit. acts of kindness] = Je *vous remercie de* toutes vos bontés.

'I *thank you for having* thought of me' = Je *vous remercie d'avoir* songé à moi.

R E P R O C H E R: 'I do not *blame him for* his ingratitude, but I do *blame him* for breaking his word' = Je ne *lui reproche* pas son ingratitude; ce que je *lui reproche* c'est d'avoir manqué à sa parole.

R É S O U D R E: 'He *resolved to act* without further delay' = Il *a résolu d'agir* sans plus tarder.

'We *are determined to* stay' = Nous *sommes résolus à* rester.

N.B. Exactly like DÉCIDER.

RETOURNER: 'While crossing the river, he fell from his horse, went to the bottom, came up again, went down again and came back once more' = En passant la rivière, il tombe de cheval: il va au fond de l'eau, il *revient*, il *retourne*, il *revient* encore.

Retourner = to *go* back, *revenir* = to *come* back. English uses 'return' in both cases.

N.B. *Se retourner*: 'He turned round' = Il *se retourna*.

RÉUSSIR: 'At last we have *succeeded in convincing* him' = Enfin nous avons *réussi à le convaincre*.

'*Have you succeeded?*' = *Y avez-vous réussi?*

Cp. SUCCÉDER.

REVENIR: for meaning see under RETOURNER.

'When *did you get back* (return)?' = A quelle heure *êtes-vous revenu*?

SAVOIR: 'I am sorry I *can't* drive a car' = Je regrette de ne pas *savoir* conduire une auto.

'I *cannot* tell you why' = Je *ne saurais* vous dire pourquoi.

SEMBLER: (1) 'He *seems to have* forgotten us' = Il *semble* nous *avoir* oubliés.

N.B. Be careful not to use a Preposition after *sembler*.

(2) 'It *seems* that we *have been* forgotten' = Il *semble* qu'on nous *ait* oubliés.

With Subjunctive when it is general or indefinite.

(3) 'It *seems* to me that he has deceived us' = Il me *semble* qu'il nous a trompés.

With Indicative when the Personal Pronoun is expressed, being more definite. Here *il me semble* = *je crois*.

SENTIR: 'I *feel* ill' = Je *me sens* malade.

SERVIR: '*What use is it to me* to know that?' = *A quoi me sert-il de* savoir cela?

'This room *serves as* a dining-room *for them*' = Cette pièce *leur sert de* salle-à-manger.

N.B. *Se servir de* = 'to use.'

S O N G E R: '*What* are you *thinking of*?—I am not *thinking of* anything' = *A quoi songez*-vous?—Je ne *songe à* rien.

S O U H A I T E R: 'I *should like* this marriage *to take place*; I hope it will' = Je *souhaite* que ce mariage *se fasse*; j'espère qu'il se fera.

S E S O U V E N I R: 'I well *remember* my grandfather' = Je *me souviens* bien *de* mon grand-père.
    'I *remember having been* introduced to your parents' = Je *me souviens d'avoir été* présenté à vos parents.
Cp. RAPPELER.

S U C C É D E R: 'In 1910 George V *succeeded* Edward VII' = En 1910 Georges V *succéda à* Édouard VII.
    N.B. 'Succeed' = 'come after' = *succéder à*; otherwise = RÉUSSIR.

S U R V I V R E: 'He has *outlived* all his friends' = Il a *survécu à* tous ses amis.

T Â C H E R: 'I was *trying to be* funny and thought I was succeeding' = Je *tâchais d'être* drôle et je croyais y réussir.

T A R D E R: 'He is *long in coming*' = Il *tarde à venir*.
    'I *was longing to* see you' = Il *me tardait de* vous voir.

T E N I R: 'The old man *was standing* at his door' = Le vieillard *se tenait* à sa porte.
    'I am *anxious to* see him again' = Je *tiens à* le revoir.
    'This child *takes after* his father' = Cet enfant *tient de* son père.

U S E R: 'My small brother soon *wears out* his shoes' = Mon petit frère *use* vite ses souliers.
    '*Use* this remedy; do not *abuse it*' = *Usez de* ce remède; n'*en abusez* pas.

V A L O I R: 'It *would be better* to go away' = Il *vaudrait mieux* s'en aller.

'He *had better go* away' = Il *vaut mieux* qu'il s'en *aille* [also = Il ferait mieux de s'en aller].

V E I L L E R: '*See that* the porter *does* not notice you' = *Veillez à ce que* le concierge ne vous *voie* pas.

V E N I R: '*Did* you walk or drive?' = Est-ce que vous ÊTES *venu* à pied ou à cheval?

'We *have just heard* he has arrived' = Nous *venons d'apprendre* qu'il est arrivé.

'He *had just sold* his house' = Il *venait de vendre* sa maison.

V O U L O I R: 'I *should very much like* to learn to swim' = Je *voudrais bien* apprendre à nager.

'Do you *want me to teach* you to play tennis?' = *Veux-tu que* je t'*apprenne* à jouer au tennis?

'I *wish I had* some' = Je *voudrais* en *avoir*.

§ 45.　SOME CONJUNCTIONS

A F T E R (*après que*):
The rule for the agreement of tense is as for *quand*.

A S:
Often to be turned by *tout en* with the gerund in *-ant*: '*As* they spoke' = *Tout en* parlant.

A S S O O N A S (*dès que, aussitôt que*):
The rule for the agreement of tense is as for *quand*.
See W H E N, below, and the diagrams on p. 93, § 50. For 'as' in 'rich *as* he is,' etc., see H O W E V E R, p. 88, § 49.

E I T H E R . . . O R (*ou . . . ou*):
When they are in any way emphasized, they are strengthened by the addition of *bien*. N.B. 'Nor I *either*' = Ni moi *non plus*.

I F (*si*):

1. When *si* means 'whether' and asks a question, it may be followed by the Future or by the Future in the Past: Je me demande *s*'il *viendra* demain.

2. When *si* expresses a condition, it can be followed only by the Present (and Perfect) or the Imperfect (and Pluperfect), according as the Verb of the main clause is Present or Past. Thus, S'il FAIT beau, nous *sortir*ONS, S'il FAISAIT beau, nous *sortir*IONS. It is a very serious error to say in such cases, S'il 'fera' (or 'ferait') beau.

3. When *que* is used to avoid repeating *si* it takes the Subjunctive: Si le malade se réveille et *qu*'il *ait* besoin de quelque chose.

4. Never use the Past Historic with *si*, when it means 'if.'

O R: see E I T H E R.

T H O U G H (*bien que* or *quoique*):

They take the Subjunctive. For 'though' in a phrase like 'Great though he is,' see under H O W E V E R, p. 88, § 49.

E V E N T H O U G H, E V E N I F (*quand même*):

This takes the Future in the Past, even when the Verb of the main clause is a Present: Quand même il *dirait* la vérité, on ne le croirait pas; Quand même la chose *serait* vraie, il n'est pas bon d'en parler.

W H E N:

1. As a Conjunction of time 'when' = *quand, lorsque*. If it is a Relative Conjunction referring to 'day,' 'moment,' etc., 'when' = *où*: Le *jour où* vous lui donnerez son congé, vous verrez ce qu'il pense de vous; C'était *l'heure* tranquille *où* les lions vont boire. With UN *jour*, however, *que* is used.

2. French uses the Future where English uses the Present even when futurity is clearly implied. Care must be taken to use the same tense as in the main

clause: 'I *shall see* you when you *come* back to-morrow'
= Je vous *reverrai* quand vous *reviendrez* demain. See
also the diagram, p. 92, § 50.

Similarly, the Future tense is used when the main
Verb is in the Imperative, since futurity is implied.

3. After conjunctions like *quand, lorsque, dès que*
(also *à peine que*), when the Verb in the main clause
is a Past Historic, the Past Anterior must be used.
This rule is absolute: Lorsque son mari nous *eut*
répondu, elle nous *quitta*. Remember that 'when'
referring to 'scarcely' (*à peine*) is *que* not *quand*.

4. In the second of two clauses linked by *et* it is
customary either to repeat *quand*, etc., or else to
substitute *que* for it, e.g. *Quand* l'hiver viendra et
qu'il fera froid....

WHEREAS (*alors que, au lieu que*):
Often *tandis que*.

WHILE (*tandis que*):
Not *pendant que*, unless it introduces an expression
of time only, without any implication of contrast.
After both these conjunctions the usual tense is, naturally, the Imperfect.

§ 46. SOME ADVERBS

POSITION OF ADVERBS

The general rule is that the Adverb *follows* the Verb
as closely as possible: 'I *always say*' = Je *dis toujours*.
In compound tenses the auxiliary counts as the Verb
and therefore the Adverb comes immediately after it:
'You *have done well*' = Vous *avez bien fait*.

Adverbial expressions of time and place are usually
put at the beginning of the sentence in French.

AGAIN:
Often turned by *re-*: 'He began *again*' = Il *re*-
commença; 'He sat down *again*' = Il se *r*assit; 'He set
off *again*' = Il *re*partit.

AT LEAST:

1. Making a restriction: Il le croit, *du moins* il le dit.

2. Stating a minimum: Il gagne *au moins* trois livres par semaine.

ENOUGH:

Remember the construction, which is as for TOO, namely, *pour*: 'He is clever enough *to* understand that' = Il est assez intelligent *pour* comprendre cela.

JUST: see p. 77, § 44, under VENIR.

NOW (at the present moment) = *maintenant*, or *aujourd'hui*:

Maintenant cannot be used of the Past; use *alors* or *déjà*: 'Charles was *now* brought to Whitehall' = *Alors* Charles fut amené à Whitehall; 'George III was *now* old' = Georges III était *déjà* vieux.

Introducing a new paragraph: '*Now*, it happened that' = *Or*, il arriva que....

NOW AND AGAIN (every now and then) = *de temps en temps* or *de temps à autre*.

ONLY:

1. *ne...que*. The *que* must be placed immediately before the word it modifies, i.e. where 'only' ought to be in English: 'He makes *only* £2 a week' = Il *ne* gagne *que* deux livres par semaine.

2. When 'only' modifies a Verb, *faire* must be used: 'She *only* smiled' = Elle *ne fit que* sourire. Or the phrase *se contenter de* may be employed: Elle *se contenta de* sourire.

QUICKLY:

Not 'vitement' which is vulgar, but *vite*: 'Come *quickly*' = Venez *vite*.

RATHER:

1. *assez*: 'He is *rather* tall' = Il est *assez* grand.

2. *plutôt*: 'He is, if anything, too tall' = Il est *plutôt* trop grand.

N.B. *Plutôt que* can be followed by *de* + Infinitive: '*Rather than give up* my ambitions, I would blow my brains out' = *Plutôt que de renoncer à* mes ambitions je me brûlerais la cervelle.

S O:

Notice the order of words: 'so great a man' = *un si grand* homme. The same form is used to translate 'such a great man.' It is a common error to use *tel* here. For 'So' introductory, beware of using 'Si.' Use *aussi* and invert, or else *donc* without inverting: '*So I went away*' = *Aussi suis-je parti*, or else *Je suis donc parti*.

S T I L L:

Often *toujours* rather than *encore*.

T H E N:

'At that time' = *alors*; 'after that' = *puis*; 'next' = *ensuite* (usually following on *d'abord*); 'therefore' = *donc*.

T O O:

The construction with an Infinitive is as for *assez*; see under E N O U G H.

V E R Y:

Beware of saying 'très beaucoup.'

§ 47. NEGATIVES

In the negative formulas a more essential element than *pas*, *rien*, *nul*, *aucun*, etc. is NE. In some cases it is used alone, e.g. after *ni* and with *saurais* and *puis*, [though *peux* requires *pas*]: Je *ne saurais* vous le dire; Je *ne puis* y répondre [but Je *ne peux* PAS m'absenter]. So also *n'eût été* = 'but for,' 'if it had not been for.' *Ne* therefore must not be left out, as only too often happens when the more prominent but really less essential part of the negative formula has come at the beginning of the sentence: *Nul* parmi ses nombreux amis NE connaissait son passé; *Pas* un de ces héros NE recula.

The negative idea is no doubt strongly enforced by *pas*, but that fact must not betray us into using it unnecessarily or wrongly, as with *nul, aucun, personne, rien* or *jamais*. The only safeguard against this frequent error is to make it a rule, whenever you write down *nul, aucun, personne, rien* or *jamais*, to look whether you have not inadvertently also used *pas*. It is always a wise precaution to re-read the sentence and strike out the double negative which may easily have escaped notice, especially if the negatiyes occur at some distance from each other.

Similarly, in *non pas* the only essential element is *non*: C'est bien lui et *non* son frère. In such cases *non pas* may also be used, for greater emphasis, but not *pas* alone, which belongs to loose conversational style.

'Not only' is *non* (not *pas*) *seulement*, and no inversion takes place in French.

Ne pas is placed before an infinitive: 'Etre ou *ne pas* être'; J'aime mieux *ne pas* le savoir.

Do not overlook the negative required after a Comparative Affirmative: Il est plus riche que vous *ne* le croyez. After a Comparative Negative, however, *ne* must not be inserted: Il n'est pas plus riche qu'il l'était.

PERSONNE. Remember that *personne* can be an object or a subject and also, though this is mentioned elsewhere (§ 40), that the mood in a relative clause following on *personne* is the Subjunctive: 'There is nobody who knows that' = Il n'y a personne qui *sache* cela; 'I could find nobody to tell me' = Je ne trouvai personne qui *pût* me le dire.

RIEN. In addition to the fact already mentioned that *ne* must not be forgotten, nor *pas* added, and that an adjective depending on it takes *de*, a point demanding

attention is its place *before* the Infinitive and the Past
Participle: 'I have seen nothing' = Je n'ai *rien* vu;
N'osant *rien* demander, et n'ayant *rien* reçu.

§ 48. SOME PREPOSITIONS

1. The French tendency to be explicit necessitates
the use of Prepositions where English can dispense
with them, e.g. 'a few hundred yards from the station'
= *à* quelques centaines de mètres de la gare. They
must also be repeated after *et* and the like: 'He
remembered Marseilles *and* its crowded streets' = Il se
souvenait de Marseille *et de* ses rues encombrées.

2. The most common error is to strain the French
Prepositions. They have not as much force as ours
and often require to be supplemented by a Participle:
'a house *near* the bridge' = une maison *située près du*
pont. An English Preposition may require a Prepositional phrase in French. Thus 'from' may have
to be variously rendered: '*From* the tower one could
see...' = *Du haut de* la tour on voyait...; 'Tell him
from me that...' = Dites-lui *de ma part* que...;
'merchants *from* abroad' = des marchands *venus de*
l'étranger; '*from* to-morrow' = *à partir de* demain.

3. Many Verbs being Transitive in French, though
Intransitive in English, care must be taken not to add
a French Preposition inadvertently. Such are: *chercher, demander, écouter, regarder*: 'I am looking *for* a
friend' = Je *cherche* un ami. The most frequent cause
of error in these cases is an intervening phrase: 'Listen,
my friends, *to* what I am going to say' = Écoutez, mes
amis, ce que je vais dire.

The following points require special attention:

ABOUT:

à propos de, au sujet de. With a Personal Pronoun these phrases are turned thus: 'about him' = à son propos; 'I have written to them *about you*' = Je leur ai écrit *à votre sujet.*

N.B.   *Vers* deux heures; *environ* trois cents soldats; Il était *sur le point* de s'en aller.

BECAUSE OF:

à cause de: 'He was very unpopular *because of* his pride' = Il était très impopulaire *à cause de* son orgueil.

par suite de = as a consequence of: '*Because of* his misfortunes, he gave up all his social ambitions' = *Par suite de* ses malheurs, il renonça à toutes ses ambitions mondaines.

BEFORE:

(of time) *avant*: 'before the Flood' = *avant* le déluge;

(of place) *devant*: 'before witnesses' = *devant* témoins.

N.B.   When 'before' (of time) is an Adverb, it is usually *auparavant*: 'I had never seen him before' = Je ne l'avais pas vu *auparavant.*

BUT FOR:

sans: '*But for* the war we should have made our fortune' = *Sans* la guerre nous aurions fait fortune.

BY:

'followed (accompanied) by' = suivi (accompagné) *de.*

FOR:

The chief difficulty is in connection with expressions of time.   The use of *pendant, depuis* and *pour* may be illustrated thus: Nous sommes restés à Londres *pendant* six mois; Nous sommes à Folkestone *depuis* trois semaines, et demain nous allons à Paris *pour* trois mois.

FROM (see above, § 48, 2):

'from...to,' often *depuis...jusqu'à*: Le front s'étendait *depuis* la mer *jusqu'à* la frontière suisse.

IN:

After a superlative, *de*: 'Françoise de Sévigné was the prettiest girl *in* France' = la plus jolie fille *de* France.

de (of time): 'at ten *in* the morning' = à dix heures *du* matin;

'*in* the castle' (garden, drawing-room), generally *au* château, *au* jardin, *au* salon, rather than *dans le*. The distinction is: 'Mon frère est *au* jardin,' but 'Mon frère se promène *dans le* jardin.' Similarly '*in* the country' usually = à la campagne;

'*in* the midst of' = *au* milieu de;

'*in* spring' = *au* printemps;

'*in* the service of Germany' = *au* service de l'Allemagne;

'*in* a loud voice' = *d*'une voix forte;

'*in* this way' = *de* cette façon;

'*in* one's hand' = à la main;

'*in* the reign of Louis XIV' = *sous* le règne de Louis XIV;

'*in* my opinion' = à mon avis;

'to take an interest *in* something' = s'intéresser à quelque chose;

'one *in* a hundred' = un *sur* cent.

Distinguish *en* expressing duration and *dans* expressing a point in Future Time: Le voyage de Londres à Paris se fait *en* huit heures; J'irai à Paris *dans* huit jours = in a week's time.

'*In* three days he had grown tired of it' = *Au bout de* trois jours il en avait assez;

'In' often = 'in the course of,' and is to be translated then *au cours de*: 'In his long pilgrimage' = *Au cours de* son long pèlerinage.

NEAR:

près is more precise and matter-of-fact than *auprès*: J'habite *près de* la gare, but Je voudrais vivre *auprès de* vous.

O F:

Often *parmi* or *d'entre*: beaucoup *parmi* eux; quelques-uns *d'entre* eux.

'What has become of her?' = Qu'est-elle devenue?

O N:

Omitted with expressions of time: 'On the 16th June' = Le 16 juin; 'on the evening of the 21st March' = le 21 mars au soir; 'early on the morrow' = le lendemain de bonne heure.

N.B. 'on this occasion' = *en* cette occasion; 'on this side' = *de* ce côté; 'That depends only on you' = Cela ne dépend que *de* vous. For 'on' in 'to play *on* a musical instrument,' use *de*: jouer *du* piano.

T O:

When = 'right up to,' *jusqu'à*.

T O W A R D S:

Literally = *vers*: 'He was going *towards* the station' = Il se dirigeait *vers* la gare; often *du côté de*: Le docteur s'en alla *du côté du* village;

(of feelings) *envers*: Il est charitable *envers* les pauvres.

W I T H:

Expressing an attendant circumstance, is generally to be left untranslated: 'The regiment advanced *with* fixed bayonets' = Le régiment s'avança, baïonnette au canon.

When 'with' introduces some distinctive characteristic, it is to be translated by *à*: Connaissez-vous l'homme *aux* cheveux gris, la dame *au* chapeau bleu?

ayant must not be neglected: 'a house *with* a garden' = une maison *ayant* un jardin;

'*with* a firm step' = *d'*un pas ferme; '*with* a loud voice' = *d'*une voix forte;

(of influence): 'to have influence *with* the King' = avoir de l'influence *auprès du* roi;

'angry *with* someone' = fâché *contre* quelqu'un;

'to fill, cover, etc. with' = remplir, couvrir *de*: La terre était couverte *de* neige.

§ 49. MISCELLANEOUS

A L L:

In such expressions as 'All of us' the 'of' must never be translated: 'All of us are here' = *Nous* y sommes *tous.* (Note the order of the words.)

In accordance with the general principle that the Relative is not omitted in French: 'He gave them all he had' = Il leur donna tout *ce qu'*il avait. N.B. 'All who were present at the meeting' = Tous *ceux qui* ont assisté à la réunion.

Bear in mind that 'all' is often adverbial = 'quite.' In this case it is to be translated by *tout; tout* is invariable before a vowel, but agrees when it comes before a feminine Adjective beginning with a consonant, e.g. 'Quite astonished, *all* trembling, she replied,' etc. = Tout étonnée, tout*e* tremblante, elle répondit, etc.

A N, A N N É E:

jour, journée; matin, matinée; soir, soirée: The general principle is that the form in *-ée* gives the idea of duration, e.g. Qu'avez-vous fait de votre *matinée*? or of a space of time which can be divided up, e.g. Les quatre saisons de l'*année*; but sometimes either form may be used, e.g. le nouvel an, la nouvelle année; l'an dernier, l'année dernière; tout le jour, toute la journée. Only one can be used in certain expressions, e.g. Il y a bien des *années* = 'Many years ago,' but these are matters of usage, not of grammatical rule.

A S I F:

Beware of using *comme si* where *comme* is sufficient, i.e. where no clause follows: 'He disappeared *as if* by magic' = Il disparut *comme* par enchantement.

B E T T E R, B E S T:

Do not forget that *meilleur* is the comparative or superlative of *bon; mieux* of *bien*: 'Leave *well* alone' = Le *mieux* est souvent l'ennemi du *bien.*

E N J O Y:

jouir de, to be used sparingly, e.g. 'He knows how

to *enjoy* life' = Il sait *jouir de* la vie; 'In the country children *enjoy* more liberty than in towns' = A la campagne les enfants *jouissent de* plus de liberté que dans les villes.

Much more often 'to enjoy' is rendered otherwise: 'Did you enjoy your walk?' = Avez-vous fait une bonne promenade? 'Did you enjoy yourself?' = Vous vous êtes bien amusé? 'Did you enjoy the play?' = Le spectacle vous a-t-il plu?

FEW:

peu de = 'not many': 'Few people believe it' = *Peu de gens* le croient; *quelques* = 'some,' 'more than one': il y a *quelques* années; *peu nombreux* = 'far from numerous.'

FIRST:

As Adjective = *premier*: 'He went out *first* and came back *last*' = Il sortit *le premier* et rentra *le dernier*.

As Adverb = *d'abord*: '*First* he went out, then he came back again' = *D'abord* il sortit, puis (ensuite) il revint.

FOR:

As Preposition = *pour*, which governs a Noun or an Infinitive.

As Conjunction = *car*, which introduces a new clause.

HOWEVER:

'*However* rich he is (may be)' = *Quelque* (or *si*) riche qu'il *soit*; 'Rich *as* (though) he is' = *Tout* riche qu'il *est* (or *soit*).

INVERSION:

Inversion takes place after: *à peine*, 'scarcely'; *aussi*, 'and so'; *en vain*, 'in vain'; *peut-être*, 'perhaps' (except when followed by *que*); *toujours*, 'yet.'

It is also frequently found in relative clauses: 'The vase in which this verbena is dying' = Le vase où *meurt* cette verveine.

Inversion is not to be used after *jamais* or *non seulement*: 'Never *did I* see' = Jamais *je n'ai* vu.

LEAVE:

quitter = 'to take leave of, go away from': 'I have just *left* my friends' = Je viens de *quitter* mes amis; 'He *left* home at the age of twenty' = A vingt ans il a *quitté* la maison paternelle;

laisser = 'to leave behind': 'He has *left* a widow and three children' = Il a *laissé* une veuve et trois enfants;

abandonner = 'to leave to its fate': 'The captain was the last to *leave* the ship' = Le capitaine fut le dernier à *abandonner* le navire;

partir = 'to go away' (from some place): 'I *am leaving* on Monday morning' = Je *pars* lundi matin.

LIE:

se coucher = 'to lie down' (denotes action).

The Past Participle *couché* gives the state: 'We found him *lying* on the grass' = Nous l'avons trouvé *couché* sur l'herbe; 'After waking he *lay* for some time thinking over his plans' = Après s'être réveillé il *resta couché* assez longtemps à méditer ses projets.

Distinguish: il *se couchait* = 'he used to lie down, go to bed'; il *était couché* = 'he was in bed'; il *s'était couché* = 'he had gone to bed.' Je *coucherai* à Douvres = 'I shall sleep at Dover'; La mère *couche* ses enfants = 'puts her children to bed.'

LITTLE:

Remember that 'little,' when = 'small,' is *petit*: 'a little loaf, a roll' = un *petit* pain.

When = 'a small quantity of,' is *un peu de*: 'Give us a little bread' = Donnez-nous *un peu de* pain.

ONE:

Not to be translated in sentences like 'The struggle was a desperate one' = La lutte fut acharnée. '*The one* who (which)' = *Celui* qui.

PAR:

In translating such phrases as 'on a fine summer evening,' 'one cold winter night,' remember *par*: *par* un beau soir d'été, *par* une froide nuit d'hiver. The practical rule is: Use *par* when the weather is described.

P E O P L E :

le peuple = 'the nation': 'Je désire que mes cendres reposent au bord de la Seine, au milieu de ce *peuple* français que j'ai tant aimé' (Napoléon);

'*people* say' = *on* dit;

'many *people* say so' = beaucoup de *gens* le disent;

'young *people*' = les jeunes *gens* (often = 'young men,' as opposed to *les jeunes filles*).

'There were a great many *people* there' = Il y avait là beaucoup de *monde*.

R E S T :

When 'rest' = 'that which remains,' it is *le reste*, e.g. *le reste* de ma vie.

When 'rest' = 'those who remain,' it is *les autres*, e.g. 'He stayed, the rest went off' = Lui resta, *les autres* partirent.

R I D E :

'He can *ride*' = Il sait *monter à cheval*.

aller à cheval = '*to go on* horseback,' opposed to, e.g. *aller en* auto, *à* bicyclette.

Often translated by some such Verb as *s'éloigner* = 'to ride away,' *s'approcher* = 'to ride up'; when 'on horseback' is implied.

S I T :

s'asseoir = 'to seat oneself,' 'sit down': Asseyez-vous = 'Sit down.'

The Past Participle *assis* translates 'sitting' (state): 'She *sat* (i.e. was sitting) by the fireside' = Elle *était assise* au coin du feu.

Often 'sit,' 'sat' is translated by *rester* with or without *assis*: 'The others rose, he sat still' = Les autres se levèrent, lui *resta assis*.

Distinguish: il *s'asseyait* = 'he used to sit down'; il *était assis* = 'he was sitting' (seated); il *s'était assis* = 'he had seated himself' (sat down).

SOMETHING:

Although *chose* is feminine, *quelque chose* is masculine. Note the construction when an Adjective follows: 'something good' = *quelque chose* DE *bon*. Similarly 'nothing good' = *rien* DE *bon*.

STAND:

se tenir debout = 'to stand' with emphasis on the standing position. Often *se tenir* alone is sufficient: 'He was *standing* at the door' = Il *se tenait* à la porte; *se lever*: il *se leva* = 'he *stood up*'; il *s'arrêta* = 'he *stood still.*'

'Stand!' = *Arrêtez!*

Of inanimate objects *se dresser* and *s'élever* are generally used: Le monument *s'élève* (se dresse) au bord de la grand'route. Of trees, *croître* may be said: Un arbre *croissait* près de la maison.

TAKE:

While 'take' is often *prendre*, e.g. *prendre* le train, *prendre* son temps, it may have to be translated by another Verb: 'to take a walk, step' = *faire* une promenade, un pas; 'to take one's dinner' = *manger* son dîner; 'Take this letter to the post' = *Portez* cette lettre à la poste; 'Take these gentlemen to the office' = *Conduisez* ces messieurs au bureau; 'He is taking the horses to the water' = Il *mène* les chevaux à l'abreuvoir; 'How long do you *take to* get here?' = Combien de temps *mettez*-vous *à* venir?'

THE MORE:

'the more...the more' = *plus...plus*; 'the less... the less' = *moins...moins*: 'The more you make, the more you spend' = *Plus* on gagne, *plus* on dépense; *Plus* vous travaillerez activement, *plus* vous serez heureux.

THERE:

With an Impersonal Verb: 'There is, are' = *Il y a* or *Il est*, always singular. 'There came soldiers' = *Il* vint des soldats.

WALK:

marcher denotes the physical act of walking: Cet enfant commence à *marcher*; Il *marche* très vite;

aller à pied = 'to go on foot' (not by train, car, etc.);
se promener = 'to go for a walk,' 'take a stroll for pleasure or exercise.'

Often another Verb is used, e.g. 'He walked in' = Il entra; 'He walked on' = Il continua son chemin, se remit en route; 'He walked quickly away' = Il s'éloigna rapidement.

WHOEVER, WHATEVER:

'Whoever said that...' = Qui que ce soit qui ait dit cela...; or, often = *Quiconque* or *Celui qui* a dit cela; 'Whatever your opinions may be...' = *Quelles que soient* vos opinions...; 'Whatever I do, wherever I go, the end is always the same' = Quoi que je fasse, où que j'aille, la fin est toujours la même.

YES, NO:

In polite French it is customary to add *Monsieur, Madame*, etc., to *oui* or *non*, when in English such a use of 'Sir,' 'Madam,' would be very formal.

§ 50.　DIAGRAMS SHOWING THE SEQUENCE OF TENSES (INDICATIVE MOOD)

The following diagrams will be found useful as a supplement to our notes on AS SOON AS, WHEN, etc.

P = Past; N = now (present moment); F = Future.
NP = Past time; NF = Future time.

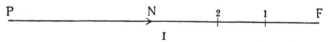

'When I have read[2] this book, I will lend[1] it to you' = Quand j'aurai lu[2] ce livre, je vous le prêterai[1].

Note. Both Verbs refer to the Future but the action described in 2 must be complete (Perfect) before that of 1 happens.

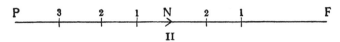

II

'He said[3] that he would lend[1] me the book as soon as he had read[2] it' = Il dit[3] (a dit) qu'il me prêterait[1] le livre dès qu'il l'aurait[2] lu.

Note. This is the reported (Indirect) form of **I**. The Future becomes Future in the Past and the Future Perfect becomes Future Perfect in the Past. If 1 and 2 are in *NP* the person who promised has forgotten his promise, if in *NF* the promise still holds good.

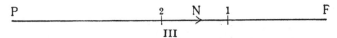

III

'I have read[2] the book. I shall lend[1] it to you' = J'ai lu[2] le livre. Je vous le prêterai[1] *or* Je vais vous le prêter.

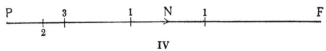

IV

'He said[3] that he had read[2] the book and that he would lend it to me' = Il dit[3] qu'il avait lu[2] le livre et qu'il me le prêterait[1].

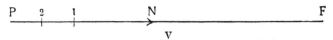

V

'As soon as he had read[2] the book he lent[1] it to me' = Dès qu'il eut lu[2] (a eu lu) le livre, il me le prêta[1] (a prêté).

Note. Eut lu and *prêta* are in Historic, Narrative style; *a eu lu, a prêté* in Conversational style.

PASSAGES FOR TRANSLATION

SECTION I

MODEL LESSON I

1. 'The water you seek springs from a well in a castle where an old fairy lives,' the Dwarf went on. 2. 'That you may be able to go safely, I will give you an iron wand, and two little loaves of bread. 3. When you come to the castle, strike the iron door three times with the wand, and it will open. 4. Inside, you will find two lions, with their mouths wide open ready to eat you. 5. But if you throw them the bread, they will let you pass. 6. Then you must run as fast as you can to the well and take some of the magic water before the clock strikes twelve. 7. If you stay after that hour, the door will shut upon you for ever.'

1. 'The water you seek springs from a well in a castle where an old fairy lives,' the Dwarf went on.

'The water you seek.' Before turning such a phrase as this into French, you must always supply the missing Relative Pronoun. English 'which' can be left out, but French *que* cannot. This is a rule to which there are no exceptions, and we must therefore say *L'eau* que *vous cherchez*.

'springs from a well in a castle.' When you do not know the French for a word, look it up in the Vocabulary at the end of this book. There you will find two Verbs which are used of water 'springing,' *sourdre* and *sortir*. One of these will be more familiar to you than the other, and it will be safer to choose it. You will have learnt its present tense by heart, 'Je sors, tu sors, *il sort....*' The Verb *sourdre* is worth knowing, for it is not uncommon and may very easily occur in a passage of Unseen Translation. If you know the part of it which corresponds to *il sort*, namely *il sourd*, you may use it, but the simpler verb *sortir* is just as good here as *sourdre*.

'where an old fairy lives.' 'A fairy' is *une fée*; 'a witch' is *une sorcière*. But *une fée* and *une sorcière* convey very much the same meaning in French and are often confused with each other, and when we say 'witch' the French often say *fée*.

For 'to live' there are several French words, *vivre, habiter, demeurer*, and naturally there is some difference in their meaning: *vivre* is the opposite of *mourir*; it means to be alive, e.g. *Après Waterloo Napoléon vécut plusieurs années. Habiter* and *demeurer* are much alike; *habiter* is to 'be an inhabitant' of a town or a house: *Les parents de Napoléon habitaient la ville d'Ajaccio. Demeurer* is less precise and less common-place; it means 'to dwell': *Tout près de la vieille église demeurait le meunier* = 'Hard by the old church dwelt the miller.' The most suitable word here is thus *demeurer*: *où une vieille sorcière demeurait*. But this phrase, though quite correct, could be improved upon. In Relative Clauses inversion is frequent, and our phrase would sound better, and look more French, if it ran thus, *où demeurait une vieille sorcière*.

'went on': *continua*; or *reprit*—if 'went on' means that the Dwarf had been interrupted and was now resuming his speech. Whenever phrases like 'he said,' 'they replied,' 'he continued' are used parenthetically in the middle of a speech, inversion is obligatory in

French. 'It is for me,' he said, 'a great pleasure' = '*C'est
pour moi*,' disait-il, '*un grand plaisir*.' 'No,' they
replied.... = '*Non*,' répondirent-ils....

Our sentence will thus run: '*L'eau que vous cherchez
sort d'un puits dans un château où demeure une vieille
fée*,' reprit le nain.

2. 'That you may be able to go safely, I will give
you an iron wand, and two little loaves of bread.'

'That you may be able to.' 'That' means 'in order
that,' and expresses purpose; in French it is *afin que*
or *pour que*. Both these Conjunctions take the Subjunctive. The tense of the Subjunctive is the Present
when the Verb of the main clause is a Present, or a
Future, as here, and we must therefore say *Afin que vous
puissiez*.

'go safely.' For 'go,' *aller* alone is not quite enough.
French is usually more explicit than English. Here 'to
go' means not 'to go away,' 'to go anywhere you
please,' but to go to a particular place already mentioned, to the castle. A French writer feels the need
of completing the expression and stating the destination, and says Y *aller*.

'safely.' The usual French for this is *en sûreté*, but
that phrase generally implies *remaining* safely where
one is, i.e. *être en sûreté*, e.g. *Nous ne sommes pas ici
en sûreté* = 'We are not safe here.' To arrive *safely* is
arriver *sain et sauf*. But a more suitable phrase for
our present purpose is *sans danger*.

'I will give you.' The Simple Future tense is not
nearly so common in ordinary French conversation as
it is in the school grammars. In nine cases out of ten
when the immediate future is meant, a Frenchman
says not *Je vous* donnerai, but *Je* vais *vous donner*, and

that is certainly what our Dwarf would have said, had he been speaking French.

'an iron wand': *une baguette de fer*. The material of which an object is made is usually expressed by means of *de*, e.g. *un chemin de fer*, 'an iron road,' 'a railway.'

'and two little loaves of bread.' Literal translation is here out of the question. We cannot possibly say *et deux petits pains de pain*. In the first place, *un petit pain* is not usually 'a little loaf,' but 'a morning roll,' and in the second place, it is unnecessary to tell the reader that *des pains* are made of—*pain*! That can be left to the imagination and it is only when a 'loaf' is made of something else that the material has to be stated, e.g. *un pain de sucre* = a sugar-loaf, or *un pain de savon* = a cake of soap. Fortunately there is another French word for 'loaf,' *une miche*, and we get round both difficulties by saying *deux petites miches*.

'Afin que vous puissiez y aller sans danger, je vais vous donner une baguette de fer et deux petites miches.'

3. 'When you come to the castle, strike the iron door three times with the wand, and it will open.'

'When you come to the castle, strike the iron door.' Some care is required as to the tense after a conjunction of time such as *quand*. It is the Future when the tense of the Verb in the main clause is a Future, or, as here, the equivalent of a Future. The Imperative 'strike' tells what will have. to be done at a future time, i.e. when the castle is reached.... We should therefore say *Quand vous viendrez, frappez*.... But is *venir* the proper verb? The French do not always use *venir* exactly as we use 'come'; *venir* means strictly to come to where the speaker is. Here *arriverez* would be more exact: *Quand vous arriverez au château, frappez la porte de fer.*

'three times': *trois fois.* Beginners are very apt to confuse *fois* and *temps.* The difference is most clearly shown by examples: e.g. 'once, twice, thrice' is *une fois, deux fois, trois fois;* as in the auctioneer's 'Going, going, gone': *Une fois, deux fois, trois fois. Adjugé!* so *la prochaine fois,* next time; *la fois suivante,* the following time; *pour la dernière fois,* for the last time. *Temps* denotes space of time, e.g. Combien de *temps?* ='How long?' whereas Combien de *fois?* ='How often?'

'with the wand': *avec la baguette,* or *de la baguette?* The distinction between *de* and *avec* is that *de* is used of less material things. To take an extreme case, we should say: *Il m'a frappé de stupeur,* but *Il m'a frappé avec un bâton.*

'and it will open': i.e. 'it will open itself': *on l'ouvrira* would quite spoil the effect. Who could *on* be? It is a magic door, opening of its own accord: thus 'Open, Sesame!' is *Sésame, Ouvre-toi!*

'Quand vous arriverez au château, frappez la porte de fer trois fois avec la baguette, et elle s'ouvrira.'

4. 'Inside, you will find two lions, with their mouths wide open ready to eat you.'

'Inside, you will find two lions.' *Dedans* or *Là-dedans* (but not *dans,* which is a Preposition, not an Adverb) *vous trouverez deux lions.*

'with their mouths open.' In such a phrase 'with' is not usually to be translated, e.g. 'She came in with her nose in the air,' *Elle entra le nez en l'air;* 'He faced death *with* a smile on his lips' = *Il affronta la mort* le sourire *aux lèvres.*

'mouths.' The mouth of a beast of prey is not *une*

bouche, but *une gueule*, notwithstanding Alfred de Vigny, who horrified the critics by speaking of *la bouche du loup*. The singular is regularly used in French in a case like this. Cp. *Les Mahométans prient*, la tête *tournée vers la Mecque* = The Mohammedans pray, with their *faces* towards Mecca.

'wide open.' The idiom is *grande ouverte*; here *grande* has the force of an Adverb, but is treated as an Adjective and agrees with *gueule*; similarly in the plural, e.g. *des fenêtres grandes ouvertes*.

'ready to eat you': *prêts* if 'ready' goes with 'lions,' *prête* if it goes with 'mouth(s),' which is less likely; *prêt* is construed with *à* and is to be carefully distinguished from *près*, which takes *de*. For 'eat,' *avaler* = 'to gobble up' or *dévorer* = 'to devour' will do very well, but *manger* is also good, being said, e.g. of the wolf in 'Le petit Chaperon rouge,' 'Little Red Riding Hood' and 'La Chèvre de Monsieur Seguin,' Et puis, le matin, le loup l'a *mangée*.

'Dedans vous trouverez deux lions, la gueule grande ouverte, prêts à vous manger.'

5. 'But if you throw them the bread, they will let you pass.'

'But if you throw.' When the Verb of the main clause is a Future, the syntax of *si* meaning 'if' is quite different from that of *quand*. While *quand* takes the Future, *si* takes the Present: *Mais si vous jetez*. See the rule, p. 78, § 45.

'them' is the indirect, not the direct object; it cannot therefore be *les*, as the thoughtless are apt to write, but must be *leur*.

'Mais si vous leur jetez le pain, ils vous laisseront passer.'

6. 'Then you must run as fast as you can to the well and take some of the magic water before the clock strikes twelve.'

'Then you must run': *Alors il faut courir* or, much better since the necessity for running will concern only one person (*vous*) and will not arise till later, *Alors il vous faudra courir*. Once again French shows its preference for explicit statement. It is also possible, though unnecessary, to use a less simple form *Alors il faudra que vous couriez.*

'as fast as you can': 'fast' is *vite*. Beware of saying 'vitement'; it is archaic or vulgar.

With *aussi...que* the syntax is as with *quand*, and here the Future is required, *aussi vite que vous pourrez*. It is not necessary however to use a Verb at all, *aussi vite que possible* being an idiomatic phrase.

'to the well': *au puits* or, more clearly, *jusqu'au puits* = right up to the well. *Alors il vous faudra courir, aussi vite que vous pourrez, jusqu'au puits.*

'and take some of the magic water.' Note that *and* usually connects parallel constructions, i.e. if we said *courir* above, we must use the Infinitive now, *prendre*; if we said *couriez*, we must now use the Subjunctive, *preniez.*

un peu de l'eau magique. N.B. 'some' = *un peu*, e.g. 'I have done *some* good,' *J'ai fait un peu de bien.*

'before the clock strikes twelve': 'clock.' There are two French words, *une pendule* and *une horloge*. *Une pendule* is a hanging or mantelpiece clock and it is highly unlikely that one is intended here; *une horloge* is an outside clock, e.g. in a tower.

With *avant que*, referring to a future event, the Subjunctive must be used and instead of saying *avant que l'horloge* sonne, French says more naturally *avant que l'horloge* ait sonné.

'twelve.' Though 'ten o'clock' is *dix heures* and 'eleven o'clock' is *onze heures*, 'twelve o'clock' is not *douze heures* (except in railway time-tables), but either *midi* or *minuit*; in this story it is no doubt *minuit*, and we translate:

'Alors il vous faudra courir, aussi vite que vous pourrez, jusqu'au puits et prendre un peu de l'eau magique avant que l'horloge ait sonné minuit (*or* avant que minuit ait sonné à l'horloge).'

7. 'If you stay after that hour, the door will shut upon you for ever.'

'stay'; stay where? We must say *Si vous y restez* (or *restez* là).

'after that hour': *cette heure* would mean 'this hour'; '*that* hour' is *cette heure-là*. Since we require *là* here, we shall prefer *y* to *là* with *restez*.

'will shut': *se fermera*, exactly like *s'ouvrira* in Sentence 3.

'Si vous y restez après cette heure-là, la porte se fermera sur vous pour toujours.'

Suggested Rendering

'L'eau que vous cherchez sort d'un puits dans un château où demeure une vieille fée,' reprit le nain. 'Afin que vous puissiez y aller sans danger, je vais vous donner une baguette de fer et deux petites miches. Quand vous arriverez au château, frappez la porte de fer trois fois avec la baguette, et elle s'ouvrira. Dedans vous trouverez deux lions, la gueule grande

ouverte, prêts à vous manger. Mais si vous leur jetez
le pain, ils vous laisseront passer. Alors il vous faudra
courir, aussi vite que vous pourrez, jusqu'au puits et
prendre un peu de l'eau magique avant que l'horloge
ait sonné minuit. Si vous y restez après cette heure-là,
la porte se fermera sur vous pour toujours.'

1. THE LITTLE BOY AND THE BEAR

A little boy had gone into the forest to[1] cut wood.
All at once he saw a bear coming[2] towards him. What
was to be done[3]? Climb up a tree? It[4] was too late.
Take to flight? It[4] was impossible. The boy took his
cap and threw it at the bear. The bear sniffed at the
cap, and during this time the boy ran away. But the
bear did not waste his time, and in a few minutes he
overtook the boy. The latter threw his coat at him,
then his waistcoat and then his tie. Each time the
bear stopped to sniff at[5] what the boy had thrown at
him. Thus the boy was[6] able to reach his mother's
house at the edge of the forest.

1 *Pour* is usually unnecessary with an Infinitive coming
directly after *aller* or *venir*, e.g. Je suis *allé chercher* du bois
dans la forêt. But when a phrase intervenes, *pour* is required.
2 Use the Infinitive or *qui*; p. 52, § 37, 2.   3 *Que faire?*
4 *Ce* or *Il*? p. 42, § 26, 2.   5 Is 'at' to be translated? p. 83,
§ 48, 3.   6 Tense?

2. THE LION HUNT

They looked up as a man came running[1] towards
the cave.

'Oho, Hickory!' called Strongarm, 'what is it?'

'A lion hunt!' shouted Hickory, and shook[1] his
spear.

Strongarm's bold face lighted up.

'Tell about it,' he said.

'A lion has come among the caves by[2] the river. He kills the people and carries off the children. The women dare not[3] go to the river for[4] water. The men are afraid to go alone to hunt. So they want help to kill the lion. They want all the strong men and the good hunters. They have sent for[4] you.'

Strongarm quickly[5] took his club and spear and went off with old Hickory. They went over[6] two hills and across[6] a stream, and came to Hickory's cave. There other men joined them[7]. All the men had clubs and spears and stone axes. They went together towards the river caves. They found[8] the lion and killed it.

Margaret A. McIntyre, The Cave Boy of the Age of Stone

1 Use *en* and the verbal form in *-ant*.　　2 Supply 'which are.'　　3 *ne...plus*.　　4 Use *chercher*.　　5 Position of the Adverb? See p. 79, § 46.　　6 *franchir* will express both 'over' and 'across.'　　7 *se joindre à.*　　8 Supply *y*.

3. PROCRUSTES' BED

Procrustes pretended to be hospitable to[1] travellers[2] and would[3] invite them into[4] the great cave in which[5] he lived, and would tell them that they should sleep[6] in his own bed. But when the traveller was in bed, he would[3] say to him: 'Every one who sleeps in my bed must fit it[7],' and if the poor man was too short[8] he would drag his[9] feet to make him longer, as he said; and if he was too long[10], he would lop his[9] feet off. Theseus conquered him, and put him into the bed, and finding that he was too long for it[11], lopped off his[9] head, for he thought it best to make an end of[12] such a[13] monster at once.

Alfred J. Church, Three Greek Children

1 *pour*.　　2 'travellers' is general; p. 23, § 12.　　3 Tense? p. 58, § 41, WOULD.　　4 Supply 'to enter.'　　5 'where'; p. 45, § 30.　　6 What were the words in which Procrustes addressed his guests?　　7 *être à sa mesure.*　　8 'small.'　　9 Use the Definite Article; p. 49, § 35, 2.　　10 'tall.'　　11 Omit 'for it.'　　12 'to make an end of' = *en finir avec*.　　13 Order of the words? p. 81, § 46, so.

4. THE PEASANT'S MISTAKE

One day an old peasant brought[1] a basket of fine apples to the castle of a certain Marquis. On[2] the stair-case he met two monkeys, dressed like[3] children, who flung themselves on his basket and proceeded to empty it. The peasant respectfully[4] took off his hat. When he came before the Marquis, the latter asked him, 'Why did you bring me a half-empty basket?' 'My Lord,' the peasant replied, 'it[5] is not my fault. My basket was quite full, but your two sons have half-emptied it.'

1 *amener* or *apporter*? p. 13, § 7, BRING.   2 *Dans.* 3 = 'as.'   4 Position of the Adverb? See p. 79, § 46.   5 *ce* or *il*? p. 42, § 26, 2.

5. MY OLD MISTRESS. i

My old mistress would[1] often say to me, 'Catherine, I am going out'; and then she would[1] be carried[2] out in her sedan. She was too feeble to[3] walk[4] to the houses of her neighbours, and could not easily get into a coach. I used to take a little basket and go by her side. We would soon stop at a cottage, into which[5] she sent me to see how the poor woman was[6]; and when I had come out again, she would say, 'Well, how does she look? Has she a[7] fire? Is there any[8] coal in the house?' Then she would send me for[9] anything that was wanted.

1 Is 'would' here = Imperfect or Future in the Past? p. 58, § 41, WOULD.   2 Use *faire* + Infinitive; p. 53, § 39, 1. 3 Preposition? See p. 81, § 46, TOO.   4 *aller à pied* or *marcher*? p. 91, § 49, WALK.   5 *où.*   6 Use *se porter.* 7 *du feu.*   8 p. 48, § 34, ANY.   9 Use *chercher.*

6. MY OLD MISTRESS. ii

And when we had come home, she would ask, 'What do you[1] think of[2] what you have seen to-day?' Then she would say, 'Catherine, poverty[3] will probably be your portion; but you have one talent which you may use for the good of others[4]. You may[5] sometimes read half an hour to a poor sick neighbour. Or you may run errands for those who have no one else to help them. Promise me, then, my child, that you will try to do what you can[6] for others[4].' Ah! there were[7] few like my dear mistress!

1 This old lady would probably have used *tu* and *toi* to her young servant.   2 *à* or *de*? p. 73, § 44, PENSER.   3 Remember what Abstract Nouns require in French; p. 23, § 12. 4 *d'autrui*; p. 46, § 32, 2.   5 Is 'may' here = 'are able' or 'will be able'? p. 57, § 41, MAY.   6 Tense?   7 Supply *en*; p. 39, § 23, 2.

7. THE BIRTHDAY PRESENT. i

'Well, this is[1] a charming present, indeed!' said the godmother. 'My Rosamond knows how[2] to make presents.'

As she spoke[3] she took hold of the basket to lift it down and show it to the company. Scarcely had[4] she touched it, when, lo! the basket fell to the ground and only the handle was left in her hand[5]. All eyes were fixed upon the wreck.

'Who can have done this?' was all[6] Rosamond could say.

Bell stood[7] silent and, while[8] every one questioned and wondered, still refused to speak.   Maria Edgeworth

1 *voici*.   2 'to know *how* to' is often *savoir* alone. 3 *Comme elle parlait* or *Tout en parlant*? p. 77, § 45, AS. 4 p. 88, § 49, INVERSION, and p. 78, § 45, WHEN.   5 'there remained only the handle in her hand'; p. 49, § 35, 2.   6 Remember the full French expression; p. 87, § 49, ALL.   7 Is the standing position emphasized? p. 91, § 49, STAND. 8 *pendant que* or *tandis que*? And Tense? p. 79, § 45, WHILE.

8. THE BIRTHDAY PRESENT. ii

At last the servants were summoned, and amongst them was Nancy, Bell's maid. When she saw what had happened to the basket, she pretended[1] to be

surprised and declared that she knew nothing of the
matter, except that she had seen her mistress put it
safely into the wardrobe that morning.

'And Miss Bell hasn't touched it either[2], ma'am,'
she said. 'I can answer for[3] her; she didn't even know
of its being[4] there. I had never mentioned it because
I knew Miss Rosamond wanted to surprise her[5].'

Maria Edgeworth

1 p. 18, § 8, PRETEND. A good expression is *jouer la surprise.*
2 p. 77, § 45, EITHER.   3 Use *de.*   4 = 'that it was.'
5 The phrase is *faire une surprise à quelqu'un.*

9. AN HONEST OLD WOMAN

So[1] the children went to[2] their grandmother and
showed her the guinea and told her how they had
found it.

The old woman was[3] very glad that they brought[4] it
to her[5], for she was sure that there had been some
mistake. She told them to go to the town and try[6] to
find out at[7] one of the inns the person who had given
it to them[5].

'Whoever gave you a guinea instead of a halfpenny
has no doubt already found out his mistake,' she said.
'All[8] you can do is[9] to go and ask for[10] the gentleman
who was reading in the carriage.'   Maria Edgeworth

1 Beware of *Si*; p. 81, § 46, SO.   2 Use *aller trouver.*
3 Tense?   4 Mood? p. 54, § 40, 2.   5 Order of the
Pronouns in French? p. 41, § 25.   6 Any Preposition used
in translating 'to go' must be repeated in translating 'try.'
7 *dans.*   8 Complete the expression; p. 87, § 49, ALL.
9 *c'est*; p. 42, § 26, 1.   10 Is 'for' to be translated? p. 66,
§ 44, DEMANDER.

10. THE MAGIC CLOAK

As a merry young huntsman was once going through[1]
a wood, a little old woman came up to him[2], and said[3],
'Good-day, good-day! you[4] seem merry enough, but
I[4] am hungry and thirsty; pray[5] give me something

to eat.' The huntsman took pity on her, and put his
hand in his pocket and gave her what he had. Then
he wanted to go his way; but she held him back and
said, 'Listen, my friend, to[6] what I am going to tell
you; I will reward you for[7] your kindness; go your
way, and after a little time[8] you will come to a tree on
which[9] you will see nine birds sitting[10] on a cloak.
Shoot into the midst of them[11], and one[12] will fall
down dead; the cloak will fall too; take it; it is a
magic cloak, and when you wear[13] it you will find
yourself where[14] you wish[13] to be.'

Grimm

1 Use *traverser* (transitive).   2 Is this *lui* or *à lui*? p. 41,
§ 24, 3.   3 To whom? French states the fact; p. 38, § 23, 1.
4 Are the Pronouns emphasized? p. 39, § 24, 1.   5 *je vous
en prie*, used parenthetically.   6 Remember that *écouter* is
transitive; p. 83, § 48, 3.   7 *de*.   8 *dans un moment.*
9 *où* or *sur lequel*? p. 45, § 30.   10 Here *posé* would be more
natural than *assis* [= 'squatting'].   11 *tirer dans le tas.*
12 Supply 'of them.'   13 Tense?   14 *là où*; p. 45, § 30.

11. A FOOLISH PRAYER

[1]King Midas having done Bacchus a service, the
god promised to grant him his first prayer. 'Grant,
O Bacchus,' said Midas, 'that all[2] I touch may turn[3]
to gold!' To see if the god had kept his promise,
Midas picked up a stone, which straightway became
an ingot of gold. Mad with joy, he tore off his sandals
and, wherever he went, he left footprints of gold. But
his joy was[4] short-lived. For[5], when hunger seized
him and he would[6] eat, the food[2] he touched turned
into gold. Then Midas realized how[7] foolish and wicked
was his prayer. He implored Bacchus to have pity on
him and take back the gift[2] he had made, and he[8],
seeing that Midas repented of his avarice, bade him
go and wash[9] in the Pactolus. The miraculous golden[10]

gift passed into the rushing stream, and from that day the waters of the Pactolus have rolled[11] down sands of gold.

1 Remember the Article; p. 23, § 12.   2 Complete the expression; p. 87, § 49, ALL.   3 Use *changer en*. The Subjunctive, without *pouvoir*, is sufficient.   4 Tense? p. 59, § 42, 4.   5 Beware of *pour*; p. 88, § 49, FOR.   6 'would' is here the Past tense of 'will' = 'wish'; p. 58, § 41, WOULD. 7 'how' = 'how much.' The French order of words is 'how much his prayer was foolish.'   8 'he' is accented; p. 40, § 24, 1.   9 *laver* alone is not enough; p. 61, § 43, 1.   10 Turn by 'the gold of this miraculous gift.'   11 Tense?

12. THE TEMPTED SOLDIER

A worthy soldier had saved a good deal of money out of[1] his pay; for he worked hard, and did not spend all[2] he earned in eating[3] and drinking, as many others did[4]. Now, he had two comrades who were great rogues, and wanted to rob him of his money, but behaved towards him in a friendly way. 'Comrade,' said they to him one day, 'why should we stay here shut up in this town like prisoners, when you, at any rate, have earned enough to live upon[5] for[6] the rest of your days in peace and plenty, at home by your own fireside?' They talked so often to him in[7] this manner that he at last said he would go and try his luck with them.

Grimm

1 *sur*.   2 Supply the Relative.   3 *à* with Infinitive. 4 The order in French is 'as did many others.'   5 *pour en vivre*.   6 Omit 'for.'   7 Preposition? p. 85, § 48, IN.

13. SNOW-DROP

It was in the middle of winter, and the big flakes of snow were falling thick. The young Queen sat[1] working[2] at[3] the open window, the frame of which was made of the finest ebony; and as she was watching the flakes turning in the air, she pricked her finger[4] with her needle, and three tiny[5] drops of blood fell upon the snow. Then she gazed thoughtfully upon the red drops which spotted the white snow, and said, 'Would that[6] my little daughter may be as white as that snow, as red as the blood, and as black as the ebony window-frame!' And so[7] the little girl grew up: her skin was as white as snow, her cheeks as rosy as the blood, and her hair as black as ebony; and she was called Snow-drop.   Grimm

1 = 'was seated'; p. 90, § 49, SIT.   2 *à* + Infinitive; p. 52, § 37, 2.   3 Use *auprès de*, to avoid repeating *à*.   4 *se piquer le doigt*.   5 'tiny drops' = *gouttelettes* (f.).   6 Use *pouvoir* in the Subjunctive; p. 53, § 40, 1.   7 *c'est ainsi que*.

14. GREEN CABBAGES

The Swallow spoke of those beautiful, warm countries, where bunches of grapes, large and heavy, hang on[1] the vines; where the air is so balmy, and[2] the mountains are tinged with various hues, such as are never known[3] here.

'Ah! but they have not our green cabbages!' said the Hen. 'I remember, one summer, I[4] and all my chickens lived[5] in the country, and we could go into a garden full of green cabbages. Oh, how green they were[6]! I cannot imagine anything[7] more beautiful!'

'But one head of cabbage looks exactly like another,' said the Swallow; 'and then we often have wet weather here!'

'One gets accustomed to that,' said the Hen.

'But it is[8] cold, it freezes!'

'That is good for the cabbages,' said the Hen; 'besides, it can be[8] warm sometimes. Did we not, four years ago, have a summer which lasted five weeks? It was[8] so hot, that one could hardly breathe.'

Hans Andersen

1 *de*.   2 Supply 'where.'   3 Avoid the Passive; p. 47, § 33, 2.   4 Remember the accented form.   5 Tense and Person?   6 The French order is 'how much they were green.' 7 Remember the construction; p. 48, § 34, 2 ANYTHING.   8 Use *faire*.

15. TOO MANY REASONS

A King was visiting the chief cities of his kingdom. He[1] was a good King and all his subjects loved him. In every town[2] he visited, the bells were rung[3] and cannon fired[3] in his honour. At last he came to a little town, where the bells rang merrily, but no cannon was heard[4]. The Mayor and Corporation were waiting for[5] him at the town gate, and the Mayor began his speech. 'Sire, we are happy to welcome your Majesty. The inhabitants of this town well know that it is the custom to fire cannon, but we have been unable to do so for the following fifteen reasons[6].' Then the Mayor drew a large manuscript from his pocket, and began to read. 'In the first place[7], Sire, we have no cannon. ...In the second place...' 'Thank you, Mr Mayor,' said the King, laughing heartily, 'your first reason is sufficient. I excuse you the other fourteen.'

1 *C'était* or *Il était?* p. 42, § 26, 2.   2 Supply the Relative. 3 Avoid the Passive; p. 47, § 33, 2.   4 *se faisait entendre.* The negative requires attention; p. 81, § 47.   5 Omit 'for'; p. 83, § 48, 3.   6 The French order is 'the fifteen reasons following.'   7 *En premier lieu.*

16. THE PURPLE JAR. i

Rosamond was very sorry that her mother wanted[1] nothing. Presently, however, they came to a shop which appeared to her far more beautiful than the rest[2]. It was a chemist's shop, but she did not know that.

'Oh, mother, oh!' cried she, pulling her mother's hand; 'look, look! blue, green, red, yellow and purple! Oh! mamma, what[3] beautiful things! Won't[4] you buy some of these?'

Still her mother answered as before[5]. 'Of what use[6] would they be to me, Rosamond?'

'You might put flowers in them, mamma, and they would look so pretty on the chimney-piece. I wish I had[7] one of them.'

'You[8] have a flower-pot,' said her mother, 'and that is not a flower-pot[9].'

Maria Edgeworth

1 Mood? p. 54, § 40, 2.   2. Not *le reste*; p. 90, § 49, REST.
3 p. 45, § 31, 3.   4 Use *aller*; p. 57, § 41, WILL.   5 An Adverb here; p. 84, § 48, BEFORE.   6 Use *servir à*; p. 75, § 44, SERVIR.   7 Use the Infinitive; p. 77, § 44, VOULOIR.
8 Rosamond may have said *vous* to her mother (see p. 39, § 23, 3), but would her mother have said *vous* to Rosamond?
9 Use 'one' to avoid the repetition; p. 39, § 23, 2.

17. THE PURPLE JAR. ii

'But it would make a nice flower-pot, mamma, you know.'

'Perhaps if you were to see[1] nearer, if you were to examine it, you might be disappointed.'

'No, indeed, I'm sure I should not[2]; I should like it exceedingly.'

Rosamond continued to look back at the purple vase till she could[3] see it no longer[4].

'Then, mother,' said she after a pause, 'perhaps[5] you have no money.'

'Yes[6], I have[7].'

'Dear me, if I had money I would buy roses and boxes and buckles and purple flower-pots and everything.' Rosamond was[8] obliged to pause in the middle of her speech.

'Oh, mamma, do[9] stop a minute for me. I have got a stone in my shoe; it hurts me very much.'

Maria Edgeworth

1 The Imperfect of *voir* gives the whole sense of 'were to see.'
2 *je suis sûre que non*.   3 Mood and Tense? p. 55, § 40, 5.
4 *le (la) voir plus longtemps*.   5 Use either *peut-être* with Inversion, or else *peut-être que* without.   6 *Si*.   7 Supply *en*; p. 39, § 23, 2.   8 Tense?   9 Use *donc* or *je t'(vous) en prie*.

18. THE DAISY AND THE LARK. i

Listen to my story!

In¹ the country, close by the road-side, there stands²
a little white-washed cottage—you must certainly have
seen it. In front is a little garden full of flowers. Last
summer there grew³ on a bank close to this garden,
amidst the green grass, a little Daisy.

The little flower thought that no one saw her, hidden
among the grass. She was quite contented: she
turned⁴ towards the sun, looked at it, and listened to
the Lark who was singing high in the sky.

The little Lark expressed clearly all⁵ the flower felt
in silence. And she looked to the happy bird who could⁶
fly and sing; it⁷ did not distress her that she could⁸ not
do the same⁹.

Hans Andersen

1 Preposition? p. 85, § 48, IN.   2 Use *se trouver*.   3 It
will make better French to transfer 'grew' to the end of the
phrase 'amidst the green grass.'   4 *tourner* or *se
tourner*?   5 Complete the expression; p. 87, § 49, ALL.
6 *pouvoir* or *savoir*? p. 56, § 41, CAN. Tense?   7 *cela*.
8 Use, instead of *que* + Subjunctive, *de* + Infinitive; p. 21,
§ 10.   9 The phrase is *en faire autant*.

19. THE DAISY AND THE LARK. ii

Next morning¹, when our little flower, fresh and
cheerful, again² spread out her white petals in the
bright sunshine, she heard the voice of a bird; but
he³ sang so mournfully. Alas! the poor Lark had good
reason to be sad; he³ had been caught and put into
a cage close by the open window.

The little Daisy would willingly have helped him,
but how could⁴ she? Ah, that she knew not. She
quite forgot how⁵ beautiful was all around her, how
pretty her own leaves were. Alas! she could⁶ think
only of the imprisoned bird—whom she was powerless
to help.

All at once two little boys came out of the garden; one[7] of them had a knife in[8] his hand. They went up to the little Daisy, who could not imagine what they wanted.

Hans Andersen

1 *Le lendemain matin.*   2 *de nouveau.* Remember the position of the Adverb in French; p. 79, § 46.   3 Gender? The Noun to which a Personal Pronoun refers is that which immediately precedes it. In this paragraph the first 'he' stands for 'bird' = *oiseau* (m.), and the second 'he' stands for 'lark' = *alouette* (f.).   4 Here 'could she?' might = 'was she able to?' or 'should she be able to?' Select *pouvait* or *pourrait* according to what you take to be the sense of 'could.'   5 *comme.*   6 Is there the same doubt here as in note 4, about the sense of 'could'?   7 *l'un.*   8 Preposition? p. 85, § 48, IN.

20. THE DAISY AND THE LARK. iii

'We can cut a nice piece of turf here for the Lark,' said one[1] of the boys: and he began to cut deep all round the Daisy, leaving her in the centre.

'Tear[2] out the flower,' said the other boy: and the little Daisy trembled with[3] fear: for she knew that if she were torn[4] out she would die, and she wished so much to live and go into the cage to keep the Lark company.

'No, leave it!' said the first, 'it looks so pretty'; and so she was put[4] into the Lark's cage.

But the poor bird lamented loudly the loss of his freedom and dashed against the iron[5] bars; and the little flower could not speak—could not say a single word of comfort to him, though she wished very much to do so. Thus passed[6] the whole morning[7].

Hans Andersen

1 *l'un.*   2 Second person singular or plural? p. 39, § 23, 3.   3 *de.*   4 Avoid the Passive; p. 47, § 33, 2.   5 Preposition? Model Lesson I, p. 97.   6 *passer* or *se passer*? p. 72, § 44, PASSER.   7 *matin* or *matinée*? p. 87, § 49, AN, ANNÉE, etc.

21. THE DAISY AND THE LARK. iv

'There is no water here!' sang the captive Lark;
'everybody has gone out and I am forgotten; not a
drop of water to drink and my throat is dry and
burning. Alas! I must die; I must leave the sunshine,
the green trees and all the beautiful things God has
created!' and then he thrust his beak into the grass
in order to refresh himself a little—and his eye[1] fell
upon the Daisy, and the bird greeted her and said,
'Thou[2], too, must wither here, poor little flower! They
have given me[3] thee, with the piece of green turf
around thee, instead of the whole world[4] which I
possessed before[5]! Every little blade of grass henceforth is[6] to be to me[7] a green tree, every white petal
a fragrant flower! Alas! thou only[8] remindest me of
what I have lost!'

Hans Andersen

1 Here, as often, 'his eye' is *son regard*.   2 Use the
accented form.   3 Use *à moi*.   4 *le vaste monde*; *tout le
monde* would mean 'everybody.'   5 An Adverb; p. 84, § 48,
BEFORE.   6 Use *devoir*.   7 *pour moi*.   8 See p. 80, § 46,
ONLY, 2.

22. THE DAISY AND THE LARK. v

'Oh! if only I could comfort him!' thought the
Daisy; but though she could[1] not move a single petal,
the fragrance which came from her was sweet and
fresh. The bird noticed it, and although, panting with[2]
thirst, he tore[1] the green blades of grass, he did not
touch[3] the flower.

Evening fell, and yet no one came to bring the poor
bird a drop of water. His song became a mournful
wail and at last he fell dying on the bottom of the cage.

The boys did not come till[4] the next morning: and
when they saw the bird was dead, they wept bitterly.
They put him into a pretty box and buried him in the
garden.

But the piece of turf which contained the Daisy was thrown into the street; no one thought of her, who had most pitied the little bird and who had[5] so much wished to comfort him.

Hans Andersen

1 Mood? p. 55, § 40, 5.   2 *de.*   3 *toucher* is intransitive and takes *à.*   4 *avant.*   5 Turn by 'would have.'

23. THE SPANIARD AND THE INDIAN. i

A Spanish traveller had met an Indian in the midst of a desert. Both were on horseback. The Spaniard, who was afraid his horse could[1] not carry him much further, asked the Indian, who had[2] a younger and stronger one, to make an exchange. He refused, as was right[3]. The Spaniard picked a quarrel with him; they came to blows[4]; but the Spaniard being well armed, easily seized[5] the horse he coveted, and continued his journey. The Indian followed him into the nearest town, and laid his complaint before the Judge. The Spaniard had[6] to appear and bring[7] the horse; he maintained that the Indian was not speaking the truth, that the horse belonged to him, and that he had reared it.

1 Mood? p. 54, § 40, 2 (*d*).   2 Supply *en*; p. 39, § 23, 2. 3 *comme de raison.*   4 Use *en venir aux mains.*   5 Use *s'emparer de*, or *se saisir de.*   6 Use *devoir.* Tense?   7 Beware of *apporter*; p. 13, § 7, BRING.

24. THE SPANIARD AND THE INDIAN. ii

There was no proof of the contrary, and the Judge was about[1] to dismiss both parties[2] when the Indian exclaimed, 'The horse *is* mine, and I will[3] prove it.' He at once took off his cloak, suddenly covered the horse's head with it[4], and, addressing the Judge, said, 'Since this man declares he reared[5] this horse, command him to say which eye he is blind in[6]!' The Spaniard, not wishing to seem[7] to hesitate, immediately replied,

'In the left eye.' Thereupon the Indian, uncovering the horse's head, said, 'He is not blind, either in the left eye or the right.' The Judge, convinced by so ingenious a proof, awarded him the horse.

1 p. 84, § 48, ABOUT.   2 See p. 36, § 18.   3 This is the Immediate Future; p. 57, § 41, WILL.   4 *en.*   5 Use the Infinitive; p. 21, § 10.   6 *de quel œil il est borgne.*   7 Remember that an Infinitive after *sembler* takes no Preposition.

25. THE DAUGHTER'S RETURN

At the close of a pleasant April day Mr Atkins sat[1] at his kitchen fire, with[2] Charley upon his knee[3]. 'Wife,' said he to Mrs Atkins, who was busy preparing the evening[4] meal, 'is it not a year since[5] Annie left home?'—'Yes, it is just a year, and I should not be surprised[6] if she should come this week.' 'Perhaps[7] she will not come[8] at all,' said Mr Atkins with a gloomy look; 'she has not written very often. I suppose she has sense enough[9] to know that no news is better than bad news[10], and having nothing pleasant to tell about herself, she has decided to tell us nothing at all.'

'Pa, the stage-coach has stopped[11] here,' cried little Charley, and he bounded from his father's knee. The next moment the room rang with the shout of 'Annie has come!' In a few moments more[12] she was in her mother's arms.

1 was seated'; p. 90, § 49, SIT.   2 Do not say *avec*; *tenant* is better; p. 86, § 48, WITH.   3 Use the plural.   4 See Model Lesson II, p. 125.   5 'it is a year since' = *il y a un an que.* Make this phrase interrogative and negative. 6 Use *s'étonner que* + Subjunctive.   7 Use *peut-être* with Inversion or, more simply, *peut-être que* without Inversion. 8 In this case 'come,' since it means 'come home,' would be more naturally *revenir* than *venir*; see Model Lesson III, p. 160. 9 Turn as if 'enough of good sense.'   10 Turn by 'it is better to have no news than bad news.'   11 Use the Reflexive; p. 61, § 43, 1.   12 *Encore quelques moments, et.*

26. ALI BABA AND THE FORTY THIEVES. i

One day, when[1] Ali Baba was in the forest, and had just[2] cut enough wood to[3] load his asses, he saw at a distance a great cloud of dust, which seemed to be approaching. He observed it very attentively and soon distinguished a troop of horsemen coming[4] briskly on; and though they[5] did not talk of robbers in that country[6], Ali Baba began to think they might prove so[7], and without considering[8] what would become of[9] his asses, he resolved to save himself[10]. He climbed a large thick tree and placed himself in the middle, from whence he could see all that passed[11] without being[8] seen; and this tree stood[12] at the foot of a rock which rose very high above it and so steep that nobody could climb it.   *The Arabian Nights*

1 Here 'when' is a Relative Adverb, referring to 'day'; p. 78, § 45.   2 p. 77, § 44, VENIR.   3 Construction of the Infinitive? p. 80, § 46, ENOUGH.   4 Use a Relative Clause; p. 52, § 37, 2.   5 Is 'they' definite enough to be = *ils*? or is it = *on*? p. 47, § 33, 2.   6 p. 14, § 7, COUNTRY.   7 *qu'ils pourraient bien en être.*   8 Construction after *sans*? p. 52, § 38, 1.   9 For the construction, see p. 67, § 44, DEVENIR. 10 Use *se mettre en sûreté* or *sauver sa peau.*   11 *passer* or *se passer*? p. 72, § 44, PASSER. Tense? Is it 'all that *was* going on' or 'all that *would be* going on'?   12 p. 91, § 49, STAND.

27. ALI BABA AND THE FORTY THIEVES. ii

The horsemen, who were all well mounted and well armed, came to the foot of this rock and there dismounted. Ali Baba counted forty of them and, by[1] their looks and equipment, never doubted[2] they were thieves. And he was not mistaken; for they were a troop of banditti who, without doing any harm in the neighbourhood, robbed at a distance and made[3] that place their rendezvous. Each man tied his horse to a bush, and hung about his neck a bag of corn which he had carried behind the saddle. Then each of them

took off his portmanteau[4], which seemed to be very
heavy as if it were full of silver or gold. One[5], who
seemed[6] to be their captain, approached the face of
the rock and said in[7] a loud voice: 'Open[8], Sesame!'
As soon as he had uttered[9] these words, a door
opened[8]; and after he had[9] made all his troop go in
before him, he followed them and the door shut[10]
again of itself. *The Arabian Nights*

1 *d'après*. 2 Construction? p. 67, § 44, DOUTER. 3 Turn
as if = 'made of.' 4 'portmanteau' has here its older sense,
which French *portemanteau* (m.) also had = a case carried
behind the saddle. 5 *L'un d'eux.* 6 Remember that
after *sembler* the Infinitive takes no Preposition. 7 Preposition? p. 85, § 48, IN. 8 *ouvrir* or *s'ouvrir*? see Model
Lesson I, p. 98. 9 Tense? p. 79, § 45, 3, WHEN. 10 *fermer*
or *se fermer*? see Model Lesson I, p. 98.

28. ALI BABA AND THE FORTY THIEVES. iii

The robbers stayed some time within the rock and
Ali Baba, who feared[1] that one of them[2] might[3] come
out and catch[1] him if he should endeavour[4] to make
his escape, was obliged to[5] sit[6] patiently in the tree.

At last the door opened again and the forty robbers
came out. The captain had gone in last[7] and he came
out first[7], and stood[8] by the entrance of the cavern
to see them all pass by[9] him; and then Ali Baba heard
him[10] make the door close by pronouncing[11] these
words, 'Shut, Sesame!' Every man went and un-
fastened his horse and mounted again. When the
captain saw them all ready, he put himself at their
head and they returned the same way[12] they came.

Ali Baba did not immediately quit his tree: 'For,'
said he to himself, 'they may have[13] forgotten something and come back again and then I shall be taken.'
He followed them with his eyes as far as he could see
them. Then he came down and, perceiving[14] the door
concealed among the bushes, he stood[15] before it and

said, 'Open, Sesame!' The door instantly flew wide
open. *The Arabian Nights*

1 Remember the construction; p. 54, § 40, 2. 2 *l'un
d'eux.* 3 Here 'might' is not to be translated. 4 Tense?
p. 78, § 45, 2, IF. 5 *à* or *de*? p. 72, § 44, OBLIGER.
6 'remain'; p. 90, § 49, SIT. 7 '*the* last...*the* first.'
8 Use *se tenir.* 9 Use *devant.* 10 Case of the Personal
Pronoun? p. 69, § 44, FAIRE. 11 Beware of *par*; p. 52, § 38, 2.
12 'the same way'; say *du même côté.* 13 *ils peuvent avoir
oublié.* 14 *apercevoir* or *s'apercevoir*? p. 63, § 44. 15 Use
se placer.

29. ALI BABA AND THE FORTY THIEVES. iv

Ali Baba, who expected to find a dark, dismal grotto,
was very much surprised to find a well-lighted vault
full of gold and silver and rich silk stuffs. He did not
stay long to[1] consider what he should do but went
immediately into the cave and, as soon as he was[2] in,
the door shut again. But this did not disturb him for
he knew the secret to[3] open it again. He never looked
at the silver but made the best use of his time in[1]
carrying out as much of the gold coin, which was in
bags, as his three asses could carry. When he had
done, he collected his asses, which had wandered away,
and when he had loaded them with[4] the bags, laid the
wood on them in such a manner that[5] they could not
be seen. Then he stood[6] before the door and pronounced
the words, 'Shut, Sesame!' and the door closed after
him. It had shut itself while he was within but remained open while[7] he was out. He then drove his
asses back[8] to town and arrived at nightfall, and got
home without anyone seeing[9] the bags of gold hidden
under the faggots. *The Arabian Nights*

1 *à* + Infinitive; p. 52, § 37, 2. 2 Tense? p. 77, § 45, AS
SOON AS. 3 *pour.* 4 *de.* 5 Does *de façon que* require
here the Indicative or the Subjunctive? p. 56, § 40, 7. 6 Use
se placer. 7 *tant que.* 8 How can 'drove back' be most
neatly rendered? p. 79, § 46, AGAIN. 9 *sans que* + Subjunctive.

30. A SPLENDID PRESENT

As they drove down[1] the avenue, under the arching trees[2], the Earl was rather[3] silent. But Fauntleroy was[4] not. He talked about the pony. What colour was it? How big was it[5]? What was its name? What did it like to eat best? How old was it? How early in the morning might[6] he get up and see it?

'Dearest[7] will be so glad!' he kept saying. 'She will be so much obliged to you for being[8] so kind to[9] me! She knows I always liked ponies so much, but we never thought[10] I should have one. There was a little boy on[11] Fifth Avenue who[12] had one[13], and he used to ride out[14] every morning and we used to take a walk past[15] his house to see him.

'I think you must be the best person in the world,' he burst forth at last. 'You are always doing good, aren't you?—and thinking about other people. Dearest says that[16] is the best kind of goodness; not to think about[17] yourself[18]; but to think about other people. That is just the way you are[19], isn't it?'

Frances Hodgson Burnett, *Little Lord Fauntleroy*

1 Use *descendre*; *en voiture* could be added, though perhaps unnecessary. 2 *sous la voûte des arbres.* 3 *assez* or *plutôt?* p. 80, § 46, RATHER. 4 Complete the construction; p. 38, § 23, 1. 5 *Comment était-il gros?* 6 Tense of *pouvoir?* p. 56, § 41, COULD. 7 *Chérie.* 8 'for (*de*) having been.' 9 *pour.* 10 Tense? 11 *dans.* 12 Transpose, so that the Relative may be next its Antecedent; p. 44, § 28, 3. 13 What word must be supplied? p. 39, § 23, 2. 14 It will be enough to say in French 'ride it.' 15 Use, e.g., *passer devant.* 16 p. 42, § 26, 4. 17 Preposition? p. 73, § 44, PENSER. 18 *soi-même* or *vous-même?* p. 47, § 33, 1. 19 *comme vous êtes.*

31. A TALL STORY

A traveller crossing[1] a desert was passing under a high rock when suddenly a lion sprang at him. Fortunately the lion overshot the mark, and before he could[2] recover himself, the traveller had time to get

safely away. Having to[3] return by the same route a
few weeks later, he provided himself with a rifle and
determined to take his revenge. When he was still far
from the fatal spot, he could see the lion on the same
rock, but, strange to say, every now and then the lion
disappeared and soon came again into view. The
traveller was much puzzled and wondered what the
lion could be doing. When he came nearer, he knew[4].
The lion was practising low jumps[5].

1 Use a Relative Clause; p. 52, § 37, 2.   2 Mood? p. 55,
§ 40, 5.   3 Use *avoir à*.   4 Tense?   5 Use *s'exercer au
saut en longueur*.

32. IDA'S FLOWERS. i

'My poor flowers are quite faded!' said little Ida.
'Only[1] yesterday evening they were so pretty and now
they are all[2] drooping! What[3] can be the reason of
it?' she asked of[4] the Student, who was sitting in the
armchair and whom she liked very much because he
used to tell her pretty stories. 'Why do these flowers
look so withered?' asked she again, showing him a
bouquet of faded flowers.

'Do you not know?' replied the Student. 'Your
flowers went to a ball[5] last night[6], and are tired; that
is why they all hang their heads.'

'Surely flowers cannot dance!' exclaimed little Ida.

'Of course they can dance! When it is dark, and[7]
we are all gone to bed, they jump about as merrily as
possible. They go to a ball[5] almost every night[6].'

'Do their children go to the ball too?' asked Ida.

'Yes,' replied the Student; 'the little daisies and
lilies of the valley.'

Hans Andersen

1 *Pas plus tard qu'hier.*   2 Here 'all' is adverbial; p. 87,
§ 49, ALL.   3 Adjectival, p. 45, § 31, 3, WHAT.   4 *à.*   5 French
says *aller* au *bal*, as we say 'to go to *the* theatre.'   6 *nuit* or
soir? p. 15, § 7, NIGHT.   7 What must be supplied here?
p. 79, § 45, 4, WHEN.

33. IDA'S FLOWERS. ii

Little Ida thought what the Student had told her about the flowers was very droll, and she could not leave off thinking of[1] it. She was now sure that her flowers hung their heads[2] because they were tired with[3] dancing so much the night before. So she took them to the pretty little table where her playthings were arranged. Her doll lay sleeping[4] in its cradle but Ida said to her, 'You must get up, Sophy, and be content to sleep to-night in the table drawer, for the poor flowers are ill and are going to sleep in your bed; perhaps they will be well again to-morrow.'

She then took the doll out of her bed; but that young lady looked[5] vexed because she had to give up her bed to the flowers.

Ida then laid the faded flowers in her doll's bed, drew the covering over them, and told them to lie quite still, whilst she made[5] some tea for them, in order that they might be well again next day. And she drew the curtains round the bed, that the sun might not dazzle their eyes.

Hans Andersen

1 Preposition? p. 73, § 44, PENSER.   2 Use the Singular, Model Lesson I, p. 99.   3 *d'avoir tant dansé*.   4 'slept lying.' 5 Tense?

34. IDA'S FLOWERS. iii

During the night Ida woke. She had been dreaming of what the Student had told her about the flowers. All was still in the room, the night-lamp was burning on the table, and her father and mother[1] were both asleep.

'I wonder whether my flowers are still lying in Sophy's bed?' said she. 'I should very much like to know.' She raised herself a little and looking towards the door, which stood[2] half-open, she saw that the flowers and all her playthings were just as[3] she had left them.

She listened and it seemed to her she heard someone playing softly on[4] the piano.

'Now my flowers must certainly be[5] dancing,' said she. 'Oh, how I should like to see them!' but she dared not get up for fear of waking her father and mother[1]. 'If they would only come in here!' Still the flowers did not come, and the music sounded[6] so sweet. At last she could restrain herself no longer, she must see[7] the dancing. So she crept lightly out of bed and stole towards the door of the room. Oh, what wonderful things she saw there!   Hans Andersen

1 The Possessive Adjective cannot be omitted in French.
2 'was.'   3 *exactement comme.*   4 Preposition? p. 86, § 48,
ON.   5 Use *en train de* + Infinitive; see Model Lesson II,
p. 125.   6 *avait un ton.*   7 *il fallait que* + Subjunctive.

35. IDA'S FLOWERS. iv

There was no night-lamp there but it was quite light[1] in the room, for the full moon shone through[2] the windows. All the hyacinths and the tulips stood there in two rows, whilst their empty pots might still be seen in front of the windows; they were dancing, and took hold of[3] each other by their long leaves. At the piano sat a large yellow lily which Ida thought she had[4] seen before, for she remembered that the Student had said that this flower was very like Miss Laura, and how everyone had laughed at[5] this remark. Now she herself agreed that the lily did[6] resemble this young lady, for she had exactly her way of playing, bowing her long yellow face[7] now on[5] one side, now on the other. A tall blue crocus went up to the doll's cradle and drew aside the curtains. The sick flowers which were lying there at once rose and greeted the other flowers, who invited them to dance with them. The sick flowers appeared quite well again and danced as merrily as the rest[8].   Hans Andersen

1 *il faisait très clair.*   2 *par.*   3 'to take hold of' = *se tenir.*   4 Use the Infinitive; p. 66, § 44, CROIRE.   5 Preposition? p. 86, § 48, ON.   6 Use *vraiment.*   7 *sa tête* or *son visage?*   8 p. 90, § 49, REST.

SECTION II

MODEL LESSON II

A CONVERSATION

1. 'I have been taking my evening walk with the dog,' said my father, 'and on the way I met my boy's master, Mr S. 2. We shook hands, and after walking a little further, we turned back together talking about this and that, the state of the country, the weather and the dog, which he greatly admired, though it nearly bit him when he attempted to pat its head. 3. We then began talking about the boy; it was myself who introduced that subject; I thought it was a good opportunity to learn how he was getting on, so I asked what he thought of him. 4. He hesitated at first, seeming scarcely to know what to say. 5. At length he came out with: "Oh, a very extraordinary youth, a most remarkable youth indeed, captain." 6. "Come, come," said I, feeling rather uneasy, "it is evident that you are not altogether satisfied with him. 7. I was afraid you would not be, for, although he is my own son, I see his faults quite well; but do tell me what particular fault you find with him, and I will do my best to make him alter his conduct."'

Scottish Education Department, Higher Leaving Certificate Examinations, 1925.

1. 'I have been taking my evening walk with the dog,' said my father, 'and on the way I met my boy's master, Mr S.'

'I have been taking my evening walk.' The first difficulty is the idiom. As in so many other cases, French uses *faire*. 'To take a walk' is faire *une promenade*. The second difficulty is the verbal form. *J'ai fait ma promenade* will not be a sufficient translation. That would mean 'I have taken,' or 'I took,' my walk and would not quite render 'I have *been* taking.' Sometimes no doubt the English progressive form is adequately rendered by the simple French tense, e.g. 'I am reading' may be merely = *Je lis.* But often there is more in the English than that. Thus 'We were removing when the war broke out' may be not, *Nous déménagions*, but *Nous étions en train de déménager*, quand la guerre éclata. Here *Je viens de faire ma promenade* or *Je reviens de ma promenade* gives the fuller sense of the English phrase.

'evening' is *du soir*, exactly as in '*Pâle étoile* du *soir*,' or in *le train* du *soir*.

'on the way': not of course *sur la route*, which means 'on the *road*,' nor *en route*, which implies proceeding to a fixed destination, 'on the march' towards a certain objective, and not merely being out for a walk. A nearer approach to the precise meaning is the idiomatic *chemin faisant*, but it is not quite right here. It usually suggests 'doing something else at the same time,' taking something 'in one's stride'; thus *chemin faisant, je songeais que...* is a natural expression, but *chemin faisant, j'ai rencontré quelqu'un*, would be a rather odd one. For our sentence *en chemin* is better, being free from any of these implications.

'I met.' The tone is conversational and demands not the literary, formal, dry-as-dust Past Historic, *je rencontrai*, but the more homely *j'ai rencontré*.

'my boy's master.' We have seen (p. 12, § 7) that *garçon*, unless when qualified (e.g. *un* petit *garçon*), seldom translates 'boy.' The context suggests that *fils* is meant; if so, it should be used. The 'master' might be either a school-master = *un maître d'école*, or else the boy's employer, *son patron*. As a matter of fact he was *son patron*, but there is nothing in the passage itself to show this and *un maître* has both senses.

'Je viens de faire ma promenade du soir avec le chien,' dit mon père, 'et en chemin j'ai rencontré le maître de mon fils, M. S.'

2. 'We shook hands, and after walking a little further, we turned back together talking about this and that, the state of the country, the weather and the dog, which he greatly admired, though it nearly bit him when he attempted to pat its head.'

'We shook hands.' The simplest form of the expression is 'I shook hands with him,' in French *Je lui ai donné* (or *tendu* or, more cordially, *serré*) *la main*. The reflexive form of this is *Nous nous sommes donné la main*, where it must be remembered that *main* is the direct, and *nous* the indirect, object of *donné*, and that therefore *donné* does not take the plural *s*. The expression most likely to occur to a French speaker is, however, *Nous avons échangé des poignées de mains*. Could a candidate fairly be expected to know such idioms? He certainly could not arrive at them by reasoning. But reasoning power is not the only thing that examiners have to test. They have to test also knowledge of French, and it is obvious that we must possess a stock of ready-made expressions before we can hope to translate properly. There is only one way to acquire them, and that is to learn them by heart.

The same remark applies to 'walking a little further.' The translation offered by a good candidate might be *après avoir marché un peu plus loin*. But that is not the correct French translation: *faire un petit bout de chemin* is the normal equivalent of the English phrase. Neither *se promener* nor *marcher* suits nearly so well; *se promener* means to take a walk for pleasure; we know already that the speaker was only out for a walk and we do not wish to hear it again; *marcher* is the physical act of walking as opposed to *courir*, etc.; *aller à pied* is walking as opposed to driving or riding; it would not occur to us that the speaker came home by any other means of locomotion and we resent being told what we can perfectly well imagine. 'After doing something' in French is never '*après faire*,' but always *après* avoir *fait quelque chose* and that fact (mentioned p. 52, § 38) must now be learned once for all.

'we turned back together.' Neither *retourner*, 'to go back,' nor *se retourner*, in 'to turn round,' is suitable here. A useful expression is *rebrousser chemin*, but it would not come in very naturally, though correct enough and idiomatic. It often happens that what appears at first a good idiomatic expression is in reality not so appropriate as a simpler phrase. The simplest and the best plan is to say *nous sommes rentrés ensemble*.

'talking about this and that.' French writers do not usually say *parlant de ceci et de cela*. Why not? There is no answer to that question. It is simply not said, and we must find a colloquial expression which *is* said. There is no way to find one except by ransacking our memories. If suitable expressions are there, such as *parlant de la pluie et du beau temps*, or *parlant de choses et d'autres*, well and good. If not, there is nothing for it but to paraphrase as best we can. Bricks cannot be made without straw. Neither can French passages be composed without French phrases. We must stock our memories with useful phrases, one by one, until we have a sufficient supply. Till then we are liable to be caught unprepared, and thrown back on sorry makeshifts.

'the state of the country.' This phrase is very vague. The subject of conversation may, for all we know, have been the state of the crops, the political situation, settled or unsettled conditions in the business or the labour world, etc. According as we interpret the words, we shall say *l'état des récoltes* or *la condition du pays*. As regards the construction of 'state' (and also 'weather' and 'dog'), has 'about' to be understood? If so, we must say *de l'état* and repeat *de* before the other two words. Or are we to suppose that the speaker pauses, as it were, after 'this and that' and gives examples of what 'this and that' turned out to be? In that case it would be well to supply a connecting phrase in French such as *par exemple* or *telles que*, or else to put a semi-colon after *d'autres*.

'the weather.' If they spoke about the weather generally, this would be *du temps*; if they meant that evening only, it would be best to say *du temps qu'il fait*.

'and the dog, which he greatly admired.' The only point to note here is the position of the Adverb in French (see p. 79, § 46): *qu'il a* beaucoup *admiré*.

'though it nearly bit him.' The chief danger here is that of forgetting that *quoique* requires the Subjunctive. The usual idiom for 'nearly' + Verb is *faillir*, as in the famous remark of Louis XIV, '*J'ai failli attendre*.' Thus, we say *quoiqu'il ait failli le mordre*. If ambiguity is feared, *l'animal* can be substituted for *il*.

'when he attempted to pat its head.' The exact French for 'to pat' would be *tapoter*, or *donner de petites tapes*, but when we 'pat,' the French 'stroke,'

i.e. *flatter*, to smooth down with the 'flat' of one's hand,
or *caresser*. To translate the phrase as *caresser sa tête*
would be quite correct, but *lui caresser la tête* is better,
because more idiomatic.

'Nous nous sommes donné la main, et après avoir
fait un petit bout de chemin, nous sommes rentrés
ensemble, parlant de choses et d'autres, des récoltes,
du temps, et du chien, qu'il a beaucoup admiré, quoiqu'il ait failli le mordre quand il a essayé de lui caresser
la tête.'

3. 'We then began talking about the boy; it was
myself who introduced that subject; I thought it was
a good opportunity to learn how he was getting on,
so I asked what he thought of him.'

'We then began talking': *Puis nous nous sommes mis
à parler* is less formal (something like 'we fell a-talking,'
vulgarly, 'we got talking') than *Puis nous avons com-
mencé à parler*.

'about the boy': *du garçon* generally means 'about
the waiter'; *de* notre *garçon* or *de* notre *fils* seems to
be required. The fact must not be overlooked that
'introduced' is in the 1st person, since the 'who'
refers to 'myself.' For 'to introduce' (a subject) *introduire* is less commonly used than *mettre sur le tapis*.

For 'I thought it was a good opportunity' it would
be incorrect to say 'Je croyais que c'était une bonne
occasion.' That would mean 'I thought [but afterwards
found out that I was wrong] that,' etc. *Je trouvais*
is not open to that objection. *Cela me paraissait une
bonne occasion* is perhaps the most natural expression.

For 'how he was getting on' *quel progrès il faisait*,
or *comment cela allait*, or *comment il travaillait (se con-
duisait)* will do. If *aussi* is used for 'so' Inversion will
be necessary. Beginners are strongly tempted to use

si when translating 'so'; they must resist this temptation, save in expressions like 'so fast' = *si vite*, 'so big' = *si gros*; 'so' = *si*, only before an Adjective or an Adverb.

'Puis nous nous sommes mis à parler de notre fils; c'est moi-même qui ai mis ce sujet sur le tapis; cela me paraissait une bonne occasion d'apprendre comment il travaillait; aussi lui ai-je demandé ce qu'il pensait de lui.'

4. 'He hesitated at first, seeming scarcely to know what to say.'

For 'hesitated' the use of the Past Historic is justifiable, as at this point the tone almost becomes narrative. The normal position for such an Adverb of time in French being the beginning of the sentence, it is best to transpose: *D'abord il a hésité, semblant savoir à peine ce qu'il devait* (or *fallait*) *dire* or, much better, *que dire*.

5. 'At length he came out with: "Oh, a very extraordinary youth, a most remarkable youth indeed, captain."'

'At length he came out with.' 'At length' and 'came out with' suggest that the tone of the French here should now become narrative and that *s'écria* will be more appropriate than *s'est écrié*.

For 'very extraordinary' *extraordinaire* is quite enough, because French seldom uses *très* with a very strong adjective like *extraordinaire* or *affreux*.

'captain.' To military titles soldiers prefix *mon* when they address their officers, e.g. *mon lieutenant, mon capitaine*, and men who have been in the Army often continue the practice in civil life. Otherwise, the form of address is *Monsieur le capitaine* or, familiarly, to a personal acquaintance, *capitaine*.

'Enfin, il s'écria: "Oh, c'est un jeune homme extraordinaire, en effet un jeune homme des plus remarquables, capitaine."'

6. '"Come, come," said I, feeling rather uneasy, "it is evident that you are not altogether satisfied with him."'

It is perhaps unnecessary to translate 'feeling'; *me sentant* could be omitted. For 'evident' *clair* is more exact than *évident*, which means 'obvious.' For 'satisfied' *satisfait* is correct, but *content* is more characteristically French: cp. Napoleon's order after Austerlitz: '*Soldats, je suis* content *de vous.*'

'"Allons, allons," dis-je, un peu inquiet, "il est clair que vous n'êtes pas tout à fait content de lui."'

7. '"I was afraid you would not be, for, although he is my own son, I see his faults quite well; but do tell me what particular fault you find with him, and I will do my best to make him alter his conduct."'

'I was afraid you would not be': in full = *Je craignais bien que vous ne le fussiez pas*, but much more simply, and better, *J'en avais bien peur*.

'I see his faults.' *Je vois* or *j'aperçois* will do, but *je me rends compte de* is clearer. 'Faults' are not mistakes made by the boy, i.e. *ses fautes* (f.), but weaknesses in his character, his 'failings,' i.e. *ses défauts* (m.). When translation results in such a repetition as J'en avais *bien* peur, car, *bien* qu'il soit mon fils, je me rends *bien* compte, etc., the translator's resources are not exhausted. There are other words than *bien que* and *bien*, viz. *quoique* and *parfaitement*.

'what particular fault you find with him.' On the analogy of phrases like *Je lui trouve de l'esprit; Je vous*

croyais plus de courage; Je ne lui trouve aucun défaut
= 'I find no defect in him,' we shall say here: *quel
défaut particulier vous* lui *trouvez.*

'to make him alter his conduct.' If *changer* were a
transitive Verb and taking a direct object, then *lui*
would have been required, not *le*, as in, e.g. *Je* lui *ai
fait faire un habit.* But here *changer* is construed with *de*
[e.g. *changer de train*] and its object is an indirect one.

'"J'en avais bien peur, car, quoiqu'il soit mon fils,
je me rends parfaitement compte de ses défauts, mais
dites-moi, je vous en prie, quel défaut particulier vous
lui trouvez et je ferai de mon mieux pour le faire
changer de conduite."'

Suggested Rendering

'Je viens de faire ma promenade du soir avec le
chien,' dit mon père, 'et en chemin j'ai rencontré le
maître de mon fils, M. S. Nous nous sommes donné la
main, et après avoir fait un petit bout de chemin, nous
sommes rentrés ensemble, parlant de choses et d'autres,
des récoltes, du temps, et du chien, qu'il a beaucoup
admiré, quoiqu'il ait failli le mordre quand il a essayé
de lui caresser la tête. Puis nous nous sommes mis à
parler de notre fils; c'est moi-même qui ai mis ce sujet
sur le tapis; cela me paraissait une bonne occasion
d'apprendre comment il travaillait; aussi lui ai-je demandé ce qu'il pensait de lui. D'abord il a hésité,
semblant savoir à peine que dire. Enfin, il s'écria: "Oh,
c'est un jeune homme extraordinaire, en effet un jeune
homme des plus remarquables, capitaine." "Allons,
allons," dis-je, un peu inquiet, "il est clair que vous
n'êtes pas tout à fait content de lui. J'en avais bien

peur, car, quoiqu'il soit mon fils, je me rends parfaitement compte de ses défauts, mais dites-moi, je vous
en prie, quel défaut particulier vous lui trouvez et je
ferai de mon mieux pour le faire changer de conduite."'

86. WASHERWOMEN IN FAIRYLAND

As Jack was thinking of[1] jumping on shore, he saw
two little old women approaching[2] and gently driving
a white horse before them.

The horse had[3] panniers, one on[4] each side; and
when his feet were in the water he stood still[5]; and
Jack said to one of the old women, 'Will you be so
kind as to tell me whether this is[6] Fairyland?'

'What does he say?' asked one old woman of[7] the
other.

'I asked if this was Fairyland,' repeated Jack, for
he thought the first old woman might have been[8] deaf.
She was very handsomely dressed in[9] a red satin gown,
and did not look in the least[10] like a washerwoman,
though it afterwards appeared[11] that she was one[12].

Jean Ingelow, *Mopsa the Fairy*

1 Construction of the Verb? p. 73, § 44, PENSER.   2 Alter
to 'saw approaching two...women who,' etc.   3 Use *porter*.
4 Preposition? p. 86, § 48, ON.   5 p. 91, § 49, STAND.
6 *c'est ici.*   7 *à.*   8 'was perhaps.'   9 *de.*   10 'in
the least' = *le moins du monde.*   11 Mood? p. 55, § 40, 5.
12 Supply *en*; p. 39, § 23, 2.

87. BEAUTIFUL STOCKINGS

The little woman went on[1] knitting, and Jack began
to eat the[2] breakfast.

'I wonder what has become of[3] my stockings,' said
Jack.

'You will never see[4] them any more,' said the old
woman. 'I threw them into[5] the river, and they
floated away[6].'

'Why did you⁷?' asked Jack.

The little woman took no notice⁸; but presently she had finished a beautiful pair of stockings, and she handed them to Jack, and said⁹:

'Is that like the pair¹⁰ you lost?'

'Oh no,' said Jack, 'these are much more beautiful stockings than mine¹¹.'

'Do you like them as well¹²?' asked the fairy woman.

'I like them much better,' said Jack, putting them on⁹. 'How clever you are¹³!'

'Would you like to¹⁴ wear these,' said the woman, 'instead of yours?'

She gave Jack¹⁵ such a strange look when⁹ she said this, that he was afraid to take them, and answered:

'I shouldn't like to wear them if you think I had better not¹⁶.'

Jean Ingelow, *Mopsa the Fairy*

1 See p. 65, § 44, CONTINUER.   2 'his.'   3 Is 'of' to be translated? p. 67, § 44, DEVENIR.   4 Use *revoir*.   5 *à*.
6 Use *aller au fil de l'eau*.   7 Supply 'do that.'   8 Turn by 'did not reply.'   9 Use *en* with the verbal form in *-ant*.
10 Turn by 'Is this pair like that which.'   11 See p. 49, § 35, 3.   12 'as well' = *autant*.   13 The French order is 'How you are clever!'   14 Use *aimer* + Infinitive.
15 *lança à Jack*.   16 Turn by 'I should not do so'; p. 57, § 41, SHOULD.

38. TOM THUMB

Tom Thumb soon showed himself to be¹ a clever little fellow, who always knew what he was about². One day, as the woodman was getting ready to go into the wood to cut fuel, he said, 'I wish I had³ someone to bring the cart after me, for I must make haste.' 'Oh, father!' cried Tom, 'I will take care of that; the cart shall be in the wood by the time you want it.' Then the woodman laughed, and said, 'How can that be⁴? You cannot reach up to the horse's bridle.' 'Never mind that⁵, father,' said Tom; 'if my mother will⁶ only harness the horse I will get into his

ear, and tell him which way to go.' 'Well,' said the
father, 'we will try for once.'   Grimm

1 Use *se révéler comme*. Tense?   2 'was doing.'   8 Use
vouloir with the Infinitive; p. 20, § 10.   4 *se faire*.   5 *Ne
vous en tourmentez pas.*   6 Tense? p. 57, § 41, WILL.

89. THE GOLDEN WINDOWS

All day long the little boy worked hard, in field and
barn and shed, for his people[1] were poor farmers, and
could not pay a workman; but at sunset there came
an hour that was all his own[2], for his father had given
it to him.

Then the boy would go[3] up to the top of a hill, and
look across at another hill that rose some miles away.
On this far hill stood a house with windows of clear
gold and diamonds. They shone and blazed so that it
made the boy wink[4] to[5] look at them; but, after a
while, the people in the house put up the shutters, as
it seemed[6], and then it looked like any[7] common
farm-house.

The boy supposed they did this because it was
supper-time; and then he would go[8] into the house and
have his supper of bread and milk, and so[9] to bed.

Laura E. Richards, *The Golden Windows*

1 Here = *ses parents*.   2 *qui était toute à lui*.   8 Tense?
p. 58, § 41, WOULD.   4 p. 69, § 44, FAIRE.   5 Omit 'to
look at them.'   6 *lui semblait-il*. Note the Inversion used in
a parenthesis.   7 p. 48, § 34, ANY.   8 Use *rentrer*; see
Model Lesson III, p. 160.   9 'went' is enough.

40. MY FIRST MONTHS

The first place that I can[1] well remember, was a
large pleasant meadow with[2] a pond of clear water in it.
Some shady trees leaned over it, and rushes and water-
lilies grew at the deep end[3]. Over the hedge on one
side we looked into[4] a ploughed field, and on the other
we looked over a gate at our master's house, which

stood by the roadside; at the top of the meadow was a plantation of fir trees, and at the bottom a running brook overhung by a steep bank[5]. In the day time[6] I ran by my mother's side, and at night I lay down close by her. When it was hot[7], we used to stand by the pond in the shade of the trees, and when it was cold, we had a nice warm shed near the plantation.

Anna Sewell, *Black Beauty*

1 Mood? p. 54, § 40, 4.   2 'in which there was'; p. 45, § 30.   3 *au bout où l'eau était le plus profonde.*   4 'we saw.'   5 'which a steep bank overhung (*surplomber*); p. 43, § 28, 1 and p. 88, § 49, INVERSION.   6 *Le jour.*   7 Remember the idiom with *faire.*

41. ALL'S WELL THAT ENDS WELL. i

An honest working-man was returning[1] to a certain city by the evening[2] train after a hard day's work in the country. He sat[3] all alone in the compartment, peacefully smoking[4] his pipe. At the last station before[5] the terminus, a lady came in, holding in her arms a little dog. The strong smell of tobacco pleased neither the lady nor her dog, and she requested the workman, rather sharply, to stop smoking. He pointed out that it was a smoking compartment, that the train was half-empty, that she had had plenty of time to choose her compartment, that there were first-class carriages as well as thirds, and that in any case they would arrive at their[6] destination in a few minutes.

1 p. 16, § 7, RETURN.   2 Model Lesson II, p. 125.   3 'was sitting.'   4 Turn by 'and was smoking.'   5 *avant*, not *devant*, because = 'before they came to' and suggesting time rather than place.   6 Omit 'their.'

42. ALL'S WELL THAT ENDS WELL. ii

These remarks, however, made the lady very angry. She opened both windows[1] and, when the little dog began to sneeze, she lost her temper and, snatching the man's pipe, flung it out of the window. Thereupon he², too, lost his temper, seized the little dog and threw him after the pipe—which³ was of course a very wicked thing to do⁴. A few minutes later, the train drew up in the station, and the lady and the workman were explaining matters to the station-master when suddenly they saw the little dog come⁵ trotting up, wagging his tail and proudly carrying the pipe in his mouth.

1 To 'open the window' of a railway carriage is *baisser la glace.*   2 Use the accented form.   3 p. 44, § 28, 4.   4 'thing' = *action* (f.); 'to do' is not to be translated.   5 *s'en venir à eux.*

43. THE FLIGHT OF THE MERMAID. i

Dick was no sooner gone than¹ Mrs Fitzgerald set about cleaning up the house, and, chancing to pull down² a fishing-net, she found, in a hole in the wall, her own magic cap.

She took it out and looked at it, and then she thought of³ her father, the king of the waves, and her mother the queen, and her brothers and sisters, and she felt a longing to go back to them.

She sat down on a little stool and thought over the happy days she had spent under the sea; then she looked at her children, and thought on the love and affection of poor Dick, and feared it⁴ would break his heart to lose her. 'But,' says she, 'he won't lose me entirely, for I'll come back to him again, and who can blame me for⁵ going to see my father and mother after being⁶ so long away from them?'

T. C. Croker, *The Lady of Gollerus*

1 Use *à peine...que.*   2 Use the Present Participle and *par hasard.*   3 Preposition? p. 73, § 44, PENSER.   4 *cela.*   5 *de* + Infinitive.   6 What must be supplied with *après*? p. 52, § 38, 1.

44. THE FLIGHT OF THE MERMAID. ii

She got up and went towards the door, but came back again to look once more at the child that was sleeping in the cradle. She kissed it gently, and as she kissed it, her eyes filled with tears, which fell on its[1] rosy cheek. She wiped away the tears and, turning to her eldest child, the little girl, told her to take good care of her brothers, and to be good herself till she came back[2]. She then went down to the shore. The sea was lying[3] calm and smooth and she thought she heard[4] a faint sweet singing inviting her to come down[5]. All her old feelings came flooding over her mind, Dick and her children were at the instant forgotten, and, placing the magic cap on her head, she plunged in.

Dick came home in the evening, and, missing[6] his wife, he asked Kathleen, his little girl, what had become of[7] her mother, but she could not tell him[8].

T. C. Croker, *The Lady of Gollerus*

1 Is there danger of ambiguity? 2 Must a Verb be used? p. 21, § 10. 3 Use *s'étendre*. 4 Use the Infinitive construction; p. 20, § 10. 5 Where? Complete the expression; p. 39, § 23, 2. 6 'not finding.' 7 'what her mother had become'; p. 67, § 44, DEVENIR. 8 Complete the construction of the Verb; p. 38, § 23, 1.

45. THE TWO PEARS

A famous gardener, called Thouin, had a pear-tree which used to bear fruit[1] of[2] extraordinary size. One year it produced only two pears, but they were enormous. Thouin decided to send them to the celebrated naturalist Buffon, who lived in[3] the same district. When they were nice and[4] ripe, Thouin placed them in a basket and told a young gardener to carry them, with a letter, to Buffon. It was in the height[5] of summer and the heat was overwhelming. The messenger, being very thirsty, gave way to temptation and ate one of the pears. Reaching his destination, he delivered the letter and the remaining pear. Buffon read the letter and asked, 'But where is the other pear then?' 'The other one?' replied the unhappy young man—'I have eaten it!' 'Ah!' cried Buffon, 'such a fine[6] pear! How could you do it?' 'I did it like this, sir,' said the young man, and with these words[7] he grabbed the second pear and ate it.

1 French uses the plural.   2 Must any word be supplied? p. 23, § 11.   3 For Verbs = 'to live,' see Model Lesson I, p. 95.   4 Use *bien*; p. 21, § 10.   5 *au plus fort de l'été.* 6 Not *tel*; see p. 81, § 46, so.   7 *ce disant.*

46. HIPPOCLIDES' DANCE. i

Clisthenes, Tyrant of Sicyon, had only one daughter, but she was exceeding fair. He wished to marry[1] her to the noblest and the best young man in[2] all Greece, and he made proclamation[3] at the Olympic Games that young men of high degree who thought themselves worthy of her should appear at Sicyon within sixty days. There came[4] twelve suitors, and for[5] a whole year they were the guests of Clisthenes, who wished thus to compare them with each other and try their learning, their strength and skill in games, but particularly their breeding. The two who best pleased him were Megacles and Hippoclides, both of Athens, and of these he seemed to prefer Hippoclides.

1 Is this = *épouser* or = *marier*? p. 15, § 7, MARRY.   2 Preposition? p. 85, § 48, IN.   3 Use *faire proclamer.*   4 Use the impersonal third singular.   5 Preposition? p. 84, § 48, FOR.

47. HIPPOCLIDES' DANCE. ii

At length the great day came[1] when Clisthenes must make his choice. He sacrificed a hundred oxen[2] and invited all the citizens of his capital to be present with the suitors at a splendid feast. When the feast was[3] over and the guests were sipping their wine, the twelve vied one with another in displaying their wit and learning, and by common consent Hippoclides outstripped his rivals. At last, being tired of talking,

he called a musician and bade him play upon[4] the
flute. He struck up a dance-tune and Hippoclides
began to dance. He was much pleased with himself[5],
for he could[6] dance beautifully[7], but Clisthenes was not
pleased, and watched him with[8] a sombre look. Then
Hippoclides, the better[9] to show his skill, mounted
upon the table and danced again[10], first[11] in[12] the Attic
manner and next in the manner of the Spartans, and
at last stood upon his head, and with his legs dangling
in the air kept time to[13] the music.

1 Change the order to 'came the great day'; p. 78, § 45,
WHEN.   2 Use *faire une hécatombe.*   3 Tense? But is a
Verb necessary? p. 22, § 10.   4 Preposition? p. 86, § 48, ON.
5 In this phrase *lui* is more common than *lui-même.*   6 *pouvoir* or *savoir*? p. 56, § 41, CAN.   7 *admirablement.*   8 *de.*
9 Omit 'the.'   10 Use *se remettre à danser.*   11 *d'abord.*
12 Preposition? p. 85, § 48, IN.   13 Use *suivre le rythme de*
[notice the spelling *rythme*].

48. HIPPOCLIDES' DANCE. iii

Then Clisthenes could contain himself no longer, and
sadly exclaimed, 'Ah, Hippoclides, Hippoclides, you
have danced your wife away[1]!' And Hippoclides,
continuing to wave his legs in the air, made an answer
which afterwards became a proverb at Athens. He
said, 'Hippoclides doesn't care[2]!'
Then Clisthenes, addressing the twelve suitors, said,
'Gentlemen, I thank you for[3] the honour you have done
me. Right gladly would I make you all my sons-in-law[4].
Alas, I have but one daughter, and there are twelve of
you[5]. So must I send eleven of you away, but to each
of them[6] will I give a talent of silver, and my dear
daughter shall wed[7] Megacles.'

1 Turn by, e.g. 'by dancing you have lost your wife.'
2 Use, e.g. *Qu'importe?* or *n'en a cure,* although a modern
French Hippoclides would probably have used a more vulgar
term.   3 *de.*   4 Turn by 'have you all for sons-in-law.'
5 'you are twelve.'   6 Use *ceux-là.*   7 *épouser.*

49. NAPOLEON AND THE PRIEST

Napoleon was then at the height[1] of his glory. He had conquered half[2] of Europe. He had covered the walls of the Paris churches with[3] the flags which he had taken from[4] the enemy. He was feared abroad, worshipped in France. One day when[5] he was reviewing a regiment in the gardens of the Tuileries he noticed an elderly priest who was making great efforts in the crowd to[6] reach the front row of spectators. Napoleon drew near, made a sign to the priest, and the crowd at once made way, to let him come up. When he stood[7] before the Emperor, the latter said, 'Well, what are you looking at me for, good man?' 'Sire,' replied the priest, 'a good man is surely permitted[8] to look at a great man.' Some weeks later, the priest heard[9] with surprise that he had been made[10] a Bishop.

1 *à l'apogée* (m.).   2 'the half.'   3 Preposition? p. 86, § 48, WITH.   4 *à.*   5 Remember that 'when' relates to 'day'; p. 78, § 45, WHEN.   6 *pour.*   7 *fut* or *se trouva.* 8 Use the impersonal construction: 'it is permitted to.'   9 Use *apprendre.*   10 Use *nommé*, omitting 'a.'

50. THE BISHOP'S MISTAKE

There was once an English Bishop who was very fond of children. One afternoon, as he was going along the street in[1] London where one of his friends lived[2], he suddenly decided to pay the children a visit. He rang the bell[3], and, when the maid opened the door, asked if the ladies[4] were at home. 'Yes, my lord,' she answered, recognizing the Bishop, whom she had often seen at church. 'I know the way. Don't trouble!' said the Bishop, going quickly upstairs, for he wanted to give[5] the children a surprise. He stopped before the drawing-room door, took off his cloak, twisted it round his head, and entered on all fours[6], doing his best to[7] roar like the big lion at[1] the Zoo.

There was[8] a shrill scream, the Bishop uncovered his head as quickly as he could, and beheld two old ladies whom he had never seen before. He had gone to the wrong[9] number.

1 *de*.   2 For Verbs = 'to live,' see Model Lesson I, p. 95.
3 *sonner* alone is enough.   4 *ces dames*.   5 'to give a surprise' is FAIRE *une surprise*.   6 *à quatre pattes*.   7 *faire de son mieux pour*.   8 Tense? Say 'was heard,' using *se faire entendre*, or 'rang out,' using *retentir*.   9 Use *se tromper de*.

51. THE DOCTOR'S MISTAKE

One day a famous doctor was at work[1] in his study when his servant showed in a distinguished-looking[2] stranger. He was extremely pale, and his features expressed the completest weariness. 'Doctor,' he said, 'I have heard of[3] your great skill. Can you cure me? I am not sleeping well, eat[4] very little, and[4] take no interest in anything. I am suffering from an indescribable malady, weariness.' 'Well,' said the doctor, 'are you a rich man?' 'Fairly, I am a millionaire.' 'Then you should[5] travel, see America, Japan, China!' 'Doctor, I have already been round the world[6] several times.' 'Go and live in Paris then, go round the theatres!' 'Doctor, I have just been there[7]. I have seen everything, and was dreadfully[8] bored.' 'In that case, my dear fellow[9], I have only one piece of advice left[10] to[11] give you. You should go every night to the Grand Theatre. The famous Italian singer Velutti is there for[12] a few days. He is very funny. If you want a laugh[13], go and see Velutti!' 'Alas, doctor,' replied the stranger, 'I am Velutti!'

1 'was working.'   2 *qui paraissait très distingué*.   3 What has to be supplied in French? p. 69, § 44, ENTENDRE.   4 Is the Personal Pronoun necessary in French? p. 38, § 23, 1.
5 Use *devoir*; p. 57, § 41, SHOULD.   6 *faire le tour du monde*.
7 *j'en arrive*.   8 *bien* is sufficient.   9 *mon ami*.   10 Use *ne...plus*, as in e.g. 'I have only one cigarette *left*' = *Je n'ai plus* qu'une cigarette.   11 *à*.   12 Preposition? p. 84, § 48, FOR.   13 'want to laugh.'

52. LOG-CARRYING

Prospero had commanded Ferdinand to pile up some heavy logs of wood. Kings' sons not being much used to laborious work, Miranda soon after found the young prince almost dying with[1] fatigue. 'Alas!' said she, 'do not work so hard; my father is at[2] his studies: pray rest yourself.'

'I dare not. I must finish my task before I take[3] my rest.'

'If you will sit[4] down,' said Miranda, 'I will carry your logs the while.' But this Ferdinand would[4] by no means agree to. Instead of a help, Miranda became a hindrance, for they began a long conversation, so that the log-carrying went on very slowly.

Prospero, however, was not at his books as his daughter supposed[5], but was standing by them invisible, to overhear what they said.

Lamb, *Tales from Shakespeare*

1 *de.*   2 *à.*   8 *avant de* + Infinitive; p. 21, § 10.   4 Use *vouloir*; p. 57, § 41, WILL.   5 Complete the construction of the Verb; p. 38, § 23, 1; and invert.

53. A WICKED UNCLE

'Wherefore,' said Miranda, 'did not our enemies destroy us?'

'My child,' answered her father, 'they durst not, so great was the love that my people bore me. Antonio carried[1] us on board a ship, and when we were some[2] leagues out at sea, he forced us[3] into a small boat without mast or[4] sail: there he left[5] us to the mercy of[6] the waves. But a kind lord of my court had privately placed in the boat water, provisions, apparel and some books which I prize above all else[7].'

'O my father,' said Miranda, 'what a trouble[8] I must have been to you[9] then!'

'No, my love,' said Prospero, 'you were a[10] little angel that did preserve me. Your innocent smiles helped me to bear up against my misfortunes. Our food lasted till[11] we landed on this desert island, since when[12] my chief delight has been in[13] teaching you, Miranda, and well have you profited by my instruction.'

Lamb, Tales from Shakespeare

1 'had us carried'; p. 69, § 44, FAIRE.   2 Supply à; p. 83, § 48, 1.   3 'made us go down by force.'   4 ni.   5 p. 89, § 49, LEAVE.   6 à la merci de.   7 'are more precious to me than all the rest'; p. 90, § 49, REST.   8 Use ennui (m.). Is 'a' to be translated? p. 46, § 31.   9 Say 'caused you.' 10 'the.'   11 Mood? p. 55, § 40, 5.   12 'and since then.' 13 Use de + Infinitive.

54. LUCIUS PLEADS FOR THE LIFE OF IMOGEN

Then Lucius spoke thus to the king: 'I hear you take no ransom for[1] your prisoners, but doom them all to death: I am a Roman[2], and will[3] die like a Roman. But there is one thing for which I would entreat[3]. This boy is a Briton born[4]. Let him[5] be ransomed. He[6] is my page. Never master had a page so kind, so diligent on[7] all occasions as he. He hath done no Briton wrong[8], though he hath served a Roman. Save him if you spare no one beside.'

Cymbeline looked earnestly[9] on his daughter Imogen. He knew her not in[10] that disguise but it seemed that all-powerful Nature spake in his heart, for he said, 'I have surely seen him, his face appears familiar to me. I know not why or wherefore I say, Live, boy; but I give you your[11] life, and ask of me[12] what boon you will[13], and I will grant it you. Yea, even though it be[14] the life of the noblest prisoner I have[15].'

'I humbly thank your highness,' said Imogen.

Lamb, Tales from Shakespeare

1 de.   2 Article? p. 22, § 11.   3 Does vouloir seem to be required? p. 57, § 41.   4 Say 'by birth'; p. 22, § 11. 5 Is this = the Imperative or = 'Allow'?   6 Ce or Il? p. 42, § 26, 2.   7 Preposition? p. 86, § 48, ON.   8 Use aucun,

but with the usual precautions; p. 48, § 84.   9 *attentive-ment.*   10 *sous.*   11 Definite Article.   12 Use the dative; p. 66, § 44, DEMANDER.   13 Tense?   14 *même si.*   15 'the noblest of my prisoners.'

55. IMOGEN DISCOVERED IN THE CAVE

Bellarius entered the cave first[1] and, seeing Imogen, stopped the two youths, saying, 'Come not in yet; it[2] eats our victuals or[3] I should think it was[4] a fairy.'

'What is the matter[5], sir[6]?' asked the young men.

'It seems to me,' replied Bellarius, 'that there is an angel in our cave.'

But Imogen, hearing the sound of voices, came forth from the cave and addressed them in[7] these words: 'Good masters, do not harm me; before I entered[8] your cave, I meant to beg or buy what I have eaten. Indeed[9], I have stolen nothing, nor would I[10], though I had[11] found gold strewed on the floor. Here is money for the meat, which[12] I would have left upon the board when I had[13] made my meal, and parted[14] with prayers for the provider[15].' They refused her money with great earnestness. 'I see you are angry with[16] me,' said the timid Imogen, 'but, sirs[6], if you kill me for my fault, know that I should have died if I had not made[17] it.'   Lamb, *Tales from Shakespeare*

1 'the first.'   2 Is 'it' definite enough to be = the Personal Pronoun in French, or indefinite enough to be = *cela*? 3 *autrement.*   4 In such cases French uses the Present. 5 *Qu'est-ce qu'il y a?*   6 *Monsieur* or *Seigneur*?   7 'addressed to them these words.'   8 To use the Infinitive construction will simplify matters; p. 19, § 10. Do not forget that *entrer* is always Intransitive.   9 *En vérité.*   10 'I would not have wished to do so.'   11 *même si.*   12 Since the Relative in French must always come next its Antecedent (p. 44, § 28, 3), it is necessary to alter the English to 'Here is for the meat money which, etc.'   13 Tense?   14 'parted' = 'departed.' Whatever tense you have used in translating 'had made' is required again here.   15 'praying for my provider.'   16 Preposition? p. 86, § 48, WITH.   17 Use *commettre.*

56. THE MAGICIAN'S DESIGN. i

Aladdin, who had never been so far in his life before[1], felt very tired with so long a walk, and said to[2] the magician, 'Where are we going, [3]uncle? We have left the gardens a great way behind us, and I see nothing but mountains; if we go much farther, I do not know whether[4] I shall be able to reach the town again[5].' 'Never[6] fear, [3]nephew,' said the false uncle; 'I will show[7] you another garden which surpasses all we have yet[8] seen; it is not far off, it is but a little step; and when we come[9] there, you will say that you would have been sorry to have been so nigh it, and not[10] seen it.' Aladdin was soon persuaded; and the magician, that the way might seem shorter[11] and less fatiguing, told him a great many stories.

The Arabian Nights

1 'before' is unnecessary.   2 'asked.'   3 Supply 'my.' 4 'whether' = if. Tense? p. 78, § 45, IF.   5 *rentrer.*   6 Not *Jamais.*   7 Immediate Future; p. 57, § 41, WILL.   8 *déjà* or *jusqu'ici?*   9 Tense?   10 Use *sans* + Infinitive.   11 'to make the way appear shorter to him'; p. 69, § 44, FAIRE.

57. THE MAGICIAN'S DESIGN. ii

At last they came between two mountains of moderate height, and equal size, divided by a narrow valley[1], which was the place where the magician intended to bring Aladdin, to put into execution[2] the design which had brought him from Africa to China. 'We will go no farther now,' said he to Aladdin. 'I will show you here some very extraordinary things which nobody ever saw before[3]. While I strike fire[4], do you gather[5] up all the sticks you can see.' Aladdin found there so many dry sticks that before the magician had lighted[6] a match, he had gathered up a great heap[7]. The magician presently set them on fire[8] and when they blazed up he threw in[9] some incense which raised a great cloud of smoke. Then he pronounced several magic words which Aladdin could not understand and the earth trembled and opened and discovered a great flat stone with a brass ring to raise it up by[10]. The magician ordered[11] Aladdin to take hold of the ring and raise[12] the stone.

The Arabian Nights

1 Begin a new sentence. 2 *exécuter*. 3 Use *encore*. 4 Tense? The phrase is *battre le briquet*. 5 The Imperative will be enough. 6 Mood and Tense? 7 Supply 'of them.' 8 The phrase is *mettre le feu à quelque chose*. 9 *y*. 10 Omit 'by.' 11 Construction of the Verb? p. 72, § 44, ORDONNER. 12 Any Preposition used with the preceding Infinitive must be repeated.

58. THE SLAVE OF THE LAMP APPEARS. i

As soon as Aladdin awoke[1] he told his mother that he was very hungry and that he wanted something to eat as soon as possible. 'Alas! child,' said she, 'I have not a bit of bread to give you[2]; you ate up all I had in the house yesterday[3]; but have a little[4] patience and I shall not be long[5] in bringing you some: I have a little[4] cotton which I have spun; I will go[6] and sell it and the money I get[7] for it will buy us some food.'

'Mother,' replied Aladdin, 'keep your cotton for another time[8], and give me the lamp I brought home yesterday. I will[6] go and sell it and buy something for breakfast with the money I get for it[9].'

The Arabian Nights

1 Tense? p. 77, § 45, AS SOON AS. 2 The Second Person singular is clearly required. 3 *hier* should be placed near the verb which it modifies. 4 Remember the two senses; p. 89, § 49, LITTLE. 5 *je ne tarderai guère à* + Infinitive. 6 Immediate Future; p. 57, § 41, WILL. 7 Tense? 8 *fois* (f.) or *temps* (m.)? see Model Lesson I, p. 98. 9 Say 'that one will give me for it' (*en*).

59. THE SLAVE OF THE LAMP APPEARS. ii

Aladdin's mother took the lamp and said to her son, 'Here it is, but it is very dirty; if it were a little

cleaner, I believe it would fetch something more.' She
took a little fine sand and water to clean it with[1]; but
no sooner[2] had she begun to rub it than a hideous
genie[3] of gigantic size appeared before her, and said
to her in[4] a voice of thunder, 'What wouldst[5] thou
have? I am ready to obey thee as thy slave and the
slave of all who have that lamp in their hands[6]; I, and
the other slaves of the lamp.'

When Aladdin's mother saw this apparition, which
she was far from expecting[7], she fell in a swoon.

The Arabian Nights

1 Omit 'with.'   2 Use *à peine*. Tense? p. 78, § 45, WHEN,
and p. 88, § 49, INVERSION.   3 *éfrit* (m.).   4 Preposition?
p. 85, § 48, IN.   5 Use the Present tense.   6 *entre les
mains*.   7 Use *attendre*.

60. THE FOX AND THE FISHERMAN

The old Scottish poet John Barbour relates the
following tale. A fisherman had built himself a little
hut near the river, the[1] better to watch his nets. It
had a fireplace and only one door. One night he got
out of bed and went to look at[2] his nets. When he
returned after an hour or two, he saw in his hut by[3]
the light of the blazing fire a fox busily[4] gnawing at
a fine salmon he had caught that morning. He ran to
the door, and, drawing a sword, cried, 'Thine hour
has come, Master Fox!' Seized with[5] fear, the fox
looked round him[6] for a way out, but could find none[7],
save the door where the fisherman stood[8] with[9] the
drawn sword in his[10] hand. But he espied a mantle
on the bed, and, taking a corner of it in[11] his teeth, he
dragged it into the fire. When the fisherman saw his
mantle in danger, he rushed to save it, and the fox
ran out at[12] the door.

1 Omit 'the.'   2 The technical term is *visiter*.   3 *à*.
4 *en train de*, or *occupé à* + Infinitive.   5 Preposition? p. 86,
§ 48, WITH.   6 It is necessary to work in a phrase like *pour
trouver* or *cherchant*.   7 Supply *en*; p. 39, § 23, 2.   8 See
p. 91, § 49, STAND.   9 Is a Preposition necessary in French?

p. 86, § 48, WITH.   10 Preposition? p. 85, § 48, IN. Does French use the Possessive Adjective in such a case? p. 49, § 35, 2. 11 *entre*.   12 *par*.

61. FLINT

'The man has gone to old Hickory's for fire,' she told her father.

'Um,' said Flint, 'he might have rested[1] his legs. I can get[2] fire from stones[3].'

'From stones!' cried Burr, her face white.

The old man quietly pulled[4] two stones from his bag. One was flint[5], the other was quartz. He took[6] dry leaves from[6] his bag and rubbed them between his hands and laid them on a rock. Over the leaves he held the two stones and began to strike the one with[7] the other.

Burr and the boys watched[8] with scared faces.

'The fire man[9]—will he not be angry?' she asked.

Flint said nothing. He was striking the stones together. A spark came[10]! then another and another[11]! He kept on striking very fast until the sparks came like a flame[12] and caught[13] the dry leaves. He put on more leaves and little sticks, and soon there was a good[14] fire blazing.

Margaret A. McIntyre, The Cave Boy of the Age of Stone

1 *laisser reposer*.   2 *pouvoir* or *savoir*? p. 56, § 41, CAN. For 'get' use *tirer*.   3 General, therefore not *de pierres*; p. 23, § 12.   4 Use *sortir* transitively.   5 *de silex* (m.). 6 Use *prendre...dans*.   7 *contre*.   8 *le regardaient faire*. 9 *l'homme au feu*. 10 Use *jaillir*. 11 *d'autres encore*. 12 Use *former une flamme*.   18 Use *embraser*.   14 *beau* or *bon*?

62. SIX HUNDRED YEARS AGO: MEALTIME

Agnes, recalled to her duties by seeing the soup-bowl empty[1], jumped up and took down the spit on which a chicken was roasting at the fire. Chickens were dear at that time[2] of the year, and this one had cost three farthings. People helped themselves in those days[3]

in[4] a very simple manner. Agnes held the chicken on
the spit to the Bishop, who cut from it with his own[5]
knife the part he preferred; then she served the
chaplain and Muriel in[4] the same way, and lastly cut
some off for herself and Avice[6]. Finally, when little
was left beside[7] the carcase, she opened the back door,
and bestowed the remains on[8] Manikin the turnspit
dog, which, released from his labours, had sat[9] on the
hearth-stone licking[10] his[11] lips[12] knowing that his reward would come.

Emily Satah Holt, *Our Little Lady*

1 Turn by 'that the soup-bowl was empty.' A literal French
translation would mean 'the empty soup-bowl.' 2 p. 17,
§ 7, TIME. 3 *en ce temps-là*. 4 Preposition? p. 85, § 48,
IN. 5 Does *propre* seem necessary here? p. 49, § 35, 3.
6 Repeat the Preposition. 7 Use *ne...plus guère*, as in note
10 to Passage 51, p. 142. 8 The phrase is *faire cadeau de
quelque chose à quelqu'un.* 9 'had remained sitting.' 10 Use
à + Infinitive. 11 Does French employ the Possessive Adjective in such a case? p. 49, § 85, 2. 12 A dog has not *des
lèvres*, but *des babines* (f.).

63. TRAVELLING IN THE SEVENTEENTH
CENTURY

Farmer[1] Lavender was not quite so ready to let
Jenny go as Mrs Jane was[2] to ask it. Bristol seemed
to him a long way off[3]. In those days[4] people made
their wills[5] before they took a journey of a hundred
miles; and no wonder[6]. The roads were so bad that
men had frequently to be hired[7] to walk beside a
gentleman's carriage, and push it to either side[8], when
it showed a tendency to topple over[9]; and oxen were
sometimes fetched[7], to pull the coach out of a deep
quagmire of mud[10]. So Farmer Lavender shook his
head, and said, 'he[11] didn't know, no, he didn't[12],
whether he'd let his little maid[13] go.' But Mrs Jane
was determined—and so was[2] Jenny; and between
them[14] they conquered[15] the farmer.

Emily Sarah Holt, *The Gold that Glitters*

1 p. 23, § 12.   2 Remember that the sense of *être* requires to be completed; p. 38, § 23, 1.   8 *bien loin*.   4 *En ce temps-là*.   5 Use the singular.   6 *il n'y avait rien d'étonnant à cela*.   7 Avoid the Passive; p. 47, § 33, 2.   8 *d'un côté ou de l'autre*.   9 *verser*.   10 'a quagmire of mud' = *un bourbier*.   11 Use the accented form.   12 *non, pas du tout*.   13 *sa petite* is enough.   14 'between them' = *à elles deux*.   15 Use *avoir raison de*.

64. A GENEROUS BOY

'You see[1] Michael had the fever—'

'Who's Michael?' asked the Earl.

'Michael is Bridget's husband, and they were in great trouble. When a man is sick and has twelve children, you know how it is[2]. And Michael has always been a sober man. And Bridget used to come to our house and cry. And the evening Mr Havisham was there, she was in the kitchen crying[3] because they had almost nothing to eat and couldn't pay the rent; and[4] I went in to see her, and Mr Havisham sent for me and he said you had given him some money for me. And I ran as fast as I could into the kitchen and gave it to Bridget; and that made it all right[5]; and Bridget could scarcely believe her eyes[6]. That's why I'm so obliged to you.'

'Oh!' said the Earl in his deep voice, 'that[7] was one of the things you did for yourself, was it? What else?'   Frances Hodgson Burnett, *Little Lord Fauntleroy*

1 Not of course *Vous voyez que*, but the parenthetical exclamation *Voyez-vous*.   2 *ce que c'est*.   3 *à* + Infinitive; p. 52, § 37, 2.   4 This 'and,' and some others, could be omitted.   5 *cela a tout arrangé*.   6 *en croire les yeux*.   7 p. 42, § 26, 4.

65. A QUESTION OF NATIONALITY

In the course of the conversation, he reached[1] the Fourth of July[2] and the Revolution, and was just[3] becoming enthusiastic[4], when he suddenly remembered something and stopped very abruptly.

'What is the matter?' demanded his grandfather.
'Why don't you go on?'

Lord Fauntleroy moved rather uneasily in his chair.
It was evident to the Earl that Lord Fauntleroy was
embarrassed by the thought which had just occurred
to him[5].

'I was just thinking that perhaps you mightn't like
it,' he replied. 'Perhaps someone belonging to you[6]
might have been there. I forgot you were an Englishman[7].'

'You can go on,' said my lord. 'No one belonging to
me[8] was[9] there. You forgot you[10] were an Englishman
too.'

'Oh! no,' said Cedric quickly. 'I'm an American.'

'You are an Englishman,' said the Earl grimly[11].
'Your father was an Englishman.'

It[12] amused him a little to say this[13], but it did not
amuse Cedric.

'I was born[14] in America,' he protested. 'You have
to be an American if you are born in America. I beg
your pardon for contradicting[15] you. Mr Hobbs told
me, if there were another war, you know, I should
have to—to be an American.'

The Earl hated America and Americans, but it
amused him to see how serious this small patriot was[16].
He thought that so good an[17] American might make a
rather good Englishman when he was[18] a man.

Frances Hodgson Burnett, Little Lord Fauntleroy

1 Use en venir à.   2 For numbers, etc. in dates, see p. 38,
§ 22.   3 Omit 'just.'   4 Use s'enthousiasmer.   5 Use se
présenter à son esprit.   6 quelqu'un des vôtres.   7 p. 22,
§ 11; p. 8, § 4, 1.   8 Form a phrase of the same type as in
note 6.   9 Complete the negative; p. 81, § 47.   10 Accented;
repeat the Pronoun; p. 39, § 24, 1.   11 d'un ton sardonique.
12 Cela.   13 Use faire cette remarque.   14 French uses the
Past Indefinite.   15 The construction is de + avoir.   16 Turn
'how much...was serious.'   17 p. 81, § 46, so.   18 Tense?
See p. 93, § 50.

SECTION III

MODEL LESSON III

THE ESCAPE OF PRINCE CHARLES

1. After thus escaping death, Prince Charles lived for a time in a hut constructed in a deep thicket on the side of a mountain called Ben Alder. 2. Here he enjoyed a security which he had not known for months, until the 18th of September, when he heard that two French ships had arrived at Lochnannagh, to carry him and others of his party to France. 3. He sailed on the 20th, and landed two days later near Morlaix in Brittany. 4. His short but brilliant expedition had attracted the attention and admiration of all Europe for a period of thirteen months and a few days, five months of which had been engaged in the most perilous and fatiguing adventures that have ever been related in history or romance. 5. During his wanderings, his secret was intrusted to hundreds of people of every age and condition; but none was found, even among the poorest peasants, who thought for an instant of obtaining wealth by betraying the unhappy fugitive.

Scottish Universities Entrance Board
Preliminary Examinations, September, 1925.

1. After thus escaping death, Prince Charles lived for a time in a hut constructed in a deep thicket on the side of a mountain called Ben Alder.

'After thus escaping death.' The candidates who translated this passage into French as part of their University Entrance Examination probably did not think it very difficult. Nor is it. But many were the papers in which the first four words of the English produced four grievous mistakes in French. '*Après échapper* (or *échappant!*) *ainsi le morte*' was a common rendering. It was not a very promising start. However sympathetic the Examiner may have been and whatever system of marking he may have adopted, the marks awarded could not be very high if candidates continued in this strain, capping each English word with one elementary error in French. Even if the rest of their translation had been perfect, which it was not, this unhappy start would have sadly reduced the total marks. It may therefore be worth while to look at this short English phrase carefully and examine its difficulties. They are not really very profound.

'After' is always a danger-signal. It is true that when it is followed by a Noun, there is nothing to fear, but when it is followed by a Verb, or by the verbal form in -ing, the translator must proceed warily. Since there is no need for a finite Verb here, the rules affecting *après que* do not concern us for the moment, and we have merely to remember a very simple fact, viz. that 'after' with the verbal form in -ing is translated in French by *après* with *avoir* (or *être*). The fact which our candidates overlooked is that when we say, 'After seeing you' the French say *Après vous* avoir *vu.* We too can, and frequently do, say 'After *having seen* you,' but this form, which in English is optional, is in French obligatory. The reason is that the French mind, as usual, insists on making the facts perfectly clear. We need not, however, trouble ourselves with reasons, for the usage is a fixed one and the rule must be obeyed, reason or no reason. Whether our French friends have settled this matter in a better way than ourselves is a question on which a good deal could be said—but not in the Examination Room. Whether we like it or not, *après vous avoir vu* is what the French have said from time immemorial; *après vous voir* is *not* French, and anyone writing it in an examination paper loses marks. 'After escaping' is, then, in French *Après* avoir *échappé*.

Échapper is a Verb which is not to be used lightly. Some Verbs have but few peculiarities and can be employed by beginners without much risk of error. Such a Verb is *éviter*, by which anyone who is suspicious of *échapper* could quite well translate 'escape': thus, 'to escape punishment' is *éviter la punition*, 'to escape danger' is *éviter le danger*. The reason why some candidates did not use *éviter* to translate 'escaping death' was no doubt that they knew a better word, *échapper*. But before they could claim any credit for choosing a more suitable word than rivals who had probably been wise in their generation and played for safety in contenting themselves with the good enough, but not perfect, *éviter*, they should have made sure of *échapper*'s little peculiarities. Words are like tools. There is a right way—and several wrong ways—of using them. *Échapper* will suit our purposes admirably, but on one condition, viz. that *à* is used along with it. Here *échapper* requires *à* (cp. p. 68, § 44); 'to escape punishment' is *échapper* à *la punition*, and 'to escape danger' is *échapper* au *danger*. But that is no reason for saying here, as so many candidates did, *échapper au mort*, or *échapper à la morte*. It is true that there is a French word *le mort*. But it means 'the dead man.' There is also another French word *la morte*. But it means 'the dead woman.' The Examiner, though no doubt delighted to see that so many candidates knew one or other of these words, could allow no marks for

either, because the English has 'death' and the French
for that is *la mort*. Why is *mort* feminine? Because
the Latin *mors* is feminine: *la vie* is feminine, and it
would be rather remarkable if two words so continually
contrasted and occurring together in the same phrases
—*la vie et la mort*, etc.—were of different genders. It
would be such a remarkable fact that all the school
grammars would speak about it, and so burn it into
our memories that we should make no mistake about it.
But, *mort* being not masculine, but feminine, we must
make up our minds to remember the gender by
whatever means we can devise, e.g. by repeating to
ourselves over and over again *la vie et la mort, La Mort
et le Bûcheron, La mort a des rigueurs à nulle autre
pareilles*, or...*Après avoir ainsi échappé à la mort!*—
which will also remind us of the proper position of the
Adverb in such a phrase.

'Prince Charles lived for a time in a hut.' With
titles of rank *le* is required, and a small letter is
generally used instead of a capital, e.g. *le maréchal
Foch*. We should therefore say here le *prince Charles*,
which would be quite satisfactory for examination
purposes. But it often happens that the French have
given a somewhat unfamiliar name to historical
personages, places and things. In *Jean Sans Terre*
John Lackland is barely recognizable; *la bataille de
Senlac* is that of Hastings; *Hochstaedt* is Blenheim; *La
Société des Nations* is the League of Nations. The
person whom we know as 'Prince Charlie' is called
by Voltaire, his contemporary, *Charles-Édouard* or *le
prince Édouard* and later French historians follow
suit.

'lived.' We need have no hesitation about the
proper tense. It is clearly not a case for the Imperfect

(Past Continuous). We are not entering on a description of the life led by Prince Charlie in his hut, but merely stating that he spent some time in it, and the Past Historic is the proper tense for the statement of such fact. The possible translations are, thus, *vécut* or *habita* or (seeing that an expression of time follows) *passa*. Of these, *vécut* seems the best; *passa* is a close enough translation, but *habita* is not, because it would suggest that he 'dwelt,' 'was in residence,' in the hut, as when we say *Louis XIV habita Versailles*.

'a hut': not so much *une chaumière*, a *thatched* cottage, as the yet more modest shelter called *une cabane* or even *une hutte*, which is even smaller than *une cabane*; e.g. *une hutte de charbonniers, de pâtres*, etc. [charcoal-burners, shepherds].

'constructed in a deep thicket.' The usual translation of this was *construite* (though many forgot to make the Participle agree) *dans un* bois (taillis, maquis) *épais*. This is correct, but could be made more French by several minor changes. Thus, 'constructed' is here rather *bâtie* than *construite*, which generally denotes a more substantial building; for *dans*, treading too closely on the heels of another *dans*, *au milieu de* might well be substituted. Very few candidates knew the most suitable word for 'thicket,' *fourré*, but no Examiner would attach much importance to that. In *un fourré épais* the two *é*-sounds make an unpleasant hiatus, and it is more natural French to say *un épais fourré*. For 'thicket' *un taillis* and *un hallier* are often good translations, but they are not very appropriate here, *un taillis* being a copse composed of trees which are periodically cut down for sale and *un hallier* being generally spoken of in connection with deer and other game which take refuge in it.

'on the side of a mountain called Ben Alder.' Both
sur la pente, i.e. the slope of a hill, and *sur le versant*,
i.e. the slope of a mountain or of a mountain-range,
are possible renderings; but *au flanc* is preferable, as
being perhaps slightly more exact and certainly more
expressive. 'Ben' requires *le*. Just as the French say
le Mont Blanc, le Mont Saint-Bernard, they say also
le Ben Alder, etc.

2. Here he enjoyed a security which he had not
known for months, until the 18th of September, when
he heard that two French ships had arrived at Lochnannagh, to carry him and others of his party to
France.

'Here': in a past description such as this, 'here' is
as regularly translated by *là* as 'now' is by *alors*.

'enjoyed.' This is also a Verb requiring caution.
It is construed with *de*, e.g. *Il* jouissait *alors* de *la
faveur du roi* = 'At that time he enjoyed royal favour.'
The best safeguard against error is to learn the Verb
once for all as *jouir de*, not merely as *jouir*.

'security': not quite *tranquillité* (f.) 'peace of mind,'
but rather *sécurité* (f.) 'safety from attack.'

'which he had not known for months.' Two points
must be borne in mind: (1) 'for' in such a case is
depuis; (2) with *depuis* the Present, or the Imperfect
(Past Continuous), is generally the proper construction. Thus 'I *have known* her for a long time' is
always *Je la* connais *depuis longtemps*, and 'I *had
known* her for a long time' is *Je la* connaissais *depuis
longtemps*. In both cases the action is considered as
still continuing. According to the ordinary grammatical rule, we should therefore translate our phrase:
Là il jouit d'une sécurité qu'il ne connaissait pas depuis

des mois. For such a translation, no marks of course would be deducted. The Examiner would be only too thankful to see two important grammatical rules so faithfully observed. But all the same it is not natural French. French writers describing in the historical manner events long past generally look back on the action as a completed whole and would normally express the fact in this particular instance as *une sécurité qu'il n*'avait *pas* connue *depuis des mois.*

'until the 18th of September.' It is surprising to see how easily young people forget a very simple rule. In dates, cardinal numbers, not ordinals, must be used, with the solitary exception of *premier*, 'of' must be left untranslated, and the name of the month is usually spelled with a small letter. The rule is simple enough, and yet small indeed was the number of candidates who applied it and wrote correctly *jusqu'au* 18 *septembre.*

'when': *quand* and *lorsque* are useful conjunctions, but they will not translate every use of 'when.' No doubt 'He was singing when I came in' is *Il chantait* quand *j'entrai*, and there is no harm in substituting *lorsque* for *quand* when it sounds better or avoids an unpleasant repetition of *quand*. But if 'when' relates not to a Verb but to a Noun it must be rendered by *où* or *que*. Thus, 'the day *when* I was to leave' is *le jour* où *je devais partir*. Similarly, 'until the 18th of September when' is *jusqu'au* 18 *septembre* où... or *jusqu'au* 18 *septembre*, jour où....

'he heard that two French ships had arrived.' Followed by a subordinate clause, 'heard' is usually *entendit dire* [never, be it noted, *entendit* alone]; *entendit dire*, meaning 'heard say,' is not, however, very appropriate here, because we may be quite sure that

Prince Charlie did not pick up so important an item of news in the course of conversation. The despatch of the ships which were to take him away had been arranged beforehand with the French government and the Prince 'learned' = *sut* or *apprit* or, more probably, 'was informed,' *reçut la nouvelle* that they had duly arrived.

navire: 'ship' is feminine in English, and, whether for that reason or for others, most candidates made *navire* feminine. But it is masculine, e.g. *un beau navire*.

'had arrived.' Everyone knows that verbs of motion like *aller, venir, arriver*, etc. are construed with *être*. But not everyone applied that knowledge in the hour of trial and said *étaient arrivés*.

'to carry him and others of his party to France.' 'Carry' is an English touch which we can hardly expect to find in French:

> '*Carry* the lad that is born to be King
> Over the sea to Skye';

porter would seem odd; *amener* is better, but *ramener* better still. The Prince had started from France and was going *back*; for a Frenchman, to bring someone to France is to bring him *back*, bring him *home*, and *ramener* would spring unconsciously to his lips. For the same reason, *ramener* and *en France* being closely associated in his mind, he would naturally link them together in the sentence and leave the French for 'him and others of his party' to the end. The French for 'and others of his party' will be *et quelques-uns de ses partisans* (or *adhérents*, or, better, *compagnons*, which is both simpler and more expressive, since the devoted little party were *compagnons d'infortune*, 'companions in misfortune'); 'others' is *d'autres*, which, however, is difficult to work into the French sentence. The usual words for 'his party' are unsuitable here: *son parti* means 'his political supporters'; *sa suite* would not include the Prince himself; we could say *quelques membres de sa suite* but not *d'autres de sa suite*; *sa bande*, or even *sa petite bande* might faintly suggest that the fugitives were bandits. It will be enough to give the sense and translate somewhat freely: *et quelques-uns de ses compagnons*.

But what is to be done with these words? Since by a rule of French grammar *le* must precede the Verb, the first part of our phrase must be *pour le ramener en France*, and we cannot tack on to it *et quelques-uns de ses compagnons*. It would be quite easy to do so if we substituted for *et* either *avec* or *ainsi que*. But it is possible to retain *et* by repeating *le* in its accented form, *lui*, and saying *pour le ramener en France, lui et quelques-uns de ses compagnons*. This usage (in which both the *le* and the *lui* are necessary; see p. 40, § 24, 2) should be carefully noted.

3. He sailed on the 20th, and landed two days later near Morlaix in Brittany.

'He sailed': *Il mit à la voile*, but not *Il fit voile*, which is said of ships and *Il* would be interpreted here as = *Le navire*; *il partit* is a natural enough rendering, the context showing that the Prince went by sea; *il s'embarqua* is, however, the stock expression, although, strictly speaking, less accurate than *partit*, because a person who 'sailed' on the 20th might conceivably have gone on board on the 19th, or even before then.

'on the 20th.' Here it must be recalled once again not only that the cardinal number is required but also that 'on' must be left untranslated.

'landed': *débarqua*, but with *s'embarqua* too much emphasis would be laid on embarkation and disembarkation; *aborda* is sufficient.

'near': *près de*, not *près* alone, which is used only in postal addresses.

4. His short but brilliant expedition had attracted the attention and admiration of all Europe for a period of thirteen months and a few days, five months of which had been engaged in the most perilous and fatiguing adventures that have ever been related in history or romance.

'His short but. brilliant expedition': *son expédition courte mais brillante* [note the spelling of *brillant*] or, more forcibly, *sa courte mais brillante expédition*.

'had attracted': *avait attiré* goes well with both Nouns: *attirer l'attention* is a common phrase, and so also is *attirer l'admiration*.

'of all Europe': *de toute l'Europe*; also, more rhetorically, *de l'Europe tout entière*. The fact is quite true, because Prince Charlie's expedition had among other results that of withdrawing the British Army from the Continent, but it need not be stated rhetorically.

'for a period': 'for' expressing duration of time in the past is *pendant*.

'a period': *une période* (also, though less commonly, *un période*); more simply, *pendant un* (or *l'*) *espace*.

'of thirteen months and a few days.' Although as a general rule *de* has to be repeated before the second of two Nouns which it governs, it is not to be repeated here; *treize mois et quelques jours* is considered as a unit. It is not = *une période de treize-mois et une période de quelques-jours* but *une période de treize-mois-*

et-quelques-jours; the formula in algebra would be
$p = (13 + x)$.

'five months of which had been engaged': 'of which'
refers no doubt to 'period'; *dont* always comes at the
beginning of the relative clause; 'engaged' does not
seem to mean anything more than 'spent'; the passive
form *avaient été passés* is much less idiomatic than the
reflexive *s'étaient passés*.

'in the most perilous and fatiguing adventures.' The
point to note here, besides the spelling of *fatigant*, is
that these long Adjectives would naturally be placed
after the Noun.

'that have ever been related in history or romance.'
The Subjunctive will be required because of the
Superlative *les plus périlleuses*; for 'romance' *roman*
is usually the nearest French equivalent, meaning not
only the modern novel but also the mediaeval
'romance.' Our first draft will then be *qui aient jamais
été racontées dans les histoires ou dans les romans*. This
could be improved upon by substituting the active for
the passive. The French passive should be avoided
when it is possible to do so; it lacks force and is
commonplace, often cumbrous. Let us make another
attempt, using the active this time: *que les histoires ou
les romans aient jamais racontées*. This is more direct,
more forcible, than our first draft, but is it not capable
of further improvement? Why use the plural? *les
histoires* and *les romans* = 'history-books' and 'story-
books,' and *l'histoire* and *le roman* = 'History' and
'The Novel,' without qualification. The singular makes
a stronger expression: *qu'histoire ou roman ait jamais
racontées* [or *aient*: French is not very strict about this
matter and here the Verb may be either singular or
plural]. Then might we not invert? This would give

a more characteristically French turn to our sentence
and allow us to end on the same words as in the
English: *qu'aient jamais racontées histoire ou roman*.

5. During his wanderings, his secret was intrusted
to hundreds of people of every age and condition; but
none was found, even among the poorest peasants,
who thought for an instant of obtaining wealth by
betraying the unhappy fugitive.

'During his wanderings.' There is no very exact
French equivalent of 'wanderings' in this sense, no
Noun corresponding either to *errer* or to *errant*, as in
errer par les routes, or in *le Juif errant*. *Errement* (m.)
is used only in the moral sense of straying from the
paths of rectitude; *erreurs* (f.) is open to the same
objection, except in one or two set phrases like *les
erreurs d'Ulysse*, 'the wanderings of Ulysses,' and in
elevated or archaic style, e.g. *les erreurs des nefs sur
les vastes mers*. *Une Odyssée* is a term applied to
wanderings like those of Odysseus [Ulysses], but it
would be rather 'recherché' here; *ses allées et venues* is
very prosaic. It will therefore be wise to follow the
sound rule of translating the sense, not the words:
Dans sa (better *cette*) *vie errante* or *Pendant qu'il
errait ainsi*.

'his secret was intrusted.' For the tense, the choice
lies in the first instance between Past Continuous and
Past Historic. The meaning is 'his secret was in the
keeping of,' i.e. *était confié à*, rather than 'was next
communicated to,' i.e. *fut confié à*. But a good French
writer is always ready to help out the reader; hence
the popularity of French prose in Europe. It has become
the practice to show very clearly the relation in time
between the various happenings in a story and to

make a sharp distinction in tense when the past events described took place at different times. This intrusting of Prince Charlie's secret happened long before it could be said that 'no one was found who betrayed it.' If we translate this, as we must, by *nul ne se trouva*, then we should alter *était confié* to *avait été confié* and make the relationship in time between the two happenings perfectly clear.

'to hundreds of people': *à des centaines* [beware of using *cent* or *mille* as Nouns; the French Nouns are *centaines* and *milliers*] *de personnes*—not quite *gens*, it is too vague and may be slightly offensive, rather like 'folk,' e.g. *Certaines gens voudraient le croire* = 'Some folk would like to think so.'

'of every age and condition': *de tout âge et de toute condition.* The gender of the two Nouns being different, *tout* must be used twice, first in the masculine and then in the feminine form, exactly as we must say for 'his brother and sister' *son frère et sa sœur.*

'but none was found.' 'None' is not very easy. We cannot possibly employ the ordinary term *personne*, because we have just spoken of *des centaines de personnes* and the repetition would be intolerable. If we use *aucun*, we must put it in the feminine, to make it agree with *personne* understood. Fortunately there is another word for 'no one,' namely *nul*; *nul* is often used by itself and would not be associated in the reader's mind with *personnes* in the preceding phrase.

'was found': this states the final result of the search. The sequence of events was this: (*a*) A search took place; (*b*) then a negative result followed, i.e. Past Historic, *nul ne se trouva.* The *ne* must not be forgotten after *nul*.

'even among the poorest peasants': *les plus pauvres*

paysans is neater than *les paysans les plus pauvres*, and why use five words when four will suffice? The rule that *pauvre*, when it means the opposite of *riche*, follows the Noun is not absolute.

'who thought for an instant of obtaining wealth.' Many of the candidates who took this paper probably knew as well as the Examiner that in a relative clause whose Antecedent is a negative like *personne*, *aucun* or *nul*, the Verb is in the Subjunctive, e.g. *il n'y a* personne *qui le* sache = 'There is *no one* who *knows* it.' Why, then, did they with one accord use the Indicative? Probably because their attention was distracted by the intervening phrase 'even among the poorest peasants.' But surely it is unwise ever to use a Relative Pronoun without bearing in mind what its Antecedent is, or to place a Verb in a relative clause without first reflecting that its number and person depend entirely on the Antecedent. Here, then, we require the Imperfect Subjunctive: *qui pensât* or *qui songeât*. Either would suit, but whenever 'think' can be replaced by 'dream,' *songer* is the better translation. The distinction is: *Je n'y ai jamais pensé* = 'I never considered the matter'; *Je n'y ai jamais songé* = 'The thought never crossed my mind.'

'of': both *penser* and *songer* take *à* with a dependent infinitive.

'obtaining wealth': *obtenir de la richesse* is not in common use, but *s'enrichir* is.

'by betraying the unhappy fugitive': *malheureux* is more commonplace than *infortuné*, which is the time-hallowed epithet for hapless Kings and Princes. Thus, late at night on the 29th August, 1346, the Keeper of the Château de la Broye was awakened by a knocking at the gate and in reply to his question 'Qui heurte à cette heure?' a voice was heard in the darkness, 'C'est l'*infortuné* roi de France'—Philip VI, fleeing, wounded and alone, from the stricken field at Crécy. Both *malheureux* and *infortuné* add little to the sense of the Noun *fugitif* and would therefore naturally be placed before it.

Suggested Rendering

Après avoir ainsi échappé à la mort, le prince Édouard vécut quelque temps dans une cabane bâtie au milieu d'un épais fourré au flanc d'une montagne appelée le Ben Alder. Là il jouit d'une sécurité telle qu'il n'en avait pas connue depuis des mois, jusqu'au 18 septembre, où il reçut la nouvelle que deux navires français étaient arrivés à Lochnannagh, pour le ramener en France, lui et quelques-uns de ses compagnons. Il s'embarqua le 20, et aborda, deux jours plus tard, près de Morlaix en Bretagne. Sa courte mais brillante expédition avait attiré l'attention et l'admiration de toute l'Europe pendant un espace de treize mois et quelques jours, dont cinq mois s'étaient passés dans les aventures les plus périlleuses et les plus fatigantes qu'aient jamais racontées histoire ou roman. Pendant qu'il errait ainsi, son secret avait été confié à des centaines de personnes de tout âge et de toute condition; mais nul ne se trouva, même parmi les plus pauvres paysans, qui songeât un instant à s'enrichir en trahissant l'infortuné fugitif.

66. FIONN AND THE BARD. i

Fionn asked every question he could think of[1], and his master, who was a poet, and so[2] an honourable man, answered them[3] to the limit of his ability[4].

'Why do you live on the bank of a river?' was one of these questions.

'Because a poem is a revelation, and it is by the brink of running water that poetry is revealed[5] to the mind.'

'How long have you been[6] here?' was the next query.

'[7]Seven years,' the poet answered.

'It is a long time[8],' said wondering[9] Fionn.

'I would wait twice as long for[10] a poem,' said the bard.

'Have you caught good poems?' Fionn asked him.

'The poems I am fit for[11],' said the mild master. 'No person can get more than that.'

James Stephens, Irish Fairy Tales

1 *imaginer.*   2 'and so' = *donc* alone.   3 *y*, not *leur*, which is only personal.   4 *dans la mesure de sa compétence.* 5 Use the Reflexive form.   6 Tense?   7 The Preposition must be repeated.   8 *C'est bien long.*   9 *intrigué.* 10 *pour trouver.*   11 *dont je suis digne.*

67. FIONN AND THE BARD. ii

'Would you have got as good poems by the Shannon or the Suir or by sweet Ana Lifé?'

'They are good rivers,' was the answer. 'They all belong to good gods.'

'But why did you choose this river out of all the rivers?'

'I would tell you anything,' said Finegas, 'and I will tell you that.'

'A prophecy was made to me,' Finegas began. 'A man of knowledge foretold that I should catch the Salmon of Knowledge in the Boyne Water.'

'And then?' said Fionn eagerly.

'Then I would have All Knowledge.'

'And after that?' the boy insisted.

'What should there be after that?' the poet retorted.

'I mean, what would you do with All Knowledge?'

'A weighty question,' said Finegas smilingly. 'I could answer it if I had All Knowledge, but not until then. What would you do, my dear?'

'I would make a poem,' Fionn cried.

'I think too,' said the poet, 'that that is what would be done.'
James Stephens, *Irish Fairy Tales*

68. ON THE SEA-SHORE

Now it befel that, on the very shore, and over the very rocks where Tom was sitting with his friend the lobster, there[1] walked one day the little white lady, Ellie herself, and with her a very wise man—Professor P—.

Ellie and he[2] were walking on the rocks, and he was showing her one in[3] ten thousand of all the beautiful things which are to be seen[4] there. But little Ellie was not satisfied with[5] them at all; and at last she said honestly, 'None of these things interest me, because they can't play with me or talk to me. If there were little children now in the water, as there used to be[6], and[7] I could see them, I should like that. I know there used to be children in the water, and mermaids[8] too, and mermen[9]. I saw them all in a picture at home, of[10] a beautiful lady sailing in a car drawn by dolphins[11], and babies flying round her, and one sitting on her lap; and the mermaids swimming and playing, and the mermen trumpeting on conch shells[12].'
Kingsley, *The Water-Babies*

1 Omit 'there.'   2 Accented form.   3 Preposition? p. 85, § 48, IN.   4 'which one may see there.'   5 'they did not at all satisfy little Ellie.'   6 Supply *en* as usual (p. 39, § 23, 2) and add *autrefois* to make the meaning quite clear.   7 Repeat the conjunction. Mood? p. 78, § 45, IF. 8 *néréides*.   9 *tritons*.   10 *de* will be insufficient; say *qui représente*.   11 *attelé de dauphins* (m.).   12 Use *souffler dans des conques* (f.).

69. THE LOBSTER IN THE CAGE

But what had become of little Tom?

He slipped off the rocks into the water, as I said before. But he could not help thinking of little Ellie.

He thought about her all that day and longed to have her to play with; but he had very soon to think of something else.

He was going along by the rocks, when he saw a round cage of green withes; and inside it, looking very much ashamed of himself, sat his friend the lobster, twiddling his horns.

'What! have you been naughty, and have they put you in the lock-up?' asked Tom.

The lobster felt a little indignant at such a notion, but he was too depressed in spirits to argue; so he only said, 'I can't get out.'   Kingsley, *The Water-Babies*

70. TOM'S PUNISHMENT

The old fairy said nothing at all about the matter, not even[1] when Tom came next day with the rest for[2] sweetmeats. He was horribly afraid of coming; but he was still more afraid of staying away[3], and being suspected. He was dreadfully afraid, too, lest there should be no sweets left[4], and lest the fairy should inquire who had taken them. But, behold! she pulled out as many as before[5], which[6] astonished Tom, and frightened him still more.

And, when the fairy looked him in the face[7], he shook from head to foot; however, she gave him his share like[8] the rest, and he said to himself that she could not have found[9] out what he had done.

But when he put the sweets into his mouth, they made him so sick that he had[10] to get away as fast as he could.   Kingsley, *The Water-Babies*

1 *pas même quand.*   2 Supply an Infinitive.   3 Use *s'absenter.*   4 The phrase for 'there *are* no sweets left' is *il ne reste plus de bonbons.*   5 'as last time.'   6 What is the antecedent of 'which'? p. 44, § 28, 4.   7 *entre les deux yeux.*   8 Remember that 'like' is a Preposition, but *comme* is an Adverb. Therefore we must say *comme aux autres.* 9 What were the words Tom actually said to himself? p. 56, § 41, COULD, 2.   10 Use *devoir.*

71. IN THE SNOW

'I have been here nearly seven years,' he said,
'and, if you want to know anything about the place,
I can tell you. If you are able to walk, I can show you
some lovely spots, where you will not be bothered with
people. I can take you to a snow fairy-land. If you
are sad, you will find comfort there. In the silent snow
forests, if you dig the snow away, you will find the
tiny buds nestling in their white nursery. If the sun
does not dazzle your eyes, you may always see the
great mountains piercing the sky. These wonders have
been a happiness to me. You are not too ill but that
they may be a happiness to you also.'

'Nothing can bring me much happiness,' she said,
and her lips quivered. 'I have had to give up so much;
all my work, all my ambitions.'

'You are not the only one who has had to do that,'
he said sharply. 'You will find that things arrange
themselves.'   Beatrice Harraden, *Ships that pass in the Night*

72. JOINVILLE AND SAINT LOUIS. i

When the King asked his Barons whether, in[1] their
opinion, he should[2] return to[3] France or remain in
Egypt, they all said[4] that he had lost too many
Knights and with one accord advised return[5]. But I[6]
said, 'Let[7] the King remain, and Knights will come
from beyond the sea[8] in such great numbers[9] that he
can[10] fight for another[11] year. And thus will be
delivered the poor prisoners who were taken in[12] God's
service and in his[13], and who will never be set free
if he goes[14] away.' There was no man there but[15] had
a friend in captivity, and all fell a-weeping[16]. But
after the Council certain Knights came and mocked
me, saying: 'The King would indeed be mad did he
not[17] follow your advice against the whole Council of
the Realm!' At dinner the King made me sit[18] beside

him, as he always did[19]. He spoke not a word to me
during dinner, and I thought that he was angry
with[20] me.

1 Preposition? p. 85, § 48, IN.   2 Use *devoir*.   3 Preposition? p. 8, § 4.   4 Order of the words? p. 87, § 49, ALL.
5 *le retour*.   6 Is 'I' accented or not?   7 Do not use
laisser; p. 53, § 40, 1.   8 'from beyond the sea' = *d'outre-
mer*.   9 French uses *nombre* (m.) in the singular.   10 Tense?
11 *encore un* or *un autre*? p. 47, § 32, 4.   12 Preposition?
p. 85, § 48, IN.   13 p. 49, § 35, 3.   14 Tense? p. 78, § 45,
IF.   15 'but had' = 'who had not'; p. 54, § 40, 3.   16 *se
prirent tous à pleurer*.   17 The 'not' is ironical.   18 In
the construction after *faire* the Reflexive form is not used.
19 Complete the construction; p. 88, § 23, 1.   20 Preposition? p. 86, § 48, WITH.

73. JOINVILLE AND SAINT LOUIS. ii

While the King was hearing grace, I went to a window
in a corner and put my arms through the iron bars, and
thought that if the King went away I should go to the
Prince of Antioch my kinsman and remain in his
territory until help should reach me, to set the prisoners
free. As I stood there, someone came and laid his two
hands upon my head. And I thought it was Master
Philip of Anemos, who that day had mocked me, and
I said, 'Leave me in peace, Master Philip.' With the
movement I made, a hand dropped before my eyes and
I saw by the emerald ring that it was the King's hand.
And he said, 'Move not, for I would ask you why you,
who are so young a man, spoke thus against the
greatest and the wisest of the realm. Tell me, should
I do a wrong thing if I went away?'—And I answered,
'So help me God, Sire, yes.'—'If I remain,' he said,
'will you?' And I said I would. 'Now be of good
cheer,' he said, 'for I am grateful for your counsel.'

74. DR JOHNSON'S LETTER TO A LITTLE GIRL

The 10th of May, 1784

My dearest[1] Miss Jenny,

I am sorry that your[2] pretty letter has been[3] so long without being answered[4]; but, when I am not very well, I do not always write plain enough for young ladies. I am glad, my dear, to see that you write[5] so well, and[6] hope that you mind[7] your pen, your book, and your needle, for they are all necessary. Your books will give you knowledge, and make you respected[8]; and your needle will find you useful employment when you do[9] not care to read. When you are[9] a little older, I hope you will be[7] very diligent in learning[10] arithmetic; and, above all, that through your whole life you will carefully say your prayers and read[11] your Bible.

I am, my dear, your most[12] humble servant,

Sam. Johnson.

1 *Ma bien chère.*   2 The second person *plural* seems the more appropriate.   3 'has remained.' Mood? p. 54, § 40, 2. 4 'unanswered' is *sans réponse*.   5 What does 'write' depend on? On 'glad' or on 'see'?   6 Repeat the Pronoun. 7 'mind' = 'do not forget.' Mood? p. 69, § 44, ESPÉRER. 8 Active or Passive Infinitive? See Model Lesson II, p. 132. 9 Tense? p. 78, § 45, WHEN, 2.   10 Use *mettre beaucoup de zèle à* + Infinitive.   11 Remember that the tense used for 'say' is required also for 'read.'   12 *très.*

75. WILD ELEPHANTS

The elephants of a herd seldom roam far from each other, and even when one strays from its comrades the tiger, notwithstanding his agility and strength, will hardly venture to attack it. Should he do so, the male elephant puts down his head and takes him on his tusks, tosses him into the air, and stands prepared to stamp upon him the instant he touches the ground. The female has no tusks, but she has the art of falling upon an enemy and crushing him by her weight. In

their native forests, therefore, elephants are invincible
to all enemies, save man. The latter, even in his rudest
state, has only to light a fire, and the monster flees
in consternation; or he digs a pit and covers it with
turf, and the animal falls into it, helpless and at his
mercy.

76. THE RENEGADE

The docility of these animals could not be better
illustrated than by the aptitude which they manifest
in the capture of[1] their wild brethren. In some parts
of India a tame elephant is taught[2] to walk on a
narrow path between two pitfalls, which are covered
with branches, and then to[3] go into the woods and
induce[4] the wild herd to come that way. He walks
slowly onward till[5] near the trap, and then hurries
away as if in sport, passing safely[6] between the pits,
while some of those which follow him are immediately
trapped[7]. It has been observed that such[8] wild
elephants as have escaped[9] the snare always pursue the
traitor with the utmost fury; and if they can overtake
him, which[10] sometimes happens, they beat him to
death[11].

1 Say 'for capturing,' and use *pour*.   2 Avoid the Passive;
p. 47, § 33, 2.   3 Repeat the Preposition.   4 Turn by
e.g. 'to attract the wild herd in that direction.'   5 Might
not 'till' be omitted? p. 21, § 10.   6 *sans encombre*.   7 'fall
into the trap.'   8 'those of the.'   9 *à* or *de*? p. 68, § 44,
ÉCHAPPER.   10 Supply the antecedent to 'which'; p. 44,
§ 28, 4.   11 For 'to beat to death,' *assommer* is enough.

77. A WISE JUDGE

Once upon a time there lived two brothers named
Edmund and Alfred. One day Edmund set off to go
on a long journey, but ere he departed he went to his
brother, gave him a very valuable ring, and asked him
to take care of it till he returned. Many months passed,
and at last Edmund came home; but when he went

to his brother for the ring, the latter refused to give
it him, and declared that the ring was his. The matter
was brought before a judge, who asked Edmund where
he had given his brother the ring. Edmund replied
that they were standing under a large oak tree at the
time, but Alfred declared that he did not know of such
a tree. Then the judge asked Edmund to leave the
court, and bring a branch from the very tree. When
he had been gone a few minutes, the judge remarked
that he was a long time in returning, but Alfred said,
'Oh, my Lord, the tree is a long way off.' 'Ah!' said
the judge, 'and yet you said that you did not know
the tree. You have betrayed yourself.' He was ordered
to restore the ring, and was sent to prison.

78. ALICE FALLS DOWN THE WELL

Either[1] the well was very deep or[1] she fell very
slowly, for she had plenty of time[2] as she went down
to look about her and to wonder what was going to
happen next[3]. First, she tried to look down and make
out what she was coming to, but it was too dark to
see anything; then she looked at the sides of the well,
and noticed that they were filled with[4] cupboards and
book-shelves: here and there she saw maps and
pictures hung upon pegs. She took down[5] a jar from[6]
one of the shelves as she passed; it was labelled
'ORANGE MARMALADE[7]' but to her great disappointment it was empty: she did not like[8] to drop the jar
for fear of killing somebody, so managed[9] to put it into
one of the cupboards as she passed it[10].

Lewis Carroll, *Alice in Wonderland*

1 *Soit que...soit que* + Subjunctive.   2 The idiomatic
expression is *avoir tout le temps de* + Infinitive.   3 'next' is
not to be translated.   4 Preposition? p. 86, § 48, WITH.
5 'to take down as she passed' = *saisir au passage*.   6 *sur*.
7 *l'étiquette portait:* 'Confitures d'oranges.'   8 Use *vouloir*.
9 Use *s'arranger pour* + Infinitive.   10 *en passant*, which is
best placed before the translation of 'into one of the cupboards.'

79. THE MAD HATTER'S TEA-PARTY

The table was a large one, but the three were all
crowded together at one corner of it. 'No room! No
room!' they cried out when they saw Alice coming.
'There's plenty of room!' said Alice indignantly, and
she sat down in a large arm-chair at one end of the
table.

'Have some wine,' the March Hare said in an en-
couraging voice.

Alice looked all round the table, but there was
nothing on it but tea. 'I don't see any wine,' she
remarked.

'There isn't any,' said the March Hare.

'Then it wasn't very civil of you to offer it,' said
Alice angrily.

'It wasn't very civil of you to sit down without
being invited,' said the March Hare.

'I didn't know it was *your* table,' said Alice; 'it's
laid for a great many more than three.'

Lewis Carroll, Alice in Wonderland

80. THE KING AND THE CAT

'Who are you talking to?' said the King, coming
up to Alice and looking at the Cat's head with[1] great
curiosity.

'It's a friend of mine[2]—a Cheshire Cat,' said Alice;
'allow me to introduce it.'

'I don't like the look of it at all[3],' said the King:
'however, it may kiss my hand if it likes.'

'I'd rather not[4],' the Cat remarked.

'Don't be impertinent,' said the King, 'and don't
look at me like that!' He got[5] behind Alice as he
spoke.

'A cat may look at a king[6],' said Alice. 'I've read
that in some book, but I don't[7] remember where.'

'Well, it must be removed[8],' said the King very
decidedly, and he called to the Queen, who was passing

at the moment, 'My dear! I wish you would have[9] this cat removed![10]'

The Queen had only one way of settling all difficulties, great or small. 'Off with[11] his head!' she said, without even looking[12] round.

'I'll fetch[13] the executioner myself,' said the King eagerly, and he hurried off.

Lewis Carroll, *Alice in Wonderland*

1 What must be supplied in French? p. 23, § 11.   2 'one of my friends'; p. 49, § 35, 3.   3 The idiomatic phrase '*Sa tête ne me revient pas*' would suit well here.   4 *J'aimerais mieux pas,* or *Je n'y tiens pas.*   5 Use, e.g. *se retirer* or *se placer.*   6 The French proverb is *Un chat peut regarder l'évêque.* Is it suitable here?   7 Use *ne...plus.*   8 Use *emmener* or else *ôter de là.*   9 Mood? p. 54, § 40, 2.   10 Use *faire emmener.*   11 *Qu'on lui coupe le cou!*   12 Construction after *sans*? p. 52, § 38, 1.   13 Immediate Future; p. 58, § 41, WILL.

81. TRADING WITH SAVAGES

'Did you find any savages there?' asked Gorgo.

'O yes, and did some good trade with them.'

'But how did you understand each other? Did they talk Greek?'

'Talk Greek! no, indeed. They chattered away like so many birds or monkeys. Still, we got on very well with them. We used to put what we had to sell on the shore, and light a fire, and then go back to the ship. And when the people of the country saw the smoke, they used to come to the place, and look at the goods, and put by them so much gold as they thought they were worth. When they had done this, they went away. Then we used to land, and if the quantity of gold seemed sufficient, we took it and sailed away. But if we thought we could get more we went back to our ship and waited. Then the people used to come down, and put down some more gold, and so it went on till we were agreed.'

Alfred J. Church, *Three Greek Children*

82. JOAN AT CHINON. i

When she arrived at a village a[1] few miles[2] from Chinon in Touraine, Joan despatched a messenger to[3] the Dauphin. Some of his advisers considered her [4]a sorceress, but others[5] thought that in so sad an[6] extremity it would be rash to neglect any[7] hope of deliverance, however[8] slight it might be. At last it was agreed that[9] she should be asked[10] various questions. A favourable report having been made by her judges, Charles, after much delay, decided[11] to hear her. It was in the great hall of Chinon, lighted up for the occasion with[12] fifty torches and crowded with[12] knights and nobles, that the audience was given. The[13] better to test the truth of Joan's story, the Dauphin had dressed[14] plainly, and mingled without ceremony among[15] his courtiers, some of whom[16], magnificently attired, took the places of honour.

1 French is more explicit; p. 83, § 48, 2.   2 There are three words which translate 'miles': (a) the accurate (modern) *kilomètre* (m.) = ⅝ths of a mile; (b) the general literary *lieue* (f.) = 'league' = 2 or 3 miles; (c) *mille* (m.) [plural *milles*], on the sea. Which would best suit here?   3 *auprès de.* 4 Supply 'as.'   5 *d'autres* or *les autres*? p. 46, § 82, 2. 6 Order of words? p. 81, § 46, so.   7 p. 48, § 84, ANY. 8 p. 88, § 49, HOWEVER.   9 *convenir*, like *décider*, takes the Future in the Past.   10 Not *demander*.   11 Construction after the Verb? p. 66, § 44, DÉCIDER.   12 *de.*   13 Omit 'The,' and use *Pour* + Infinitive.   14 Intransitive or Reflexive? p. 61, § 43, 1.   15 Construction after the Verb? p. 71, § 44, MÊLER.   16 Position of *dont*? p. 44, § 29.

83. JOAN AT CHINON. ii

Neither the splendour of the scene nor the gaze of the spectators dismayed her. She advanced with a firm step, at once singled out the Dauphin and, falling on her knees before him, exclaimed: 'God give you good life, gentle Dauphin!'

'I am not he; he is there,' replied Charles, pointing

to one of his nobles. 'In the name of God, you are he,
and no other,' returned Joan. 'O most noble Dauphin!'
she continued, 'I am Joan the Maid, sent by God to
aid you and your kingdom. I am ready to take arms
against the English. And I am commanded to announce
to you that you shall be crowned in the city of Rheims.
Gentle Dauphin, why will you not believe me?'

Charles then drew her aside, and, after speaking
with her for some time in an under-tone, declared
himself in her favour.

84. THE CORONATION OF CHARLES THE SEVENTH. i

Collecting[1] ten or[2] eleven thousand men, Charles
commenced his march, followed by[3] Joan and his
bravest[4] captains, and without difficulty took Troyes
and several other towns on his way. On the evening
of the 16th of July[5], he made his triumphal entry into
the city of Rheims, accompanied by[3] a vast crowd and
followed by[3] the whole army, the Maid of Orleans
riding at his side. It was at once decided that the
Coronation should take[6] place without delay. Early
next morning the princes and prelates who had
accompanied the Dauphin assembled in the Cathedral,
but no one was looked upon with such[7] wonder and
respect as Joan, for to her[8] were attributed[9] all the
successes which had brought about this happy result.

1 Say 'After collecting'; p. 52, § 38, 1.   2 When the
numbers give the limits, the minimum and maximum, the
usual construction is *de...à*, e.g. 'a salary of ten or twelve
thousand francs' = un traitement *de* 10,000 *à* 12,000 francs.
3 Preposition? p. 84, § 48, BY.   4 'the bravest among
his captains.'   5 For the order of the words, see p. 86,
§ 48, ON, and for numerals in dates, p. 38, § 22.   6 Consult
note 9 to Passage 82, p. 178.   7 'such' = 'so much.'   8 Is
the Pronoun accented here? If so, use *c'est à...que.*   9 Avoid
the Passive, p. 47, § 33, 2.

85. THE CORONATION OF CHARLES THE SEVENTH. ii

During the whole of the solemn ceremony, Joan stood close to the altar, with her banner unfurled in her hand. Immediately the holy rites were concluded, she threw herself on her knees before the crowned monarch, her eyes streaming with tears.

'Gentle King,' she exclaimed, 'now is accomplished the will of God, that I should raise the siege of Orleans, and conduct you to your Coronation, showing you to be the king to whom belongs the kingdom of France.' It is evident that she now looked upon her mission as fulfilled, and she would willingly have retired from the gaiety of the court and the triumphs which attended her. She entreated the King to allow her to return to Domremy, but Charles would not, or dared not, let her go.

86. THESEUS SETS OUT FOR CRETE

As Prince Theseus was just going[1] on board of the ship with[2] black sails, his father spoke one last word to him.

'My beloved son,' said he, grasping the prince's hand, 'you observe that the sails of this vessel are black, as they ought to be[3], since it is making a voyage of sorrow and despair. Now, since I am very old, I know not whether I can[4] survive until the vessel shall return[5]. But as long as[6] I live[4] I shall creep up daily to the top of yonder cliff to watch for a sail upon the sea. And, dearest Theseus, if by some happy chance you should escape[7] the jaws of the Minotaur, then tear down those dismal sails, and hoist others bright as the sunshine. Beholding them on the horizon, myself and all the people[8] will know that you are coming back victorious, and will welcome you back with great joy.'

Theseus promised to remember his father's words and embarked on the ship that was to[9] carry him and his companions[10] to the Island of Crete where dwelt the savage Minotaur.

Hawthorne, Tanglewood Tales

1 p. 84, § 48, ABOUT. 2 Preposition? p. 86, § 48, WITH. 3 *comme il convient.* 4 Tense? 5 Could the Verb be avoided? Is there a suitable Noun available? p. 21, § 10. 6 *tant que.* 7 Do not use the Future in the Past; p. 78, § 45, IF, 2. Construction? p. 68, § 44, ÉCHAPPER. 8 *gens* or *peuple?* p. 90, § 49, PEOPLE. 9 Use *devoir.* 10 Accented form, see Model Lesson III, p. 161.

87. ARIADNE FREES THESEUS

A little before midnight the door of the prison softly opened and the gentle Ariadne showed herself with a torch in her hand.

'Are you awake, Prince Theseus?' she whispered.

'Yes,' answered Theseus. 'Since I have so little time to live, I do not want to waste any of it in sleep.'

'Then follow me,' said Ariadne, 'and tread softly.'

What had become of the jailer and the guards Theseus never knew. But however that might be, Ariadne opened all the doors and led him forth from the dark prison into the pleasant moonlight.

'Theseus,' said the maiden, 'you can now get on board your vessel and sail away for Athens.'

'No,' answered the young man; 'I will never leave Crete unless I can first slay the Minotaur and save my poor companions and deliver Athens from this cruel tribute.'

'I knew that this would be your resolution,' said Ariadne. 'Come, then, with me, brave Theseus. Here is your own sword which the guards took from you. You will need it; and may you use it well!'

Hawthorne, Tanglewood Tales

88. CERES SEARCHES FOR PROSERPINA. i

Ceres scarcely waited to hear what the nymphs had to say before she hurried[1] off to make inquiries all through[2] the neighbourhood. But nobody could tell her anything[3] that could[4] enable the poor mother to guess what had become of Proserpina. A fisherman, it is true, had noticed her little footprints in the sand as he went homeward along the beach with[5] a basket of fish; a rustic had seen the child stooping[6] to gather flowers; several persons had heard either the rattling of chariot wheels or the rumbling of distant[7] thunder; and one old woman, while plucking herbs, had heard a scream, but thinking it was some children playing, had not taken the trouble to look up. So[8] Mother Ceres lighted a torch and set forth, resolving never to come back until Proserpina was discovered. She had not gone far before[9] she found one of the magnificent flowers which grew on the shrub that Proserpina had pulled up.

Hawthorne, Tanglewood Tales

1 For 'before' substitute 'and,' which simplifies matters. 2 'in all.'   3 p. 48, § 34, ANYTHING.   4 Mood?   5 Is a French Preposition to be used here? See Model Lesson IV, p. 191. 6 Use the Infinitive or a Relative Clause; p. 52, § 37, 2. 7 Transfer 'distant' to 'rumbling.'   8 Beware of *Si*; p. 81, § 46, so.   9 Is it possible to avoid using *avant que*? p. 21, § 10.

89. CERES SEARCHES FOR PROSERPINA. ii

All night long, at the door of every cottage and farmhouse, Ceres knocked, and called up the weary labourers to inquire if they had seen her child: and they stood, gaping and half asleep, at the threshold, and answered her pityingly, and besought her to come in and rest. At the portal of every palace too, she rang so loudly that the menials hurried to throw open the gate, thinking that it must be some great king or queen, who would demand a banquet for supper and a stately chamber to repose in. And when they saw only a sad and anxious woman with a torch in her

hand and a wreath of withered poppies on her head,
they spoke rudely and sometimes threatened to set
the dogs upon her. But nobody had seen Proserpina,
nor could give Mother Ceres the least hint which way
to seek her.   Hawthorne, *Tanglewood Tales*

90. PROSERPINA IN PLUTO'S PALACE

Pluto now[1] summoned his domestics, and bade them
lose no time in preparing[2] a most sumptuous banquet,
and above all things, not[3] to fail of setting a golden
goblet of the water of Lethe by Proserpina's plate[4].

'I will drink neither that nor anything else[5],' said
the maiden: 'nor will I[6] taste a morsel of food, even
if you keep me for ever in your palace.'

'I should be sorry for that,' replied Pluto, patting[7]
her cheek; for he really wished to be[8] kind but knew not
how[9]. 'You are a spoiled child, I perceive, my little
Proserpina; but when you see[10] the nice things my
cook will make for you, your appetite will quickly
come back again.'   Hawthorne, *Tanglewood Tales*

1 *alors* or *maintenant*? p. 80, § 46, NOW.   2 Translate as
if = 'bade them prepare without losing time'; p. 52, § 38, 1.
3 Position of *pas* with the Infinitive? p. 82, § 47.   4 Could
not the French for 'by Proserpina's plate' be profitably trans-
ferred to another place in the sentence?   5 *autre chose.*
6 'and I will not taste.'   7 For 'patting,' see Model Lesson II,
p. 128.   8 *se montrer.*   9 *comment s'y prendre.*   10 Tense?

91. PROSERPINA'S RETURN. i

Mother Ceres had returned to her deserted home and
was sitting disconsolately on the doorstep, with her
torch burning in her hand. She had been idly watching
it for some moments past, when, all at once, the flame
flickered and went out.

'What does this mean?' thought she. 'It was an
enchanted torch, and should have kept burning until
my child came back.'

Lifting her eyes, she was surprised to see a sudden

verdure flashing over the brown and barren fields,
exactly as you may have observed a golden hue
gleaming far and wide across the landscape from the
just risen sun.

'Does the Earth dare to disobey me?' exclaimed
Mother Ceres indignantly. 'Does it presume to be
green when I have bidden it be barren until my
daughter shall be restored to my arms?'

'Then open your arms, dear mother,' cried a well-
known voice, 'and take your daughter into them.'

And Proserpina came running, and flung herself
upon her mother's bosom.   Hawthorne, *Tanglewood Tales*

92. PROSERPINA'S RETURN. ii

'My child,' said Ceres, 'did you taste any[1] food
while you were in Pluto's palace?'

'Dearest[2] mother,' answered Proserpina, 'I will tell[3]
you the whole truth. Until this morning not a morsel
of food passed[4] my lips. But to-day they brought me
a pomegranate, and I was tempted to bite it. I did
not swallow a morsel, but I am afraid that six seeds
remained in my mouth.'

'Woe is me!' exclaimed Ceres. 'For each of these
six pomegranate seeds you must spend one month of
every year in the palace of that wretched King of
Darkness!'

'Do not speak so harshly of King Pluto,' said
Proserpina, kissing her mother. 'He has some good
qualities; and I really think I can[5] bear to spend six
months in his palace, if he will[5] only let me spend the
other six[6] with you. There is some comfort in making[7]
him so happy; and so, upon the whole, dearest mother,
let us be glad that he is not to keep me the whole
year round.'   Hawthorne, *Tanglewood Tales*

1 p. 48, § 34, ANY.   2 *Ma bien chère*.   3 Immediate
Future; p. 58, § 41, WILL.   4 Remember to complete the
negative; p. 81, § 47.   5 Tense?   6 Order of words? p. 37,
§ 20, 2.   7 *à* + Infinitive.

93. WALTER VISITS MR DOMBEY

On the day after, they were sitting at breakfast still praising the major when Florence came running in, her face suffused with a bright colour, and her eyes sparkling joyfully, and cried—

'Papa! papa! Here's Walter, and he won't come in.'

'Who?' cried Mr Dombey. 'What does she mean?'

'Walter, papa!' said Florence timidly, afraid of having addressed her father with too great familiarity, 'who found me when I was lost.'

'Does she mean young Gay, Louisa?' inquired Mr Dombey, knitting his brows. 'She cannot mean young Gay. See what it is.'

Mrs Chick hurried into the passage and returned with the information that it was young Gay accompanied by a very strange-looking person; and that he had said he would not take the liberty of coming in, since Mr Dombey was at breakfast, but would wait until Mr Dombey was ready to receive him.

Dickens, Dombey and Son

94. A FAITHFUL SHEPHERD'S DOG. i

James Hogg, the Scottish shepherd-poet, once had a dog called Sirrah, which was very intelligent and which he was very fond of. A story he relates shows that this dog was no[1] ordinary animal. Once about[2] seven hundred lambs which were under the shepherd's charge scampered off at midnight in three divisions across the hills, in spite of all that he[3] and a lad could do to bring them together. 'Sirrah,' cried the shepherd in distress, 'my man[4], they're a' awa'.' The night was so dark that he did not see Sirrah; but the faithful animal had heard his master's words, and he silently set off in quest of the flock.

1 'was far from being an.'   2 p. 84, § 48, ABOUT.   8 Use the accented form; p. 40, § 24, 2.   4 *mon garçon.*

95. A FAITHFUL SHEPHERD'S DOG. ii

Meanwhile the shepherd and his companion did not
fail to do all that was in their power to recover the
lambs. They spent the whole night in scouring the
hills for miles around, but of neither the lambs nor
Sirrah could they obtain the slightest trace. When the
day dawned, they realized they would have to return
to their master and inform him that they had lost his
whole flock of lambs, and knew not what was become
of them. On their way home, however, they discovered
a large number of lambs at the bottom of a deep
ravine and Sirrah standing on guard. They thought
that it was one of the three divisions. But what was
their astonishment when on counting them they found
that not one lamb of the whole flock was missing!

96. A STABLE FIRE

On[1] the other side of the yard windows were thrown
up[2], and people were shouting all sorts of things; but
I kept my eye fixed on the stable door, where[3] the
smoke poured[4] out thicker than ever, and I could see
flashes of red light; presently I heard above all the
stir and din a loud clear voice, which I knew was[5]
master's: 'James Howard, are you there?' There was[4]
no answer, but I heard a crash of something falling[6]
in the stable, and the next moment I gave a loud
joyful neigh, for I saw James coming through the
smoke leading Ginger[7] with him; she was coughing
violently and he was not able to speak.

Anna Sewell, *Black Beauty*

1 Preposition? p. 86, § 48, ON.   2 Active with *on*? or
Passive? or Reflexive? Use *ouvrir précipitamment* and note that
in France windows cannot be thrown *up*.   3 *d'où*.   4 Tense?
5 'which I recognized for that of my master.'   6 Turn by a
relative clause; p. 52, § 37, 2.   7 *Poil de Carotte*.

97. WARFARE IN LA VENDÉE

The organization of the peasant armies was peculiar. A section always remained in arms; but the mass of the army assembled and disbanded as circumstances required. When anything was to be done, the windmill sails were seen going on the hills, the horns were heard blowing in the woods and watchers set the church bells a-tolling. The country people, flocking to the church, were summoned, in the name of God and the King, to gather at a particular hour and place. All along the road women used to be waiting, telling their beads on their knees, offering provisions tó the men as they passed on to the meeting-place. After a victory or a defeat the army melted away, so much did the peasants, after a day or two's absence, long to revisit their farms and their homes.

98. THE DUSTMAN[1]. i

There is no one in the world[2] who knows[3] so many stories as the Dustman.

In the evening, when children are sitting quietly at table, or on their little stools, he takes off his shoes, comes softly[4] up-stairs, opens the door gently, and all on a sudden throws dust into the children's eyes. He then[5] glides behind them, and breathes lightly upon[6] their necks and immediately their heads become heavy. But it[7] does them no harm; the Dustman only wants the children to be quiet and they are most[8] quiet when they are in bed. They must be quiet in order that he may tell them his stories.

When the children are asleep, the Dustman sits down upon the bed. He is gaily dressed in[9] a silk coat. Under each arm he holds an umbrella: one[10], which has pictures painted upon it[11], he holds[12] over good[13] children and it makes them[14] have the most delightful dreams all night long: and the other, which has no

pictures, he holds over naughty children, so that they
may awake in the morning without having dreamed
at all.   Hans Andersen

1 *Le Marchand de Sable.*   2 *au monde.*   8 Mood?
p. 54, § 40, 3.   4 *à pas de loup*, or *sans bruit.*   5 Order of
words? p. 80, § 46, NOW.   6 *dans.*   7 *cela.*   8 *le plus.*
9 *de.*   10 *le premier.*   11 'on which pictures are painted';
p. 45, § 30.   12 What must be supplied? p. 38, § 23, 1.
13 Supply the definite Article.   14 What is the case of the
Pronoun in French? p. 69, § 44, FAIRE.

99. THE DUSTMAN. ii

'Now may I have some stories?' asked little Hialmar,
as soon as the Dustman had put him to sleep.

'We shall have no time for telling or listening to
stories this evening,' replied the Dustman. 'To-morrow
is Sunday, and by to-morrow morning all the world
must be put in order. I must go to the church-tower,
to see whether the little elves are rubbing the bells so
as to make them ring merrily. I must away to the
fields to see that the winds are sweeping the dust off
the grass and leaves. I must take down the stars in
order to brighten them.'

'Listen to me, good Mr Dustman,' said an old
Portrait, which hung by the wall near where Hialmar
was sleeping. 'Do you know that I am Hialmar's
great-grandfather? I am much obliged to you for
telling the boy stories; but you must not puzzle him.
Stars cannot be taken down and brightened; they are
solid bodies like our earth.'   Hans Andersen

100. THE WEATHERCOCK AND THE SUNDIAL

'What a[1] restless life!' moaned the Weathercock on[2]
the church tower. 'Ah! how much rather would[3] I lead
the quiet, peaceful existence of my old[4] friend, the
Dial, down below yonder on his pedestal. That *is*
a life[5]!'

'How he is chattering away up above there!' remarked the Dial; 'he almost makes me smile, though not a ray of sunshine has[6] fallen on me through the livelong day[7], alas! I often wonder what he finds to talk about. But his active life gives him[8] subjects enough, no doubt. Ah! what would I not give to be like him! But all is so different with me[9], alas! I thought I heard my own name too, just now. I will ask[10]. Halloo[11]! up above there. Did you call, my sprightly friend? Is there anything fresh[12]? Tell me, if there is. What were you talking about?'

'Nothing[13] profitable this time, good neighbour,' replied the Weathercock; 'for, in truth, you have caught me grumbling[14].' Mrs Gatty, *Parables from Nature*

1 Is 'a' to be translated? p. 46, § 31.   2 Expand to, e.g. *qui surmontait.*   3 See p. 62, § 44, AIMER MIEUX.   4 Remember the spelling before a vowel.   5 *C'est une vie, cela!* or *Voilà une vie, au moins!*   6 Mood? What auxiliary is used with *tomber*?   7 'through,' etc., *de toute la sainte journée.* 8 'makes him find'; p. 69, § 44, FAIRE.   9 *en ce qui me concerne.*   10 p. 58, § 41, WILL.   11 *Ohé!*   12 Construction of the Adjective? p. 48, § 34, ANYTHING.   13 Repeat the Preposition.   14 Use *à* + Infinitive.

SECTION IV

MODEL LESSON IV

1. At this time one of the Lords of the Council came to the Castle with a message from his brethren and demanded admittance to the Earl.   2. It was answered that the Earl was asleep.   3. The Councillor thought that this was a subterfuge and insisted on entering. 4. The door of the cell was softly opened; and there lay Argyle on his bed, sleeping, in his irons, the placid sleep of infancy.   5. The conscience of the renegade smote him.   6. He turned away sick at heart, ran out

of the Castle and took refuge in the dwelling of a lady
of his family, who lived hard by. 7. There he flung
himself on a couch and gave way to an agony of
remorse and shame.   8. His kinswoman, alarmed by
his looks and groans, thought that he had been taken
with sudden illness, and begged him to drink a cup of
sack. 9. 'No, no, that will do me no good!' 10. She
prayed him to tell her what had disturbed him.
11. 'I have been,' he said, 'to Argyle's prison.
12. I have seen him within an hour of eternity, sleeping
as sweetly as ever man did, but as for me—'

Macaulay, History of England

1. At this time one of the Lords of the Council came
to the Castle with a message from his brethren and
demanded admittance to the Earl.

'At this time': not *vers cette époque* = 'at that period
of history,' which is too wide, nor *à ce moment* = 'at
that minute,' which is too narrow a limit. The context
is that Argyle has lain down to sleep. *C'est alors que*
is near enough to what is meant, or *Sur ces entrefaites*
= 'At this juncture.'

'one of the Lords of the Council.' English or
Scottish lords are generally called in French *lords*, not
seigneurs, both the title and 'La Chambre des *Lords*'
being very well known. *Conseil* is also in current use
in such phrases, e.g. *le conseil des ministres* = 'the
Cabinet,' *le Président du Conseil* = 'the Prime Minister.'
It is therefore very natural French to say *un des lords
du Conseil*.

'came to the Castle.' The distinction between
'come' and 'go' is less strictly observed than that
between *venir* and *aller*; 'come' often encroaches on
the domain of 'go,' but *venir* implies *venir ici* and *aller*

implies *aller là*. Thus, 'I will *come* to see you to-morrow' = *J'*irai *vous voir demain*. But in the present instance *vint* is the correct term. The author has taken his readers with him into the Castle as it were. They are supposed to see these events from the inside. To say *alla au château* would be to speak as if author and readers were outside observers.

'with a message from his brethren.' This short phrase contains two lessons on the French Prepositions:

(1) It is just possible to say 'avec *un message*.' But English people when they write French are much too fond of *avec* in this sense. An *avec* which has been used merely because it has been prompted by 'with' is not likely to make idiomatic French. The normal French phrase for 'with' is often *portant*; 'with a message' is *porteur d'un message*.

(2) *De* is not nearly so precise a preposition as 'from,' because it means 'of' as well as 'from'; *un message de ses collègues* is French, of course, but it would be taken to mean 'a message of his brethren,' 'his brethren's message,' more readily perhaps than a 'message from.' In such cases *de la part de* is better, because it leaves no doubt as to the precise meaning intended.

For 'brethren,' *collègues* will do [*confrères* is usually said of humbler people than 'Lords of the Council'], but *pairs* is as correct and more dignified.

'and demanded admittance to the Earl.' 'demanded': our first draft might be *demanda à être admis*. But *demanda* is not a strong word and would not necessarily imply anything more than 'asked,' whereas the bearer of the message asked admittance as a right, and possibly with some haughtiness; *exigea* is stronger and even *ordonna* does not, in the circumstances, seem too strong. With both *exigea* and *ordonna* an infinitive construction is hardly possible and we must amplify the phrase to: *ordonna qu'on le fît entrer* (or *l'admît*).

'to the Earl': the literal *au comte* will not do; *à* is not used so abruptly as this. As usual, the English Preposition can express what the French cannot, unaided. Nor will *chez le comte* suit the case. He was not, unhappily for himself, 'at home.' The situation requires the more formal, less abrupt, *auprès de*.

Sur ces entrefaites, un des lords du Conseil vint au château, porteur d'un message de la part de ses pairs, et ordonna qu'on l'admît auprès du comte.

2. It was answered that the Earl was asleep.

'It was answered': *Il lui fut répondu* is the best translation, because the most exact. But cautious students who prefer *On lui répondit* or *On répondit* or *La réponse fut* are quite within their rights and would forfeit no marks in an examination.

'was alseep': not *était endormi*, i.e. had fallen asleep, but rather *dormait*.

Il lui fut répondu que le comte dormait.

3. The Councillor thought that this was a subterfuge and insisted on entering.

The literal rendering is correct enough: *Le conseiller pensa que c'était un subterfuge et insista pour entrer.* But it could be improved upon; *pensa...et* would be more neatly expressed by the Present Participle *pensant*; *subterfuge* (m.) is a French word, but a rare one, and *prétexte* (m.) is the usual term. In a phrase like *pensant que c'était un prétexte*, French writers find it difficult to resist the temptation to insert *ne...que*, which has become associated with *prétexte*, and the chances are that they would say here *pensant que ce n'était qu'un prétexte.* The term *insista pour entrer* is clearly suggested by the English, having an English flavour about it which it would be preferable to avoid. A few minor alterations will produce a more French-looking sentence:

Le conseiller, croyant que ce n'était qu'un prétexte, insista pour qu'on le laissât entrer.

4. The door of the cell was softly opened; and there lay Argyle on his bed, sleeping, in his irons, the placid sleep of infancy.

'the cell': *une cellule* is generally a monk's cell; a prisoner's cell, especially in the historical style, is *un cachot.*

'was softly opened.' Shall we say (1) *On ouvrit doucement la porte du cachot* or (2) *La porte du cachot s'ouvrit doucement?* The first seems the better rendering. The door of Argyle's cell did not open of its own accord like the magic door in Model Lesson I, p. 98, but was opened by someone, and from the outside. This fact weighs the scale in favour of *on,* which evokes a gaoler and his keys.

'and there lay Argyle on his bed': the English is too condensed for French taste, which prefers to express more fully the fact that 'there he saw Argyle lying on his bed.' If *voilà* had kept its original sense = 'behold there,' it would have been useful; but it has become weakened—and vulgarized.

'on his bed': there will not be much hesitation between the two words for 'lying'; *couché dans son lit* is 'lying *in* his bed,' comfortably and at home; *étendu sur son lit* is 'lying *on* his bed' in a prison cell, in chains. The ordinary expression for 'in bed' is *au lit*

(cp. *au salon, au jardin*, etc.), but it is quite unsuitable
here. There is a difference between *au lit* and *sur le lit*;
the latter = on the bed-clothes. Thus *Je suis malade,
je vais rester* au lit, but *Je suis fatigué, je vais m'étendre
un peu* sur mon lit.

'sleeping, in his irons, the placid sleep of infancy':
dormir with *sommeil* requires *de*, e.g. *dormir* d'*un
sommeil de plomb* = 'to sleep heavily,' *dormir* du *sommeil des justes* = 'to sleep the sleep of the just.'

'irons': *fers* is often used figuratively for 'chains,'
e.g. in the opening sentence of Rousseau's *Contrat
social*: *L'homme est né libre, et partout il est dans les*
fers; but it can also be used literally.

For 'placid,' *calme, paisible* or *tranquille* are equally
correct; *paisible* perhaps suits best, as *du paisible
sommeil de l'enfance* makes a well-balanced ending to
the sentence.

On ouvrit doucement la porte du cachot, et là il
vit Argyle, étendu sur son lit, dormant, dans ses fers,
du paisible sommeil de l'enfance.

5. The conscience of the renegade smote him.

For 'renegade,' *renégat* is the usual word, but there
are others worth noting: *un transfuge*, properly someone
who deserts one side and joins the other; *un tourne-
casaque*, a 'turn-coat'; and *un traître*, which is as
common a term as any in such a connection as
this.

The boldness of the English phrase 'his conscience
smote him' is not paralleled in French, possibly
because the French mind wants to *see* what happened,
and it is difficult to imagine how one's conscience could
rise and smite one; *sa conscience se troubla* (weak), or

s'éveilla or *se révolta* are the available expressions.
Here it is perhaps enough to say *La conscience du
renégat s'éveilla.*

6. He turned away sick at heart, ran out of the
Castle and took refuge in the dwelling of a lady of his
family, who lived hard by.

'He turned away': *Il se détourna* implies that he
turned away so as not to look at something unpleasant,
but remained in the cell, and is somewhat like *il
détourna la tête*; *il se retourna* implies that he turned
and made to go, which is the case here.

'sick at heart': *plein d'angoisse* or *le cœur gros*, or
le cœur serré, seem the best expressions.

'ran out of the Castle': in such expressions the
sense of the English Adverb is generally to be rendered
by a French Verb, e.g. 'to swim across a river' = traverser *une rivière à la nage*, 'to go up (come down) a
hill' = *monter (descendre) une colline*. Since 'to run
upstairs' is *monter l'escalier en courant*, we could in the
same way say *sortit du château en courant*. Or we could
use a stronger Verb, *s'élança du château*, or add an
Adverb, *sortit précipitamment du château*.

'and took refuge': *se réfugia* or *chercha refuge*.

'in the dwelling of a lady of his family': *chez* is so
delightfully convenient a word that it is a pity not to
use it. But 'in the dwelling of' is very formal and
perhaps *dans la demeure de* is therefore more appropriate. This, however, raises a difficulty. We cannot
well use *demeure* and *demeurer* in the same sentence,
and we should have to fall back on another equally
pompous phrase, *sous le toit de*, if we wished to convey
the same impression as the English. Everything considered, *chez* seems to cause the least difficulty.

'a lady of his family' is probably just *une parente*
and 'hard by' nothing more than *tout près.*

Il se retourna, le cœur serré, sortit précipitamment
du château et chercha refuge chez une parente qui
demeurait tout près.

7. There he flung himself on a couch and gave way
to an agony of remorse and shame.

Là il se jeta [*s'affaissa* = 'collapsed' and *s'affala*
= 'sank down' imply physical exhaustion] *sur un lit de
repos* [*une couche* is 'a bed' rather than 'a couch'; *un
canapé* is too modern = 'a sofa,' one might almost as
well say 'a Chesterfield'!] *et s'abandonna* [not quite *se
livra* which implies a more permanent state] *à un
paroxysme* [a rare word, which even Higher Certificate
candidates could hardly be expected to know]. They
might safely enough use *un accès* although it is incorrect, meaning a 'fit' of ague, or the like; or else
leave 'agony' untranslated, for clearly it is better to
convey the sense and say *s'abandonna au remords et
à la honte* than to lose marks by using *une agonie*
wrongly: it always means '*death*-agony,' e.g. *Il est à
l'agonie* = 'He lies at the point of death,' the same
thing as *Il est à l'article de la mort.*

Là il se jeta sur un lit de repos et s'abandonna à un
paroxysme de remords et de honte.

8. His kinswoman, alarmed by his looks and groans,
thought that he had been taken with sudden illness,
and begged him to drink a cup of sack.

'his looks': *sa mine* if pallor and drawn features are
meant; *ses regards* if the expression of the face is
intended.

'and groans': *ses* must be repeated, but *par* need

not; *gémissements* (m. pl.) are low moans, e.g. the whining of a dog; *soupirs* (m. pl.) are 'sighs' and perhaps the word is too weak here; *plaintes* (f. pl.) are 'groans of pain,' whether mental or physical.

'thought': *pensa*, i.e. reflected on the matter and formed the opinion that, or *crut*, i.e. came to believe that.

'had been taken with sudden illness': freely, *venait de se trouver mal, était tombé subitement malade*; or, more literally, *avait été subitement pris de maladie*, or, more exactly, *atteint d'une maladie subite*.

'begged': not *pria* = 'requested,' 'asked,' but *supplia*.

'a cup of sack.' The precise beverage, *du vin sec* or *du vin de Xérès*, need not be specified, nor perhaps the precise container, whether *un verre* or *une coupe*. At the present day *boire un verre de vin* has associations with 'le cabaret' and rubicund taxi-drivers, which we are better without.

Sa parente, effrayée par ses regards et ses plaintes, crut qu'il avait été atteint d'une maladie subite et le supplia de boire une coupe de vin.

9. 'No, no, that will do me no good.'

French is much more particular than English with regard to tense. The cup of sack *will* do the Councillor neither good nor harm, since he has refused it. What he really means, and would have said if he had had a logical French mind, is 'If I *were* to drink it, it *would* do me no good.' The fact must be stated so in French.

'Non, non, cela ne me ferait aucun bien.'

10. She prayed him to tell her what had disturbed him.

Elle le pria is not forcible enough; *elle le supplia* we

have already used; *elle l'implora* or, better, *elle le conjura* will suit.

'disturbed': *troubler* is to be used charily [*déranger* is the word in ordinary trivial circumstances], but it is clearly the proper word here, expressing mental disturbance.

Elle le conjura de lui dire ce qui l'avait troublé.

11. 'I have been,' he said, 'to Argyle's prison.'

'*J'ai été*,' *dit-il* [or *répondit-il*], '*dans* [more natural than *à*] *la prison d'Argyle*'; or '*Je viens*,' *dit-il*, '*de la prison d'Argyle.*'

12. 'I have seen him within an hour of eternity, sleeping as sweetly as ever man did, but as for me—'

'within an hour of eternity.' This cannot be translated literally, i.e. the literal French translation would evidently convey no meaning. When such cases arise, there are two methods of dealing with them: expansion or simplification. Expanding the phrase, we might say, e.g. *Je l'ai vu, lui qu'une heure sépare de l'éternité*, or *lui qui, dans une heure, doit entrer dans l'éternité.* Simplifying it, we could give the sense, baldly, by *une heure avant sa mort* or, picturesquely, by *au seuil de l'éternité.*

'sleeping as sweetly': *dormant aussi doucement* (or *paisiblement*) or *d'un sommeil aussi paisible.*

'as ever man did': *qu'homme a jamais dormi* or *qu'homme dormait jamais*, which is a little more terse and direct.

'but as for me—': *mais quant à moi*—or, more dramatic, *mais moi*—.

'Je l'ai vu, au seuil de l'éternité, dormant d'un sommeil aussi paisible qu'homme dormait jamais, mais moi—.'

Suggested Rendering

Sur ces entrefaites, un des lords du Conseil vint au château, porteur d'un message de la part de ses pairs, et ordonna qu'on l'admît auprès du comte. Il lui fut répondu que le comte dormait. Le conseiller, croyant que ce n'était qu'un prétexte, insista pour qu'on le laissât entrer. On ouvrit doucement la porte du cachot, et là il vit Argyle, étendu sur son lit, dormant, dans ses fers, du paisible sommeil de l'enfance. La conscience du renégat s'éveilla. Il se retourna, le cœur serré, sortit précipitamment du château et chercha refuge chez une parente qui demeurait tout près. Là il se jeta sur un lit de repos et s'abandonna à un paroxysme de remords et de honte. Sa parente, effrayée par ses regards et ses plaintes, crut qu'il avait été atteint d'une maladie subite et le supplia de boire une coupe de vin. 'Non, non, cela ne me ferait aucun bien.' Elle le conjura de lui dire ce qui l'avait troublé. 'Je viens,' dit-il, 'de la prison d'Argyle. Je l'ai vu, au seuil de l'éternité, dormant d'un sommeil aussi paisible qu'homme dormait jamais, mais moi—.'

101. THE DEATH OF LOUVOIS

Louvois had been at the head of the military administration of his country during a quarter of a century; he had borne a chief part in the direction of the wars which had enlarged the French territory, and had filled the world with the renown of the French arms, and he had lived to see the beginning of a third war which taxed his great powers to the utmost.

In spite, however, of his abilities and of his services, he had become odious to Lewis and to her who governed Lewis. On the last occasion on which the King and the minister transacted business together,

the ill humour on both sides broke violently forth.
The servant, in his vexation, dashed his portfolio on
the ground. The master, forgetting what he seldom
forgot, that a king should be a gentleman, lifted his
cane. Fortunately his wife was present. She, with her
usual prudence, caught his arm. She then got Louvois
out of the room, and exhorted him to come back the
next day as if nothing had happened. The next day
he came, but with death in his face. The King, though
full of resentment, was touched with pity, and advised
Louvois to go home and take care of himself. That
evening the great minister died.

Macaulay, *History of England*

102. A FINE OLD CITY

Gazing[1] from those heights, the eye[2] beholds a
scene which cannot fail to[3] awaken, even in the least
sensitive bosom, feelings of pleasure and admiration.
At the foot of the heights flows a narrow and deep
river, with an antique bridge communicating[4] with a
long and narrow suburb, flanked on[5] either side by rich
meadows of the brightest green, beyond which[6] spreads
the fine old city. Yes, there[7] it spreads from north to
south, with[8] its venerable houses, its numerous gardens,
its thrice twelve churches, its mighty mound, which, if
tradition speaks true[9], was raised by human hands[10] to
serve as the grave heap[11] of an old heathen king, who
sits deep within it[12], with his sword in his hand and his
gold and silver treasures about him. There is a grey
old castle upon the top of that mighty mound; and
yonder, rising[13] three hundred feet above the soil,
from among those noble forest trees, behold that old
Norman master-work, that cloud-encircled cathedral
spire.

George Borrow

1 Is it necessary to translate 'Gazing'?   2 *le regard.*
3 Construction of the Verb? p. 71, § 44, MANQUER.   4 'which
leads to.'   5 Preposition? p. 86, § 48, ON.   6 Begin a

new Clause, omitting 'which.'   7 Is 'there' = *là* or em-
phatic enough to = *c'est là que?*   8 'with' denotes here not
a characteristic but accompaniment, and is therefore not *à*
but *avec.*   9 *dit vrai.*   10 *de main d'homme.*   11 'grave
heap' = *tumulus* (m.).   12 *se tient assis dans ses profondeurs.*
13 Supply *à.*

103. WILLIAM OF ORANGE

The death of Mary forced William to recall Anne,
who became by this event his successor; and with
Anne the Marlboroughs returned to court. The King
could not bend himself to trust the Earl again; but
as death drew near he saw in him the one man whose
splendid talents fitted him, in spite of the baseness and
treason of his life, to rule England and direct the
Grand Alliance in his stead. He employed Marlborough
therefore to negotiate the treaty of alliance with the
Emperor, and put him at the head of the army in
Flanders. But the Earl had only just taken the
command when a fall from his horse proved fatal to
the broken frame of the King. 'There was a time when
I should have been glad to have been delivered out
of my troubles,' the dying man whispered to Portland,
'but I own I see another scene and could wish to live
a little longer.' He knew, however, that the wish was
vain, and commended Marlborough to Anne as the
fittest person to lead her armies and guide her counsels.

J. R. Green

104. THE RETURN FROM ELBA

It was on Sunday, 26th February[1], that Napoleon
left the little island of Elba. The force with which he
was[2] once more to change the fortunes of France
consisted of[3] only a thousand[4] men. On the 1st of
March[1] he reached Cannes, and at once began his
march towards the centre of a kingdom from which[5]
he had been but recently expelled. At first he was
coldly received by the peasants, but as he approached

Dauphiné, the[6] cradle of the Revolution, they greeted him more warmly. When he came at length to Grenoble, some of the King's soldiers came out to meet him[7], scarcely knowing whether they ought to call upon him to surrender or to open fire on his little party. Seeing their hesitation, Napoleon came forward[8] alone and unarmed, and exclaimed, 'Let him who[9] would kill his Emperor now do so!' The soldiers flung down their arms and hailed with loud cheers the general who so often had led them to victory[6]. General Marchand, the[6] commandant of Grenoble, was[10] unable to influence those who had remained in the town: they made him prisoner and delivered up the city to Buonaparte, who started[11] soon afterwards in triumph for the French capital[12].

Sir Walter Scott

1 p. 38, § 22.   2 Use *aller*.   3 Use *compter*.   4 p. 37, § 21.   5 *d'où*.   6 p. 23, § 12.   7 *à sa rencontre*. Tense? *avancer* or *s'avancer*? p. 11, § 7, ADVANCE.   9 'If anyone among you...let him,' etc.   10 Tense?   11 Use *commencer sa marche*.   12 Gender? p. 35, § 18.

105. THE BRITISH EMPIRE

Our Empire grew from the adventurous spirit of our fathers. They went forth urged by the love of adventure, by the passion for discovery, by the desire for a freer life in new countries. Wherever they went they carried with them the traditions, the habits, the ideals of their Mother Country. Wherever they settled they planted a new homeland. And though mountains and the waste of seas divided them, they never lost that golden thread of the spirit which drew their thoughts back to the land of their birth.

Even their children and their children's children—to whom Great Britain was no more than a name—a vision—spoke of it always as home. In this sense of kinship the Empire finds its brightest glory and its most essential strength.

Stanley Baldwin

106. MARSHAL NEY IMPRISONED

At Waterloo Ney led several cavalry charges against the British squares; and, after five horses had been killed[1] under him, he marched at the head of the Old Guard. He fought till night in the midst of the plain and he was[2] the last French general who left[3] the battle-field. When all was[2] lost, knowing to what dangers he was exposed, he fled to[4] Auvergne, where he found shelter in the castle of a friend at Aurillac. At[5] a dinner given by his protector, one of the guests observed a magnificent sabre. The authorities were supplied[6] with a description of it and it was recognized as the sabre of Ney. On the 5th of August the castle was searched, and the marshal taken and imprisoned.

1 Mood and Tense? p. 77, § 45.   2 Tense?   3 Say 'to leave'; p. 21, § 10.   4 Preposition? p. 8, § 4.   5 *A l'occasion de.*   6 Avoid the Passive; 'to *supply* someone *with*' is *fournir* quelque chose *à* quelqu'un.

107. THE EXECUTION OF MARSHAL NEY

During his trial he showed great calmness and when the judge who read the sentence of death came to his titles, Ney interrupted him: 'There is no need of titles now. I am Michel Ney and soon shall be but a handful of dust.' On the 7th of December, at nine o'clock a.m., he was shot in the garden of the Luxembourg. When an attempt was made to blindfold him, he tore away the bandage, and indignantly exclaimed: 'Have you forgotten that for twenty-six years I have lived among bullets?' Then turning to the soldiers, he declared that he had never been a traitor to his country and, laying his hand upon his heart, called out, with a steady voice: 'Aim true. France for ever! Fire!'

108. A RICH FIND

In the first week of July 1851 a native shepherd, employed by[1] a doctor[2] near Bathurst, discovered a large mass of gold whilst tending[3] his sheep. His

attention was first attracted by a speck of some
glittering yellow substance upon the surface of a block
of quartz, of which he broke off a portion. Then he
realized what he had found, and at once started off
home to announce the discovery to his master. As
may well be supposed[4], the worthy doctor[2] lost not a
moment. Quick as his horse could carry him, he was[5]
on the spot; and in a very short time three blocks of
quartz containing three hundredweight of gold and
worth at least £4000[6] each[7], were released from the bed
where they had rested for thousands of years, awaiting[8]
the hand of civilized man to disturb them.

1 'employed by' = 'in the service of'; p. 85, § 48, IN.
2 *médecin*, the general term, a 'medical man'; *docteur*, used in
addressing, or speaking of, a medical man whom you know.
3 Use *en* and the verbal form in *-ant.*　　4 Avoid the Passive.
5 Tense?　　6 p. 80, § 46, AT LEAST.　　7 Adjective or
Pronoun? p. 46, § 32, 1.　　8 Turn by 'waiting till...should
disturb.'

109. FIRST IMPRESSIONS OF ENGLAND

Mr W. H. Hudson, the celebrated American novelist
who spent a great part of his life in England, used to
give a delightful account of his impressions on his first
arrival, in 1869. As soon as I landed, he said, I made
up my mind to stay for a little at Southampton,
instead of going straight to London as most of the
others did. I got a room and went for a walk about the
town. And suddenly I smelt England! I asked myself
what so strange a smell could be. It was sweet and
yet there was, as it were, a touch of sourness in it, and
it seemed warm and fat and strong and pervading and
yet elusive. And I said, 'Why, this is the typical smell
of England,' and I went up one street and down
another, and sometimes I lost it, or only smelt it
faintly, and then again it came in heavy puffs, and

though so strange to me I found it very attractive. But it was only long afterwards that I knew it was the smell of a brewery!

Times, Feb. 15, 1924,
review of Morley Roberts, W. H. Hudson (adapted)

110. THE PENTLAND FIRTH

It was on[1] a charming morning towards the end of June that our vessel left[2] the port of Wick and stood out to sea[3]. The sea was beautifully green, the air mild, and not a breath of wind ruffled[4] the surface of the waters. The coast of Caithness on our left was bare and mostly level, [5]with high hills rising in the distance. In[6] two hours we were off John o' Groats, the north-eastern extremity of Great Britain, and about to[7] cross the Pentland Firth, a channel about twenty miles in length[8] and from five and a half to eight miles in breadth. The dangers of this dreaded strait arise from the meeting of the tides of the Atlantic and the North Sea. The currents and whirlpools make the crossing extremely unpleasant in[1] heavy weather[9]. But on this occasion[10] the sea was so tranquil that the smallest boat might have crossed without any risk.

1 p. 89, § 49, PAR.   2 p. 89, § 49, LEAVE.   3 'to stand out to sea' = *prendre le large*.   4 Remember to complete the negative; p. 81, § 47.   5 Omit 'with' and begin a new clause.   6 *dans* or *en* or *au bout de*? p. 85, § 48, IN.   7 p. 84, § 48, ABOUT.   8 *long de vingt milles*.   9 *le gros temps*.   10 'this time'; see Model Lesson I, p. 98.

111. THE CROSSING OF THE BERESINA

I recollect reading, in an account of the famous retreat from Moscow, how the French army, worn out, tired, and dejected, at length came to a great river over which there was but one bridge. Disorganized and demoralized as that army was, the struggle must certainly have been a terrible one—

everyone heeding only himself, and crushing through
the ranks and treading down his fellows. The writer
of the narrative, who was himself one of those who
were fortunate enough to succeed in getting over,
ascribed his escape to the fact that he saw striding
onward through the mass a great strong fellow—one of
the French Cuirassiers, who had on a large blue cloak—
and he had enough presence of mind to catch and
retain a hold of this strong man's cloak. He says,
'I caught hold of his cloak, and although he swore at
me and cut at and struck me by turns, and at last,
when he found he could not shake me off, fell to en-
treating me to leave go, I still kept tight hold of him,
and would not quit my grasp until he had at last
dragged me through.'   T. H. Huxley

112. AN UNFORTUNATE ERROR

When the Glasgow express was standing in Crewe
station at two in[1] the morning[2], a passenger called the
guard and said, 'I am going to Carlisle. I am very
tired and sleepy[3], but I am afraid I may[4] not wake up
in time. Will[5] you put me out at Carlisle?' 'Yes, sir,'
replied the guard. 'Thank you. I have a very important engagement in the morning[2] and absolutely
must[5] get out there. I am a heavy sleeper[6] and hate[7]
being disturbed, and I may be[8] very rude when you
come[5]. I am afraid I may even swear[9] at you and
resist. But pay no attention! Here's five shillings for
you! Get a few porters if you like, but put me out
on the platform at Carlisle, whatever I say.' The
guard smiled, pocketed the tip, saying, 'All right[10],
sir. You may depend on me.'

Thereupon the traveller wrapped himself up in[11]
his rug and soon fell into a deep slumber. When the
train was coming into a big station, he awoke with a
start and saw, to his horror, that the station was
Glasgow. On the platform he met the guard and
proceeded[12] to give him a piece of his mind[13]. The

guard listened patiently and, when at last the traveller had exhausted his vocabulary[14], calmly observed: 'Ay man[15], ye sweir bonny[16]. But you're naething[17] to the man we pit oot[18] at Carlisle.'

1 Use *de*.   2 *matin* or *matinée*? p. 87, § 49, AN, ANNÉE.
3 *et j'ai bien envie de dormir*.   4 Use an Infinitive; p. 21,
§ 10.   5 Tense?   6 *J'ai le sommeil très lourd*.   7 Use
détester + *que* + Subjunctive.   8 Use *il se peut que*.   9 Use
vous dire de gros mots. Construction of the Verb? p. 54, § 40, 2.
10 *Entendu!*   11 *dans*.   12 *se mit en devoir de* + Infinitive.
13 'say what he thought of him'; p. 73, § 44, PENSER.   14 *répertoire* (m.).   15 '*Oui, mon pauvre monsieur.*'   16 *joli-
ment bien*.   17 *mais ce n'est rien à côté de*.   18 Use
débarquer.

113. NELL AND HER GRANDFATHER

The supper was very good but Nell was too tired to eat, and yet would not leave her grandfather. He sat listening with a smile to all that his new friends said and it was not until they retired yawning to their room that he followed the child up-stairs.

It was but a loft divided into two compartments where they were to rest, but they were well pleased with their lodging and had hoped for none so good. The old man was uneasy when he had lain down, and begged that Nell would come and sit at his bedside as she had done so often. She hastened to him and sat there till he slept.

There was a little window, hardly more than a chink in the wall, in her room, and when she left him she opened it, quite wondering at the silence.

Charles Dickens, *The Old Curiosity Shop*

114. A PATRIARCH

'Who is this gray-haired patriarch?' asked the young men of[1] their sires. 'Who is this venerable brother?' asked the old men among themselves. But none could[2] make reply. The fathers of the people, those of[3] fourscore years and upwards were disturbed, deeming it strange that they should[4] forget one[5] of such evident authority[6], whom they must have known[7] in their early days[8]. 'Whence did he come[9]? What is his purpose? Who can this old man be?' whispered the wondering crowd. Meanwhile the venerable stranger, staff in hand[10], was pursuing his solitary walk along the centre of the street. As he drew near the advancing soldiers, and as the roll of the drum came full on his ears, he marched onward with a warrior's step, keeping time to the military music. Thus the old man advanced on[11] one side and the soldiers and magistrates on the other, till[12], when scarcely twenty yards remained between them, he grasped his staff by the middle and held it before him like a leader's truncheon. 'Stand!'[13] he cried. At the old man's word and [14]outstretched arm the roll of the drum was hushed at once and the advancing line stood still.   Hawthorne

1 à.   2 Tense? Remember to complete the negative; p. 81, § 47.   3 'who were aged eighty.'   4 Mood?   5 = 'have forgotten a man.'   6 *imbu d'une autorité si évidente.* 7 Tense? To decide the proper tense, ask yourself what 'they' actually said to themselves; see p. 58, § 41, under WOULD. 8 *au temps de leur jeunesse.*   9 Tense? What auxiliary verb is used with *venir?*   10 p. 85, § 48, IN.   11 p. 86, § 48, ON. 12 Is 'till' necessary? p. 21, § 10.   13 The military term is *Halte!*   14 Supply 'before his.'

115. AN ENGLISH BELL

I remember many years ago standing on the terrace of a beautiful villa near Florence. It was a September evening, and the valley below was transfigured in the long horizontal rays of the declining sun. And then I heard a bell, such a bell as never was on land or sea, a bell whose every vibration found an echo in my innermost heart. I said to my hostess, 'That is the most beautiful bell I have ever heard.' 'Yes,' she replied, 'it is an English bell.' And so it was. For generations its sound had gone out over English fields giving the hours of work and prayer to English folk

from the tower of an English abbey, and then came
the Reformation, and some wise Italian bought the
bell, whose work at home was done, and sent it to
the valley of the Arno, where, after four centuries, it
stirred the heart of a wandering Englishman and made
him sick for home.

Thus the chance word of a Latin inscription, a line
in the anthology, a phrase of Horace, or a 'chorus
ending of Euripides,' plucks at the heart strings and
stirs a thousand memories, memories subconscious and
ancestral.   Stanley Baldwin

116. A WALK

They crossed the water by a simple[1] bridge, in
character with[2] the general air of the scene[3]; it was a
spot less adorned than any[4] they had yet visited; and
the valley...allowed room[5] only for the stream, and
a narrow walk amidst the rough[6] coppice-wood which
bordered it. Elizabeth longed to explore its[7] windings;
but when they had[8] crossed the bridge and perceived
their distance[9] from the house, Mrs Gardiner, who was
not a great walker, could[8] go no farther, and thought[9]
only of[10] returning to the carriage as quickly as possible.
Her niece was, therefore, obliged to submit, and they
took their way[11] towards the house on the opposite
side of the river in the nearest direction[12]; but their
progress was slow[13], for Mr Gardiner, though seldom
able to indulge the taste, was very fond of fishing, and
was so much engaged in watching[14] the occasional
appearance[13] of some fish in the water, and talking to
the man[15] about them[16], that he advanced[17] but little.
                                              Jane Austen

1 *rustique.*   2 *en harmonie avec.*   3 *paysage* or *scène?*
4 *aucun.*   5 Use *offrir passage.*   6 *emmêlé* or *irrégulier.*
7 Use *en* + Definite Article.   8 Tense? p. 79, § 45, WHEN, 3.
9 'at what distance they were from.'   10 Construction of
Verb? p. 73, § 44, PENSER.   11 Use *se diriger.*   12 *par le
chemin le plus court.*   13 Simplify the English.   14 *guetter*
or *regarder?*   15 *garde.*   16 Use *en.*   17 p. 11, § 7, ADVANCE.

117. A MORNING WALK

Another bright day shining through the small casement awoke the child. At sight of the strange room she started up in alarm, wondering how she had been moved from the familiar chamber in which she seemed to have fallen asleep last night, and whither she had been conveyed. But another glance around called to her mind all that had lately passed, and she sprang from her bed, hoping and trusting.

It was yet early, and the old man being still asleep she walked out into the churchyard, brushing the dew from the long grass with her feet and often turning aside from places where it grew longer than in others, that she might not tread upon the graves.

It was a very quiet place, as such a place should be, save for the cawing of the rooks who had built their nests among the branches of some tall old trees and were calling to one another, high up in the air.

Charles Dickens, *The Old Curiosity Shop*

118. LOST IN LONDON

One night[1], I had roamed into the city, and was walking slowly in my usual way[2], musing upon a great many things, when an inquiry was addressed to me[3] in a soft, sweet voice, that struck me very pleasantly. I turned hastily round[4], and found at my elbow a pretty little girl, who begged to be directed[3] to a certain street at a considerable distance[5], and indeed in quite another quarter of the town.

'It is a very long way[6] from here,' said I.

'I know that, Sir,' she replied timidly. 'I am afraid it is a very long way, for I came from there to-night.'

'Alone?' said I, in some surprise[7].

'Oh yes, I don't mind that[8], but I am a little frightened now, for I have lost my road.'

'And what made you ask it of me[9]? Suppose I should[10] tell you wrong[11].'

'I am sure you will not do that,' said the little creature, 'you are such[12] a very old gentleman, and walk so slow yourself.'

I cannot describe how much I was impressed by this appeal.

'Come,' said I, 'I'll take[13] you there.'

Charles Dickens, *The Old Curiosity Shop*

1 *nuit* or *soir*? p. 15, § 7, NIGHT.   2 *selon mon habitude.*
3 Simplify the English first.   4 *se retourner.*   5 Use *très éloigné.*   6 'a very long way' = 'very far.'   7 'somewhat surprised.'   8 *Cela ne m'effraye pas.*   9 Accented.
10 Supply *si* and use the Imperfect.   11 Use *tromper.*
12 Beware of *tel*; p. 81, § 46, SO.   13 p. 91, § 49, TAKE.

119. THE PIECE OF GOLD

The sight of the old church and the graves about it in the moonlight, and the dark trees whispering among themselves made her more thoughtful than before. She closed the window again, and, sitting down upon the bed, thought of the life that was before them.

She had a little money, but it was very little, and when that was gone they must begin to beg. There was one piece of gold among it and she decided to hide this coin and never produce it unless their case was absolutely desperate.

Her resolution taken, she sewed the piece of gold into her dress, and going to bed with a lighter heart, sank into a deep slumber.

Charles Dickens, *The Old Curiosity Shop*

120. JEANIE DEANS

A young woman of rather low stature, whose countenance was very modest and pleasing in expression[1], though sunburnt, somewhat freckled, and not possessing regular features, was ushered into the splendid library[2]. She wore the plaid of her country, adjusted so as partly[3] to cover her head, and partly to fall back over her shoulders. A quantity of fair hair, disposed with great simplicity, appeared in front of[4] her round and good-humoured face, to which the solemnity of her errand, and her sense of the Duke's rank and importance, gave an appearance of deep awe.

She stopped near the door, and made her deepest reverence, without uttering a syllable. The Duke of Argyle advanced towards her; and, if she admired his graceful deportment and rich dress, decorated with the orders which had been deservedly bestowed upon him[5], his courteous manner, and quick and intelligent cast of countenance[6], he[7] on his part was not less struck with the quiet simplicity and modesty expressed in[8] the dress, manners and countenance of his humble countrywoman.

Sir Walter Scott, *The Heart of Midlothian*

1 Turn by 'had a very modest...expression.'   2 In French the natural order would be 'One ushered into, etc....a young woman (*jeune fille*).'   3 Turn by 'so that one part covered,' etc.   4 Use *couronner* for the whole expression.   5 'the orders which he had so well deserved.'   6 *physionomie* (f.). 7 Accented form.   8 Use a Relative Clause and invert.

121. HER FATHER'S DOOR

When no one in the house was stirring, and the lights were all extinguished, she would softly leave her own room, and with noiseless step descend the staircase and approach her father's door. Against it, scarcely breathing, she would rest her face and head, and press her lips in the yearning of her love. She crouched upon the cold stone floor outside it every night, to listen even for his breath. In her desire to win his affection she would have knelt down at his feet, if she had dared, in humble supplication.

No one knew it. No one thought of it. The door was ever closed, and he shut up within. He went out once or twice, and it was said in the house that he was very soon going on his country journey: but he lived in those rooms, and lived alone, and never saw her, or inquired for her. Perhaps he did not even know that she was in the house. Charles Dickens, *Dombey and Son*

122. THE ABBEY

Now[1] the great church, and the buildings of the Abbey where the monks lived[2], were about three miles[3] from the town, and the town stood[4] on a hill overlooking the rich autumn country: it[5] was girt about with great walls that had overhanging battlements, and towers at certain places all along the walls, and often we could see from the churchyard or the Abbey garden the flash of helmets and spears, and the dim shadowy waving of banners, as the knights and lords and men-at-arms passed to and fro along the battlements; and we could see too in the town the three spires of the three churches; and the spire of the Cathedral, which was the tallest of the three, was gilt all over, and always at night-time[6] a great lamp shone from it[7] that hung in the spire midway[8] between the roof of the church and the cross at the top of the spire. The Abbey was not girt by stone walls, but by a circle of poplar trees, and whenever a wind passed over them, were it ever so little[9] a breath, it set them all a-ripple[10]. W. Morris, *Story of the Unknown Church*

1 p. 80, § 46, NOW. 2 For 'live,' see Model Lesson I, p. 95. 3 Supply a Preposition; p. 83, § 48, 1. For 'miles,' see Passage 82, note 2. 4 p. 91, § 49, STAND. 5 *ce, il* or *elle*, or *la ville*? p. 42, § 26. 6 *nuit* or *soir*? p. 15, § 7, NIGHT. 7 Remember that the Relative must come next the Antecedent. 8 *à mi-hauteur de la flèche*. 9 'were it only a little breath' (*un petit souffle*); for 'it,' see p. 42, § 26. 10 'they began to ripple' (*onduler*).

123. A DISAGREEABLE OLD MAN

The old man had lived in the country for many years when we met for the first time. He was suspicious of everyone and did not like to be disturbed, even by the charwoman who came every day to do the housework. 'Out you go, as soon as you have finished your work,' he would say, as he watched her while he sat by the fireside. When she tried to talk to him, he would tell her to be quiet, or he would take up a book from the table and begin to read. 'Even though the truth should offend him, someone ought to tell him that this sort of life only serves to make him unhappy,' I used to say to my friend. 'Well, you will see what you can do,' he would answer, 'but I don't think you will succeed in changing his character.' I hesitated for a long time, but at last one day I did go to see him. I knocked at the door, which opened suddenly, and I saw the old man standing in front of me.

124. AN OLD GENTLEMAN

He was a good-looking gentleman of about sixty years of age. His hair was snow white, very plentiful, and somewhat like[1] wool of the finest description[2]. His whiskers were very large and very white, and gave to his face the appearance of a benevolent sleepy old lion. His dress was always unexceptionable[3]. He was not a man given to much talking, but what little he did say[4] was generally well said. His reading seldom went beyond[5] romances and poetry of the lightest description[5]. He was an accomplished judge of wine, though he never drank to excess[6]; and a most inexorable[7] critic in all affairs touching[5] the kitchen. He had much to forgive in his own family, since[8] a family had grown up around him, and had forgiven everything—except inattention to[5] his dinner. His weakness in that respect was now fully understood, and his temper[9] but seldom tried.

Anthony Trollope, Barchester Towers

1 Use *semblable à*.   2 'a very fine wool.'   3 Simplify; e.g. 'He was always dressed in an irreproachable way.'   4 *le peu qu'il disait*.   5 Simplify the English.   6 *à l'excès*. 7 *des plus inexorables*.   8 Meaning?   9 *sa bonne humeur*.

125. A DREAM

A plan occurred to me for passing the night, which I was going to carry into execution. This was to lie behind the wall at the back of my old school. I imagined it would be a kind of company to have the boys and the bedroom where I used to tell the stories, so near me; although the boys would know nothing of my being there, and the bedroom would yield me no shelter. It cost me some trouble to find out Salem House; but I found it and I lay down beside the wall, having first walked round it and looked up at the windows, and seen that all was dark and silent within.

Sleep came upon me, and I dreamed of lying on my old school-bed, talking to the boys in my room; and found myself sitting upright, looking wildly at the stars which were glistening above me. When I remembered where I was, a feeling stole upon me that made me get up, afraid of I don't know what, and walk about. But the fainter glimmering of the stars and the pale light in the sky where the day was coming reassured me, and I lay down again and slept, until the warm beams of the sun and the ringing of the morning bell at Salem House awoke me.   Dickens

126. OSBALDISTONE MEETS ROB ROY

'You are then the person who requested to meet me here at this unusual hour?'

'I am[1],' he replied. 'Follow me, and you shall know my reasons.'

'Before following you, I must know your name and purpose,' I answered.

'I am a man,' was the reply; 'and my purpose is friendly to you[2].'

'A man!' I repeated; 'that is[3] a very brief description.'

'It[4] will serve for one[5] who has no other[6] to give,' said the stranger.

'He[7] that is without name, without friends, without coin, without country, is still at least a man; and he that has all these[8] is no more[9]. You must follow me, or remain in ignorance of[10] the information which I have to give you.'

There was something short[11], determined, and even stern, in the man's manner, certainly not[12] well calculated to inspire confidence.

'What is it you fear?' he said, impatiently. 'To[13] whom, think ye, is your life of such consequence, that they should seek to bereave you of it?'

'I fear nothing,' I replied, firmly though somewhat hastily. 'Walk on—I attend you.'

Sir Walter Scott, *Rob Roy*

1 Complete the predicate; p. 38, § 23, 1.　　2 Turn by 'I have only friendly intentions.'　3 p. 42, § 26, 4.　4 When 'it' clearly stands for an immediately preceding Noun, the Personal Pronoun, and not *cela*, must be used.　5 Either *celui* or *quelqu'un*.　6 Remember *en*; p. 39, § 23, 2.　7 Remember *celui*; p. 43, § 27.　8 *tout cela*.　9 *n'est rien de plus*. 10 *continuer d'ignorer*.　11 Construction after *quelque chose*? p. 91, § 49, SOMETHING.　12 Use a Relative Clause, but alter the order of words so that the Relative may stand next to its Antecedent; p. 44, § 28, 3.　13 *Pour*.

127. IN THE ATTIC

Maggie soon thought she had been hours in the attic, and it must be tea-time, and they were all having their tea, and not thinking of her. Well, then, she would stay up there and starve herself—hide herself behind the tub, and stay there all night; and then they would all be frightened, and Tom would be sorry. Thus Maggie thought in the pride of her heart, as she crept behind the tub; but presently she began to cry again at the idea that they didn't mind her being there. If she went down again to Tom now—would he forgive her?—perhaps her father would be there, and he would take her part. But then she wanted Tom to forgive her because he loved her, not because his father told

him. No, she would never go down if Tom didn't
come to fetch her. This resolution lasted for five dark
minutes behind the tub; but then the need of being
loved, the strongest need in poor Maggie's nature,
began to wrestle with her pride and soon threw it.
She crept from behind her tub into the twilight of the
long attic, but just then she head a quick footstep on
the stairs.   George Eliot, *The Mill on the Floss*

128. THE MASTER OF RAVENSWOOD. i

'Lucy, my dear Lucy, are you safe? are you well[1]?'
were the only words that broke[2] from Sir William
Ashton as he embraced his daughter.

'I am well, sir, thank God!—but this gentleman,'
she said, quitting his arm, 'what must he think
of me?'

'This gentleman,' said Sir William Ashton, 'will,
I trust, not regret the trouble we have given him,
when[3] I assure him of the gratitude of[4] the Lord
Keeper for the greatest service which one man ever
rendered[5] to another—for[6] the life of my child—for
my own life, which he has saved by his bravery and
presence of mind. He will, I am sure, permit us to
request—'

'Request nothing of ME[7], my lord,' said the stranger,
in[8] a stern and peremptory tone; 'I am the Master of
Ravenswood.'

There was a dead pause of surprise, not unmixed
with[9] less pleasant feelings. The Master wrapped
himself in his cloak, made a haughty inclination
towards[10] Lucy, muttering a few words of courtesy,
and, turning from them, was immediately lost in the
thicket.   Sir Walter Scott, *The Bride of Lammermoor*

1 For both expressions *vous n'êtes pas blessée?* will be enough.
2 Is this a case for the Indicative or the Subjunctive? p. 54,
§ 40, 4.   3 Translate 'when' here by *puisque*.   4 *que lui*

a valu, de la part du garde du sceau royal.   **5** Mood and Tense?   **6** It is neater to turn by *avoir sauvé*.   **7** Remember that the Personal Pronoun is required twice; p. 38, § 23, 1.   **8** *de*.   **9** Say, e.g. *où la surprise se mêlait à*, etc. **10** Use *devant*.

129. THE MASTER OF RAVENSWOOD. ii

'The Master of Ravenswood!' said the Lord Keeper, when he had recovered from his astonishment— 'Hasten after him—stop him—beg him to speak to me for a single moment.'

The two foresters accordingly set off in pursuit of the stranger. They speedily reappeared, and, in an embarrassed and awkward manner, said the gentleman would not return. The Lord Keeper took one of the fellows aside, and questioned him more closely.

'He just said he would not come back,' said the man.

'He said something more, sir, and I insist on knowing what it was.'

'Why, then, my lord,' said the man, looking down, 'he said—But it would be no pleasure to your lordship to hear it, for I daresay the Master meant no ill.'

'That's none of your concern, sir; I desire to hear the very words.'

'Well, then,' replied the man, 'he said, "Tell Sir William Ashton that the next time he and I forgather, he will not be half so blithe of our meeting as of our parting."'

'Very well, sir,' said the Lord Keeper, 'I believe he alludes to a wager we have on our hawks—it is a matter of no consequence.'

Sir Walter Scott, *The Bride of Lammermoor*

130. OLD MORTALITY

According to the belief of most people, Old Mortality was lineally descended from some of those champions of the Covenant whose deeds and sufferings were his favourite theme. He is said to have held[1], at one period of his life, a small moorland farm; but he had long renounced every gainful calling[2]. In the language[3] of Scripture, he left[4] his house, his home and his kindred, and wandered[5] about until the day of his death. During[6] this long pilgrimage, he visited every year the graves of the unfortunate Covenanters who had died for their faith during[6] the reigns of the last two[7] monarchs of the Stewart[8] line. In the most lonely recesses of the mountains the moor-fowl[9] shooter has often been surprised to find him busied in cleaning the moss from the grey stones and repairing the emblems of death with which[10] these simple monuments are usually adorned, trimming[11], as it were[12], the beacon-light which was to warn[13] future generations to defend their religion even unto death.

Sir Walter Scott, *Old Mortality*

1 = 'had.' 2 *occupation rémunératrice.* 3 *Pour emprunter le langage de la Bible.*   4 Tense? p. 61, § 42, 5; *abandonner, laisser,* or *quitter?* p. 89, § 49, LEAVE. 5 *pour errer.* 6 p. 85, § 48, IN.   7 Order of words? p. 37, § 20.   8 *des Stuarts.* 9 *coq de bruyère.* 10 *dont.* 11 Use *entretenir.* 12 *pour ainsi dire.* 13 Use *appeler…à.*

VOCABULARY

*[All words in which the h is aspirated are marked thus *.]*

a, an, un, *fem.* une.
abbey, abbaye (*f.*).
ability, capacité (*f.*).
able, capable; to be able, pouvoir; avoir le moyen de, avoir l'occasion de.
about, § 48; de, sur, au sujet de, autour (de), quelque, environ; to jump about, sauter deçà, delà; to walk about, se promener de long en large.
above, au-dessus (de); above all, surtout.
abroad, à l'étranger.
abruptly, brusquement.
absence, absence (*f.*).
absolutely, absolument.
accompany, to, accompagner.
accomplish, to, faire, accomplir.
accomplished, parfait.
accord, with one, d'un commun accord.
according to, selon.
accordingly, donc.
account, récit (*m.*).
accustomed, to get, s'habituer.
across, à travers.
active, actif.
address, to, adresser, s'adresser à.
adjust, to, arranger.
administration, administration (*f.*).
admiration, admiration (*f.*).
admire, to, admirer.
adorn with, to, orner de.
advancing (*adj.*), en marche.
adventure, aventure (*f.*).
adventurous, d'aventure, aventureux.
advice, avis (*m.*); piece of advice, conseil (*m.*).
advise, to, conseiller.
adviser, conseiller (*m.*).
affection, affection (*f.*).
afraid, to be, craindre, avoir peur.
Africa, Afrique (*f.*).

after (*prep.*), après, derrière, suivant; (*conj.*), après que, quand.
afternoon, après-midi (*m.f.*).
afterwards, par la suite, plus tard.
again, § 46; de nouveau.
against, contre.
age, âge (*m.*).
agility, agilité (*f.*).
Agnes, Agnès (*f.*).
ago, *use* il y a.
agree, to, convenir (de), consentir (à).
agreed! d'accord!
aid, to, aider.
aim, to, viser; aim true, viser juste.
air, air, aspect (*m.*); in the air, en l'air.
Aladdin, Aladin (*m.*).
alarm, in, tout effrayé.
alarm, to, effrayer.
alas! hélas!
all, tout (87, § 49); not at all, pas du tout.
alliance, alliance (*f.*).
allow, to, permettre.
allude, to, faire allusion.
almost, presque.
alone, seul, tout seul.
along, le long de.
along, to go, passer dans, longer.
already, déjà.
altar, autel (*m.*).
alter, to, changer.
although, bien que, quoique.
always, toujours.
ambition, ambition (*f.*).
America, Amérique (*f.*).
American, américain.
amidst, au milieu de.
among, amongst, parmi.
amuse, to, amuser.
ancestral, *turn by e.g.* que nous tenons de nos pères.
and, et.
angel, ange (*m.*).

angrily, en colère.

angry, to be, se fâcher, être fâché; **make very angry,** mettre en fureur.

animal, animal (*m.*).

announce, to, annoncer; **announce something to someone,** mettre qqn. au courant de quelque chose.

another, un autre.

answer, réponse (*f.*).

answer, to, répondre (à).

anthology, anthologie (*f.*).

Antioch, Antioche (*f.*).

antique, ancien, antique.

anxious, inquiet, anxieux.

any, § 34; du, de la, des; aucun, le moindre; tout.

anything, § 34; **anything that,** ce qui.

apparel, habits (*m.pl.*).

apparition, apparition (*f.*).

appeal, appel (*m.*).

appear, to, paraître, apparaître, comparaître, surgir.

appearance, air, aspect (*m.*).

appetite, appétit (*m.*).

apple, pomme (*f.*).

approach, to, (s')approcher.

April, avril (*m.*).

aptitude, aptitude (*f.*).

argue, to, discuter.

Ariadne, Ariane (*f.*).

arise from, to, *turn by* être causé par.

arithmetic, arithmétique (*f.*).

arm, bras (*m.*); arme (*f.*); **in arms,** sous les armes.

arm, to, armer.

armchair, fauteuil (*m.*).

army, armée (*f.*).

around (*prep.*), autour de; (*adv.*), autour, à la ronde.

arrange, to, ranger, arranger.

arrival, arrivée (*f.*).

arrive, to, arriver.

art, art (*m.*).

as, comme, à mesure que, pendant que, au moment que, un jour que; **dressed as,** habillé en; **as...as,** aussi...que; **as many (much),** autant.

ascribe, to, attribuer.

ashamed, *honteux.

aside, à part; **draw aside,** prendre à part; **turn aside,** (se) détourner.

ask, to, demander, prier; **ask for,** demander, demander après; **ask a question,** poser une question.

asleep, endormi; **to be asleep,** dormir, être endormi.

ass, âne (*m.*).

assemble, to, (s')assembler.

assure, to, assurer.

astonish, to, étonner.

astonishment, étonnement (*m.*).

at, à.

Athens, Athènes (*f.*).

Atlantic, Atlantique (*m.*).

attack, to, attaquer.

attempt, to, essayer.

attend, to, entourer; suivre.

attention, attention (*f.*); **to pay attention,** faire attention.

attentively, attentivement.

Attic, attique.

attic, mansarde (*f.*).

attired, habillé; paré.

attract, to, attirer.

attractive, agréable.

attribute, to, attribuer.

audience (*of a king*), audience (*f.*).

August, août (*m.*).

authority, autorité (*f.*)

autumn, automne (*m.f.*).

avarice, cupidité (*f.*).

avenue, avenue (*f.*).

awake, éveillé.

awake, to, (s')éveiller, (se) réveiller.

award, to, adjuger.

away, loin; **some miles away,** à quelques milles de là.

awe, respect (*m.*).

awkward, gauche.

axe, *hache (*f.*).

baby, bébé (*m.*), petit enfant.

back (*adj.*), de derrière.

bad, mauvais.

bag, sac (*m.*).

ball (dance), bal (*m.*).
balmy, parfumé.
bandage, bandeau (*m.*).
bandit, bandit (*m.*); **banditti**, bandits (*m.pl.*).
bank (*of a river*), berge (*f.*), bord (*m.*); talus (*m.*).
banner, bannière (*f.*), étendard (*m.*).
banquet, banquet, festin (*m.*).
bar, barreau (*m.*).
bard, barde (*m.*).
bare, nu.
barn, grange (*f.*).
baron, baron (*m.*).
barren, aride.
baseness, bassesse (*f.*).
basket, corbeille (*f.*), panier (*m.*).
battlefield, champ (*m.*) de bataille.
battlement, créneau (*m.*).
be, to, être; y avoir; se trouver.
beach, plage (*f.*).
beacon-light, phare (*m.*).
beads, chapelet (*m.*).
beak, bec (*m.*).
beam, rayon (*m.*).
bear, ours (*m.*).
bear, to, porter; supporter; **bear up against**, supporter.
beautiful, beau, joli; mélodieux.
because, parce que.
become, to, devenir; se changer en.
bed, lit (*m.*), couche (*f.*); **in bed**, au lit; **to go to bed**, se coucher; **to put into bed**, coucher dans le lit.
bedroom, dortoir (*m.*).
bedside, chevet (*m.*).
befall, to, arriver.
before (*prep.*), devant, avant; (*conj.*), avant que; (*adv.*), déjà, auparavant.
beg, to, mendier; prier.
begin, to, commencer, se mettre à.
beginning, commencement (*m.*).
behave, to, se conduire.
behind, derrière.
behold, voilà.
behold, to, apercevoir, voir; **the eye beholds**, le regard embrasse.
belief, croyance (*f.*).
believe, to, croire, supposer.
bell, cloche (*f.*). See *p.* 12.
belong, to, appartenir.
beloved, bien-aimé.
below, en bas, à ses pieds.
bend, to, plier.
benevolent, débonnaire, bienveillant.
bereave, to, priver.
beseech, to, prier.
beside, à côté de, au pied de.
besides, d'ailleurs.
best (*adj.*), meilleur; (*adv.*), mieux; **to do one's best**, faire de son mieux; **it is best to**, il vaut mieux.
betray, to, trahir.
better, meilleur, mieux; **it is better to**, il vaut mieux.
between, entre.
beyond, au-delà.
Bible, Bible (*f.*).
bid, to, ordonner.
big, gros; important.
bird, oiseau (*m.*).
birth, naissance (*f.*); **of birth**, natal, de naissance.
birthday, fête (*f.*).
bishop, évêque (*m.*).
bit, morceau; **not a bit**, pas un seul morceau.
bite, to, mordre.
bitterly, amèrement.
black, noir.
blade (*of grass*), brin (*m.*).
blame, to, blâmer.
blaze, to, flamber, flamboyer; **blaze up**, flamber.
blind, aveugle; **blind in one eye**, borgne.
blindfold, to, bander les yeux.
blithe, enchanté, gai.
block, bloc (*m.*).
blood, sang (*m.*).
blow, to, sonner.
blue, bleu.
board, table (*f.*); **on board**, à bord (de); **to go on board**, s'embarquer.

boat, bateau (*m.*), barque (*f.*), esquif (*m.*). *See* p. 12.
body, corps (*m.*).
bold, *hardi.
book, livre (*m.*).
bookshelf, bibliothèque (*f.*).
boon, faveur (*f.*).
border, to, border.
bored, to be, s'ennuyer.
born, to be, naître.
bosom, sein (*m.*), cœur (*m.*).
both, deux, tous deux.
bother, to, déranger.
bottom, bas, fond, pied (*m.*); at the bottom of, au fond de.
bound, to, sauter.
bouquet, bouquet (*m.*).
bow, to (= to bend), se pencher.
box, boîte (*f.*).
boy, garçon, élève, enfant, camarade, jeune homme (*m.*). *See* p. 12.
branch, branche (*f.*).
brass, cuivre (*m.*).
brave, brave, courageux.
bravery, courage (*m.*).
bread, pain (*m.*).
break, to, *see* p. 13; **break forth**, éclater; **break from**, échapper à; **break off**, détacher.
breakfast, déjeuner (*m.*).
breath, respiration (*f.*), souffle (*m.*).
breathe, to, respirer, souffler.
breeding, éducation (*f.*).
brewery, brasserie (*f.*).
bridge, pont (*m.*).
bridle, bride (*f.*).
brief, court.
bright, brillant, clair, éclatant, ensoleillé.
brighten, to, faire briller.
brilliant, brillant.
bring, to, amener, apporter, conduire; **bring about**, aboutir à; **bring together**, rassembler.
brink, bord (*m.*).
briskly, (à, de) bon train.
Britain, Bretagne (*f.*); **Great Britain**, Grande-Bretagne (*f.*).

British, britannique, anglais.
Briton (*ancient*), Breton (*m.*).
broad, large.
brook, ruisseau (*m.*).
brother, frère (*m.*).
brow, sourcil (*m.*); **to knit one's brows**, froncer le sourcil.
brown, brun.
brush away, to, essuyer.
buckle, bouche, barrette (*f.*).
bud, bouton (*m.*).
build, to, bâtir.
building, bâtiment (*m.*).
bullet, balle (*f.*).
bunch (*of grapes, etc.*), grappe (*f.*).
burn, to, brûler.
burning, allumé; brûlant.
burst forth, to, éclater.
bury, to, enterrer.
bush, buisson (*m.*).
busied in, occupé à.
business, affaire (*f.*); **to transact business**, faire des affaires.
busy, to be, s'occuper à.
but (*conj.*), mais; (*prep.*), ne... que; **but little**, ne...guère.
buy, to, acheter.
by, par; (= near) près de.

cabbage, chou (*m.*).
cage, cage (*f.*).
calculated, well, fait.
call, to, appeler, crier, nommer; **call to mind**, (se) rappeler; **call up** (= awaken), réveiller; **call upon** (= summon), sommer.
calm, calme (*adj. & n.m.*).
calmly, paisiblement.
calmness, calme (*m.*).
can, *see* able.
cane, canne (*f.*).
cannon, canon (*m.*).
cap, bonnet (*m.*); (boy's cap), casquette (*f.*).
capital, capitale (*f.*).
captain, capitaine (*m.*).
captive, captif.
captivity, captivité (*f.*).
capture, to, capturer.
car (= chariot), char (*m.*).

carcase, carcasse (*f.*).

care, soin (*m.*); **to take care of**, soigner, se charger de, prendre soin de.

care to, to, avoir envie de.

carefully, soigneusement.

carriage, carrosse (*m.*), voiture (*f.*).

carry, to, porter, emporter; **carry off**, emporter; **carry out**, emmener, transporter.

carrying, transport (*m.*).

cart, charrette (*f.*).

case, cas (*m.*).

casement, croisée (*f.*).

castle, château (*m.*).

cat, chat (*m.*).

catch, to, arrêter, attraper, prendre, surprendre; **catch hold of, catch and keep hold of**, saisir et retenir.

cathedral, cathédrale (*f.*).

cause, to, causer, être cause de.

cavalry, cavalerie (*f.*).

cave, caverne (*f.*).

cawing, croassement (*m.*).

celebrated, célèbre.

cell, cachot (*m.*), cellule (*f.*).

centre, centre, milieu (*m.*); **in the centre**, au centre.

century, siècle (*m.*).

ceremony, cérémonie (*f.*).

Ceres, Cérès (*f.*).

certain, certain.

certainly, certainement.

chair, chaise (*f.*); (= arm-chair), fauteuil (*m.*).

chamber, chambre (*f.*).

champion, champion, *héros (*m.*).

chance, *hasard (*m.*).

change, to, changer.

channel, détroit (*m.*).

chaplain, chapelain (*m.*).

character, caractère (*m.*).

charge, charge, garde (*f.*).

chariot, char (*m.*).

Charley, le petit Charles, Charlot.

charming, charmant, délicieux.

charwoman, femme (*f.*) de ménage.

chatter, to, bavarder, jacasser.

cheek, joue (*f.*).

cheer; **of good cheer**, content; **with loud cheers**, à grands cris, avec acclamations.

cheerful, joyeux.

chemist, pharmacien (*m.*); **chemist's shop**, pharmacie (*f.*).

chicken, poulet; poussin (*m.*).

chief, le plus grand, prépondérant, principal.

child, enfant (*m.f.*), petit, petite.

chimney-piece, cheminée (*f.*).

China, Chine (*f.*).

chink, fente (*f.*).

choice, choix (*m.*).

choose, to, choisir.

chorus, chœur (*m.*).

church, église (*f.*).

church-bell, cloche (*f.*).

church-tower, clocher (*m.*).

churchyard, cimetière (*m.*).

circle, cercle (*m.*).

circumstance, circonstance (*f.*); **as circumstances required**, selon les circonstances.

citizen, citoyen (*m.*).

city, cité, ville (*f.*).

civil, poli.

civilize, to, civiliser.

claim, to, réclamer.

clean, propre.

clean (up), to, nettoyer; **clean away**, arracher.

clear, clair.

clearly, clairement.

clever, habile, intelligent.

cliff, falaise (*f.*).

climb, to, grimper (à *or* sur).

Clisthenes, Clisthène (*m.*).

cloak, manteau (*m.*).

clock, horloge, pendule (*f.*) (*see* p. 11, § 7).

close (*of day*), soir (*m.*), tombée (*f.*) du jour.

close, to, fermer.

close by, tout près (de), tout proche (de).

closely, de près.

cloud, nuage (*m.*); **cloud encircled**, couronné de nuages.

club, massue (*f.*).

coach, carrosse (*m.*), voiture
(*f.*); (=stage-coach), diligence (*f.*).
coal, charbon (*m.*).
coast, côte (*f.*).
coat, veste (*f.*); (=overcoat),
manteau (*m.*).
coin, pièce (*f.*), argent (*m.*).
cold, froid.
coldly, froidement.
collect, to, rassembler.
colour, couleur (*f.*).
come, to, venir, arriver; come
back, revenir; come down,
descendre; come forth, sortir; come in, entrer; come
on, arriver; come out, sortir;
come out again, ressortir;
come to, arriver à, atteindre;
come up, monter, (s')avancer,
arriver.
comfort, consolation (*f.*).
comfort, to, consoler; récon-
forter.
command, commandement
(*m.*).
command, to, commander; I
am commanded, on m'a
ordonné.
commandant, commandant
(*m.*).
commend, to, recommander.
companion, compagnon (*m.*).
company, compagnie, société
(*f.*); to keep company, tenir
compagnie.
compare, to, comparer.
compartment, compartiment
(*m.*); smoking compart-
ment, compartiment de fu-
meurs.
complaint, plainte (*f.*); to lay a
complaint, porter ses plaintes.
complete, complet.
comrade, camarade (*m.f.*).
conceal, to, cacher.
concern, affaire (*f.*).
concern, to, concerner.
conclude, to, terminer.
condition, condition (*f.*).
conduct, conduite (*f.*).
conduct, to (=lead), amener.

confidence, confiance (*f.*).
conquer, to, conquérir, vaincre.
conscience, conscience (*f.*).
consent, consentement (*m.*); by
common consent, d'un ac-
cord commun.
consent, to, consentir.
consequence, conséquence, importance (*f.*); it is a matter
of no consequence, peu importe, cela ne fait rien.
consider, to, considérer.
consternation, consternation
(*f.*), terreur panique (*f.*).
construct, to, construire.
contain, to, contenir.
content, to be, se contenter.
contented, content.
continue, to, continuer.
contradict, to, contredire.
contrary, contraire (*m.*).
conversation, conversation (*f.*).
convey, to, amener.
convince, to, convaincre.
cook, cuisinier (*m.*), cuisinière
(*f.*).
coppice-wood, taillis (*m.*).
corn, grain (*m.*).
corner, coin (*m.*).
coronation, sacre (*m.*).
corporation, conseillers muni-
cipaux (*m.pl.*).
cost, to, coûter.
cottage, chaumière (*f.*).
cotton, coton (*m.*).
couch, canapé (*m.*), lit de repos
(*m.*).
cough, to, tousser.
council, conseil (*m.*).
counsel, avis, conseil (*m.*).
count, to, compter.
countenance, visage (*m.*), physionomie (*f.*).
country, campagne (*f.*), pays
(*see p.* 14, § 7); paysage (*m.*);
mother-country, patrie (*f.*);
in the country, à la cam-
pagne.
countrywoman, compatriote
(*f.*).
course, cours (*m.*); of course,
évidemment; mais si!

court, cour (*f.*), tribunal (*m.*).
courteous, courtois.
courtesy, politesse (*f.*).
courtier, courtisan (*m.*).
covenant, covenant (*m.*).
covenanter, covenantaire (*m.*).
cover, to, couvrir.
covering, couverture (*f.*).
covet, to, désirer.
cradle, berceau (*m.*).
crash, fracas (*m.*).
create, to, créer.
creature, little, petit (*m.*), petite (*f.*).
creep, to, se glisser, se traîner; creep out, sortir en rampant.
Crete, Crète (*f.*).
critic, critique (*m.*).
crocus, crocus (*m.*).
cross, croix (*f.*).
cross, to, franchir, passer, traverser.
crossing, passage (*m.*); traversée (*f.*).
crouch, to, s'accroupir.
crowd, foule (*f.*).
crowd, to, serrer.
crowded (with), rempli, bondé (de).
crown, to, couronner, sacrer.
cruel, cruel.
crush, to, écraser; crush through, se frayer un chemin à travers.
cry, to, crier, s'écrier; (=weep), pleurer; cry out, s'écrier.
cuirassier, cuirassier (*m.*).
cupboard, placard (*m.*), armoire (*f.*).
cure, to, guérir.
curiosity, curiosité (*f.*).
current, courant (*m.*).
curtain, rideau (*m.*).
custom, coutume (*f.*).
cut, to, couper; (=cut out, cut up), découper; cut at, *turn by* lâcher des coups de sabre.

daily, tous les jours.
daisy, pâquerette (*f.*).
dance, danse (*f.*).
dance, to, danser.

dancing, danse (*f.*).
danger, danger (*m.*).
dangle, to, pendre; tournoyer.
dare, to, oser; I dare say, sans doute.
dark, sombre; to be dark, faire noir, faire nuit.
darkness, obscurité (*f.*), ténèbres (*f.pl.*).
dash, to, se lancer; dash to the ground, jeter à terre.
daughter, fille (*f.*).
dauphin, dauphin (*m.*).
Dauphiné, Dauphiné (*m.*).
dawn, aube, aurore (*f.*); point (*m.*) du jour.
day, jour (*m.*), journée (*f.*); next day, (le) lendemain.
dazzle, to, éblouir.
dead, mort.
deaf, sourd.
deal, a good, beaucoup.
dear, cher; my dear, mon petit, ma chère petite; dear me! mon Dieu!
death, mort (*f.*).
December, décembre (*m.*).
decide, to, (se) décider, résoudre; *see p. 66, § 44.*
decidedly, very, d'un ton décidé.
declare, to, affirmer, assurer, déclarer.
declining (*of the sun*), couchant.
decorate, to, décorer.
deed, haut fait (*m.*).
deem, to, (=think) trouver.
deep (*adj.*), gros, profond; (*adv.*), profondément.
defeat, défaite (*f.*).
defend, to, défendre.
degree, parage (*m.*).
dejected, abattu.
delay, délai (*m.*).
delight, plaisir (*m.*).
delightful, délicieux.
deliver, to, délivrer, remettre; deliver up, livrer.
deliverance, délivrance (*f.*).
demand, to, demander, exiger, ordonner.
demoralize, to, démoraliser.
depart, to, partir.

departure, départ (*m.*).
depend, to, dépendre; **depend on**, dépendre de, compter sur.
deportment, maintien (*m.*).
depressed, déprimé; **depressed in spirits**, abattu.
descended, to be, descendre.
describe, to, dire, décrire.
description, description (*f.*).
desert, désert (*m.*).
desert (*adj.*), désert.
deserted (*adj.*), désert.
deserve, to, mériter.
design, dessein (*m.*).
desire, désir (*m.*).
despair, désespoir (*m.*).
despatch, to, dépêcher.
desperate, désespéré.
destination, destination (*f.*).
destroy, to, détruire; faire mourir.
determine, to, résoudre.
determined, décidé, bien décidé.
dew, rosée (*f.*).
dial, cadran (*m.*); **sundial**, cadran solaire.
diamond, diamant (*m.*).
die, to, mourir.
different, différent.
difficulty, difficulté (*f.*); **to settle a difficulty**, aplanir, résoudre une difficulté.
dig, to, **dig away**, creuser.
diligent, actif.
dim, vague.
dinner, diner (*m.*).
direct, to, diriger.
direction, côté (*m.*), direction (*f.*).
dirty, sale.
disagreeable, désagréable.
disappear, to, disparaître.
disappointed, déçu.
disappointment, déception (*f.*).
disband, to, (se) débander.
disconsolate, désolé.
discover, to, apercevoir, découvrir.
discovery, découverte (*f.*).
disguise, déguisement (*m.*).
dismal, lugubre.

dismay, to, déconcerter.
dismiss, to, renvoyer.
dismount, to, descendre de cheval.
disobey, to, désobéir.
disorganize, to, désorganiser.
display, to, étaler.
dispose, to, disposer.
distance, distance (*f.*), lointain (*m.*); **at a distance**, au loin.
distant, lointain.
distinguish, to, distinguer.
distress, détresse (*f.*).
distress, to, affliger.
district, région (*f.*).
disturb, to, déranger, troubler.
divide, to, diviser, séparer.
division, bande (*f.*).
do, to, faire; achever, finir.
docility, docilité (*f.*).
doctor, docteur, médecin (*m.*).
dog, chien (*m.*); **to set the dogs on**, lâcher les chiens contre.
doll, poupée (*f.*).
domestic, domestique (*m.f.*).
doom, to, condamner.
door, porte, entrée (*f.*).
doorstep, seuil (*m.*) de la porte.
doubt, no, certainement, sans doute.
doubt, to, douter.
down, en bas.
drag, to, tirer, traîner.
draw, to, tirer; **draw back**, ramener; **draw near**, (s')approcher; **draw up**, s'arrêter.
drawer, tiroir (*m.*).
drawing-room, salon (*m.*).
dread, to, redouter.
dreadful, effroyable.
dream, rêve (*m.*).
dream (of), to, rêver (à).
dress, costume (*m.*), robe (*f.*).
dress, to, (s')habiller, (se) vêtir.
drink, to, boire.
drive, to, conduire, faire aller.
droll, drôle.
droop, to, languir.
drop, goutte (*f.*).
drop, to, lâcher; tomber, laisser tomber.
drum, tambour (*m.*).

dry, sec; (*of leaves, etc.*), mort.
duke, duc (*m.*).
during, pendant.
dust, poussière (*f.*).
duty, devoir (*m.*).
dwarf, nain (*m.*).
dwell, to, habiter.

each (*adj.*), chaque; (*pron.*), chacun; **each other**, l'un l'autre.
eagerly, avec empressement, vivement.
ear, oreille (*f.*).
earl, comte (*m.*).
early, de bonne heure; **how early**, à quelle heure.
earn, to, gagner.
earnestness, empressement (*m.*).
earth, terre (*f.*).
easily, facilement.
eastern, oriental, est.
eat, to, manger, avaler, dévorer; **eat up**, manger.
ebony, ébène (*m.*).
echo, écho (*m.*).
edge, bord (*m.*).
Edmund, Edmond (*m.*).
effort, effort (*m.*).
Egypt, Égypte (*f.*).
eight, *huit.
eighteen, dix-huit.
eighteenth, dix-huitième.
eighty, quatre-vingts.
(not) either...or, (ne)...ni...ni.
Elba, Elbe (*f.*).
elbow, coude (*m.*); **at my elbow**, à mon côté.
elderly, d'un certain âge.
eldest, aîné.
elephant, éléphant (*m.*).
eleven, onze.
elf, lutin (*m.*).
else, d'autre.
elsewhere, ailleurs.
elusive, insaisissable.
embark, to, s'embarquer.
embarrass, gêner, embarrasser.
emblem, emblème (*m.*).
embrace, to, serrer dans ses bras, etreindre.
emerald, émeraude (*f.*).

emperor, empereur (*m.*).
empire, empire (*m.*).
employ, to, employer.
employment, emploi (*m.*).
empty, vide.
empty, to, vider.
enable, to, permettre; *or use* faire.
enchanted, enchanté.
encourage, to, encourager.
end, bout (*m.*), extrémité (*f.*), fin (*f.*).
end, to, finir.
endeavour, to, essayer.
ending, fin (*f.*).
enemy, ennemi (*m.*).
engagement (= **appointment**), rendez-vous (*m.*).
England, Angleterre (*f.*).
English, anglais; **Englishman**, Anglais.
enjoy, to, jouir de.
enlarge, to, agrandir.
enormous, énorme.
enough, assez, bien.
enter, to, entrer (*see p.* 69, § 44); faire son entrée.
entirely, entièrement, tout à fait.
entrance, entrée (*f.*).
entreat, to, demander avec instance, supplier.
entry, entrée (*f.*).
equal, égal.
equipment, équipement (*m.*).
ere, *see* **before**.
errand, mission, commission; **to run errands**, faire des commissions.
error, erreur (*f.*).
escape, salut (*m.*); **to make one's escape**, s'enfuir.
escape, to, échapper, s'échapper (*see p.* 68, § 44); éviter (*see p.* 155).
espy, to, apercevoir.
essential, essentiel, réel.
eternity, éternité (*f.*).
Euripides, Euripide (*m.*).
Europe, Europe (*f.*).
even, même; **even though**, quand même (*see p.* 78, § 45); **even unto**, jusqu'à.

evening, soir (*m*.); soirée (*f*.).
event, événement (*m*.).
ever, jamais, toujours; **France
for ever**, vive la France!
every, chaque, tous les; **everybody, every one**, chacun,
tout le monde, tous ceux;
everything, tout; **every now
and then**, de temps à autre.
evident, clair, évident, visible.
exactly, exactement, tout à
fait.
examine, to, examiner.
exceeding, exceedingly, très,
énormément.
except, excepté, sauf.
exchange, échange (*m*.).
exclaim, to, s'écrier, s'exclamer.
excuse, to, excuser, faire grâce.
execution, exécution (*f*.); **to
carry into execution**, mettre
à exécution.
executioner, bourreau (*m*.).
exhaust, to, épuiser.
exhort, to, exhorter.
existence, existence (*f*.).
expect, to, attendre, s'attendre
à.
expedition, expédition (*f*.).
expel, to, expulser.
experience, expérience, impression (*f*.).
explain matters, to, s'expli-
quer.
explore, to, explorer.
expose, to, exposer.
express, rapide (*m*.).
express, to, exprimer.
expression, expression (*f*.).
extinguish, to, éteindre.
extraordinary, extraordinaire.
extremely, extrêmement.
extremity, extrémité (*f*.).
eye, œil; regard (*m*.).

face, face (*f*.), figure (*f*.), visage
(*m*.); tête (*f*.).
fact, fait (*m*.).
fade, to, (se) faner.
faggot, fagot (*m*.).
fail, to, laisser; manquer (*see p.*
71, § 44).

faint, faible.
faintly, faiblement.
fair, beau; (*of complexion, hair,
etc*.), blond.
fairly, assez.
fairy, fairy woman, fée (*f*.).
fairyland, pays (*m*.) des fées,
féerie (*f*.).
faith, foi (*f*.).
faithful, fidèle.
fall, chute (*f*.).
fall (down), to, tomber; **fall
back**, retomber; (=**happen**),
arriver.
false, faux, prétendu.
familiar, familier.
familiarity, familiarité (*f*.).
famous, célèbre, fameux.
far (*adj*.), lointain; (*adv*.), loin,
beaucoup; **far and wide**, au
loin.
farm, ferme (*f*.).
farmer, fermier (*m*.).
farmhouse, ferme (*f*.).
farther, plus avant.
farthing, denier (*m*.).
fast (*adv*.), vite.
fat, gras.
fatal, fatal; **proved fatal**, porta
le dernier coup.
father, papa, père (*m*.); **the
fathers of the people**, les
anciens (*m.pl*.).
fatigue, fatigue (*f*.).
fatiguing, fatigant.
fault, défaut (*m*.), faute (*f*.).
favour, faveur (*f*.).
favourable, favorable.
favourite, favori.
fear, crainte, peur (*f*.); **for fear
of**, de peur de.
fear, to, craindre, avoir peur.
feast, festin (*m*.).
feature, trait (*m*.).
February, février (*m*.).
feeble, faible, affaibli.
feel, to, éprouver, (se) sentir,
ressentir.
feeling, sentiment (*m*.).
fellow, bonhomme, gaillard,
camarade (*m*.).
female, femelle (*f*.).

fetch, to, aller chercher; rapporter.

fever, fièvre (*f.*).

few, peu; a few, quelques.

field, champ (*m.*).

fifteen, quinze.

fifty, cinquante.

fight, to, combattre.

fill, to, garnir, remplir.

finally, à la fin.

find, a rich find, trouvaille (*f.*).

find, to, trouver, fournir; find out, découvrir.

fine, beau, fin, magnifique.

finger, doigt (*m.*).

finish, to, finir, achever.

fir, fir tree, sapin (*m.*).

fire, feu; incendie (*m.*); to open fire, ouvrir le feu.

fire, to, tirer.

fireplace, foyer (*m.*).

fireside, coin (*m.*) du feu.

firm, ferme.

firmly, avec fermeté.

first (*adj.*), premier; (at) first (*adv.*), d'abord, préalablement; first-class carriage, première (*f.*).

fish, poisson (*m.*).

fisherman, pêcheur (*m.*).

fishing, pêche (*f.*).

fishing-net, filet (*m.*) de pêche.

fit, capable.

fit, to, rendre capable.

five, cinq.

fix, to, fixer.

flag, drapeau (*m.*).

flake, flocon (*m.*).

flame, flamme (*f.*).

Flanders, Flandre (*f.*).

flanked, flanqué.

flash, étincellement (*m.*); flash of light, lueur (*f.*).

flash, to, éclater.

flee, to, s'enfuir.

flicker, to, vaciller.

flight, fuite (*f.*); to take to flight, prendre la fuite.

fling, to, jeter; fling down, jeter bas.

flint, silex (*m.*).

flock, troupeau (*m.*).

flock, to, accourir en foule.

flood, to, envahir.

floor, sol (*m.*); stone floor, dalles (*f.pl.*).

flow, to, couler.

flower, fleur (*f.*).

flower-pot, jardinière (*f.*), vase (*m.*).

flute, flûte (*f.*).

fly, to, voler; fly wide open, s'ouvrir toute grande.

folk, gens (*pl.*), paysans (*m.pl.*).

follow, to, suivre.

fond of, to be, aimer.

food, aliments (*m.pl.*), nourriture (*f.*), vivres (*m.pl.*).

foolish, imprudent, insensé.

foot, pied (*m.*).

footprint, empreinte (*f.*).

footstep, pas (*m.*).

for (*prep.*), pour; (*conj.*), car.

force, force; armée (*f.*); by force, de force.

force, to, obliger (*see p.* 72, § 44).

forest, forêt (*f.*).

forester, garde-forestier (*m.*).

foretell, to, prédire.

forgather, to, se trouver face à face.

forget, to, oublier.

forgive, to, pardonner.

forth, hors de.

fortunate, heureux.

fortunately, heureusement.

fortune, destin (*m.*).

forty, quarante.

four, quatre.

fourscore, quatre-vingts.

fourteen, quatorze.

fourth, quatrième.

fox, renard (*m.*).

fragrance, parfum (*m.*).

fragrant, odorant.

frame, châssis (*m.*); broken frame (*of health*), santé faible (*f.*).

France, France (*f.*).

freckled, piqueté de taches de rousseur.

free, libre; to set free, libérer, mettre en liberté.

free, to, délivrer.

freedom, liberté (*f.*).
freeze, to, geler.
French, français.
frequently, souvent.
fresh, frais, nouveau.
friend, ami (*m.*).
friendly, amical.
frighten, to, effrayer.
fro; to pass to and fro, passer et repasser.
from, de; depuis.
front, in, par devant; **in front of**, devant.
fruit, fruit (*m.*).
fuel, des fagots (*m.pl.*).
fugitive, fugitif (*m.*)
fulfil, to, remplir.
full, plein; **to come full upon**, frapper en plein.
fully, pleinement.
funny, drôle.
fury, furie (*f.*).
future, futur.

gaiety, gaieté (*f.*).
gaily, gaîment.
game, jeu (*m.*).
gaping, bouche bée (*f.*).
garden, jardin; **(vegetable) garden**, potager (*m.*).
gardener, jardinier (*m.*).
gate, barrière, grille, porte (*f.*).
gather, to, cueillir, (se) réunir; **gather up**, ramasser.
gaze, regard(s) (*m.*).
gaze upon, to, contempler.
general, général (*m.*).
generally, généralement.
generation, génération (*f.*).
generous, généreux.
gentle, gentil.
gentleman, gentilhomme, monsieur, seigneur (*m.*).
gently, doucement.
get, to, *translate the meaning, e.g. by* amener, louer, trouver, *etc.*; **get away safely**, se sauver; **get home**, rentrer; **get into**, monter (grimper) dans; **get on with**, s'entendre très bien avec; **get out**, sortir, des-

cendre; **get over**, traverser; **get up**, se lever.
gift, don (*m.*).
gigantic, gigantesque.
gilt, doré.
gird, to, ceindre.
girl, fille (*f.*); **little girl**, fillette (*f.*).
give, to, donner, annoncer; **give up**, céder, renoncer (à).
given to, enclin à.
glad, content; **to be glad**, se réjouir.
glance, coup (*m.*) d'œil.
gleam, to, luire.
glide, to, se glisser.
glimmering, lueur (*f.*).
glisten, to, scintiller, briller.
glitter, to, étinceler.
gloomy, sombre.
glory, gloire (*f.*).
gnaw, to, ronger.
go, to, aller, s'en aller, partir, se diriger, porter ses pas; **go across**, franchir; **go back to**, regagner; **go down**, descendre; **go for**, aller chercher; **go in**, entrer; **go off**, s'en aller; **go on**, aller, continuer, reprendre; **go out**, sortir, s'éteindre; **go over**, franchir; **go to**, aller rejoindre; **go up**, monter; **go up to**, (s')approcher.
goblet, gobelet (*m.*).
God, Dieu (*m.*).
godmother, marraine (*f.*).
gold, or (*m.*).
golden, d'or, doré.
good, bien (*m.*).
good (*adj.*), bienfaisant, bon, sage.
good-day, bonjour.
good-humoured, aimable.
good-looking, beau.
goodness, bonté (*f.*).
goods, marchandise(s) (*f.*).
govern, to, gouverner.
gown, robe (*f.*).
grab, to, saisir, empoigner.
grace, grâce (*f.*); **to hear grace**, entendre les grâces.

graceful, gracieux.
grand, grand; **Grand Theatre,** Grand-Théâtre (*m.*).
grandfather, grand-père (*m.*); **great-grandfather,** arrière-grand-père (*m.*).
grandmother, grand'mère (*f.*).
grant, to, accorder, exaucer.
grape, raisin (*m.*).
grasp, to, empoigner, étreindre.
grasp, **to quit one's,** lâcher prise.
grass, herbe (*f.*).
grateful, reconnaissant.
gratitude, reconnaissance (*f.*).
grave, tombe (*f.*).
great, grand, gros, *haut; (=**much**), beaucoup de.
greatly, beaucoup.
Greece, Grèce (*f.*).
Greek, grec.
green, vert.
greet, to, saluer.
grey, gris; **grey-haired,** aux cheveux gris.
grotto, grotte (*f.*).
ground, terre (*f.*); **to the ground,** par terre.
grow, to, pousser; **grow from,** naître de; **grow up,** grandir, pousser.
grumble, to, grogner.
guard (=**watch**), garde (*f.*); garde (*m.*); (**railway**) **guard,** chef (*m.*) de train; **on guard,** en sentinelle.
guess, to, deviner.
guest, hôte (*m.f.*), convive (*m.f.*), invité (*m.*).
guinea, louis (*m.*) d'or.

habit, habitude (*f.*).
hail, to, acclamer.
hair, chevelure (*f.*), cheveux (*m.pl.*).
half, moitié (*f.*).
half (*adj.*), demi; (*adv.*), à moitié; **half-empty,** à moitié vide; **half an hour,** demi-heure (*f.*); **half-open,** entr'ouvert.
halfpenny, sou (*m.*).

hall, galerie (*f.*), grande salle.
hand, main (*f.*).
hand, to, tendre.
handful, poignée (*f.*).
handle, anse (*f.*).
handsomely, richement.
hang, to, pendre, suspendre, pencher.
happen, to, arriver.
happiness, bonheur (*m.*).
happy, heureux.
hard, dur, fort; **hard by,** tout près.
hardly, à peine, ne...guère.
hare, lièvre (*m.*); **March hare,** lièvre fou (*m.*).
harm, mal (*m.*).
harm, to, faire mal.
harness, to, *harnacher.
harshly, durement.
haste, to make, se dépêcher.
hasten, to, courir, s'empresser.
hastily, en toute *hâte, précipitamment.
hat, chapeau (*m.*).
hate, to, haïr, détester.
hatter, chapelier (*m.*).
haughtily, avec hauteur.
have, to, avoir, posséder; **to have to,** devoir, falloir, avoir à.
hawk, faucon (*m.*).
he, il, lui; **he who,** celui qui.
head, tête (*f.*).
heap, tas (*m.*).
hear, to, apprendre, entendre, entendre dire.
heart, cœur (*m.*); **to pluck at the heart strings,** faire vibrer le cœur.
hearth-stone, pierre (*f.*) du foyer, âtre (*m.*).
heartily, de bon cœur.
heat, chaleur (*f.*).
heathen, païen.
heavy, lourd, pesant; **to become heavy,** s'alourdir.
hedge, *haie (*f.*).
heed, to, penser, faire attention à.
height, *hauteur (*f.*).
helmet, *heaume, casque (*m.*).

help, aide (*f.*).
help, to, aider, secourir, servir, s'empêcher; **so help me God!** Dieu me soit en aide!
helpless, impuissant.
hen, poule (*f.*).
henceforth, dorénavant.
her (*pron.*), la, elle; **to her,** lui, à elle; (*adj.*), son, sa, ses.
herb, herbe (*f.*).
herd, troupeau (*m.*).
here, ici; **here and there,** çà et là; **here is** (**are**), voici.
herself, se; en personne, elle aussi, elle-même.
hesitate, to, hésiter.
hesitation, hésitation (*f.*).
hide, to, (se) cacher.
hideous, effroyable.
high, élevé, (bien) *haut; **high up,** là-haut.
Highness, Grandeur (*f.*).
hill, colline (*f.*); **across the hills,** dans la montagne.
him, le, lui; **to him,** lui, à lui.
himself, se; lui-même.
hindrance, obstacle (*m.*).
hint, indication (*f.*).
Hippoclides, Hippoclide (*m.*).
hire, to, louer.
his (*adj.*), son, sa, ses; (*pron.*), le sien.
hoist, to, *hisser.
hold; to take hold of, empoigner; **to keep tight hold of,** se cramponner étroitement à.
hold, to, tenir; **hold back,** retenir; **hold out,** étendre, tendre.
hole, trou (*m.*).
holy, sacré.
home, foyer (*m.*), maison (*f.*); **at home,** chez soi, à la maison; **to come home,** rentrer; **to be sick for home,** avoir la nostalgie de son pays.
homeland, patrie (*f.*).
honest, honnête.
honestly, franchement.
honour, honneur (*m.*).

honourable, honnête.
hope, espoir (*m.*).
hope, to, espérer; **hoping and trusting,** plein d'espoir et de confiance.
horizon, horizon (*m.*); **on the horizon,** à l'horizon.
horizontal, horizontal.
horn, corne (*f.*); antenne (*f.*); (= *musical instrument*), cor (*m.*).
horrible, horrible, atroce.
horror, horreur (*f.*).
horse, cheval (*m.*); **on horseback,** à cheval.
horseman, cavalier (*m.*).
hospitable, hospitalier; **to be hospitable,** se montrer hospitalier.
hostess, hôtesse (*f.*).
hot, chaud.
hour, heure (*f.*).
house, maison (*f.*); **at (to) the house(s) of,** chez.
housework, ménage (*m.*).
how, comme, comment; **how much,** combien, à quel point.
however (*adv.*), cependant, néanmoins, pourtant, toutefois; (*conj.*), de quelque façon que; *see p. 88, § 49.*
hue, couleur, teinte (*f.*).
humble, humble.
humbly, humblement.
humour, humeur (*f.*); **ill humour,** mauvaise humeur.
hundred (*adj.*), cent; (*noun*), centaine (*f.*); *see p. 37, § 21.*
hundredweight, quintal (*m.*).
hunger, faim (*f.*).
hungry, to be, avoir faim.
hunt, chasse (*f.*); **lion hunt,** chasse au lion.
hunt, to, chasser, (aller) à la chasse.
hunter, huntsman, chasseur (*m.*).
hurry, to, se *hâter; **hurry away, off,** hâter le pas, se hâter de partir, partir en *hâte.
hurt, to, faire mal.
husband, mari (*m.*).

hushed, to be, se taire.
hut, cabane, chaumière, *hutte (f.).
hyacinth, jacinthe (f.).

I, je, moi.
idea, idée (f.).
ideal, idéal (m.).
idly, paresseusement, distraitement.
if, si.
ill, malade.
illustrate, to, démontrer.
imagine, to, (s')imaginer.
immediately (adv.), immédiatement, à l'instant; (conj.), aussitôt que.
Imogen, Imogène (f.).
impatiently, avec impatience.
impertinent, impertinent; **to be impertinent,** faire l'impertinent.
implore, to, supplier.
importance, importance (f.).
important, important.
impossible, impossible.
impress, to, toucher.
impression, impression (f.).
imprison, to, emprisonner.
in (prep.), see § 48; dans, en, au bout de; (adv.), dedans.
inattention, inattention (f.); **inattention to,** les négligences (f.) à l'égard de.
incense, encens (m.).
inclination, to make an, s'incliner.
indeed, en effet, en fait, vraiment; **no, indeed,** ma foi, non, non vraiment.
indescribable, indescriptible.
India, Inde (f.).
Indian, indien.
indignant, indigné.
indignantly, indigné, avec indignation.
indulge, to, satisfaire.
infancy, enfance (f.).
influence, to, influencer.
inform, to, informer.
information, information (f.), renseignement (m.).

ingenious, ingénieux.
ingot, lingot (m.).
inhabitant, habitant (m.).
inn, auberge (f.), hôtel (m.).
innermost heart, le fond du cœur.
innocent, candide.
inquire, to, chercher, demander, demander des nouvelles, se renseigner.
inquiry, renseignement (m.); **to make inquiries,** se renseigner.
inscription, inscription (f.).
inside, à 'l'intérieur, dedans, là-dedans.
insist, to, insister; **insist on,** insister pour que + Subjunctive.
inspire, to, inspirer.
instantly, à l'instant.
instead of, à la place de, au lieu de.
instruction, enseignement (m.).
intelligent, intelligent.
intend, to, désirer, avoir l'intention de.
intention, intention (f.).
interest, to, intéresser.
interest in, to take an, s'intéresser à.
interrupt, to, interrompre.
into, (jusque) dans.
introduce, to, (a person) présenter; (a subject) mettre sur le tapis.
invincible, invincible.
invisible, invisible.
invite, to, inviter.
iron, fer (m.).
irreproachable, irréprochable.
island, île (f.).
it, ce; ceci, cela; il, elle; le, la; lui.
Italian, italien.
its, son, sa, ses.
itself, se, soi, elle-même, lui-même.

jailer, geôlier (m.).
Japan, Japon (m.).
jar, pot, vase (m.).
jaws, gueule (f.).
Joan, Jeanne (f.).

join, to, (se) joindre.

journey, voyage (*m.*); to continue one's journey, continuer sa route; go on one's country journey, faire sa tournée dans la campagne.

joy, joie (*f.*).

joyfully, de joie.

judge, juge (*m.*); to be a judge of, se connaître en.

July, juillet (*m.*).

jump, to, sauter; jump about, *see* about; jump up, se lever brusquement.

June, juin (*m.*).

just, à peine, exactement, juste, seulement, tout à fait; to have just done, venir de faire; just now, tout à l'heure.

keep, to, garder, tenir, retenir; keep on, continuer; keep saying, répéter.

kill, to, tuer.

kind, sorte (*f.*).

kind, aimable, bon, brave; to be so kind as to, avoir la bonté de.

kindness, bonté (*f.*).

kindred, parents (*m.pl.*).

king, roi (*m.*).

kingdom, royaume (*m.*).

kinship, parenté (*f.*).

kinsman, parent (*m.*).

kinswoman, parente (*f.*).

kiss, to, baiser, embrasser.

kitchen, cuisine (*f.*).

knee, genou (*m.*).

kneel down, to, s'agenouiller.

knife, couteau (*m.*).

knight, chevalier (*m.*).

knit, to, tricoter.

knock, to, frapper.

know, to, comprendre, connaître, savoir, avoir connaissance; know nothing of, ignorer; to want to know, désirer des renseignements.

knowledge, connaissance (*f.*), savoir (*m.*), science (*f.*).

label, étiquette (*f.*).

laborious, laborieux, fatigant.

labour, travail (*m.*).

labourer, laboureur, ouvrier (*m.*).

lad, garçon; jeune homme (*m.*).

lady, dame, demoiselle (*f.*).

lamb, agneau (*m.*).

lament, to, pleurer.

lamp, lampe (*f.*).

land, to, aborder (à), débarquer.

landscape, paysage (*m.*).

lap, genoux (*m.pl.*).

large, énorme, grand, gros.

lark, alouette (*f.*).

last, dernier; at last, enfin, à la fin.

last, to, durer.

lastly, enfin.

late, tard.

later, après, plus tard.

Latin, latin.

latter, celui-ci, ce dernier.

laugh, to, rire; to laugh at, rire de.

lay, to, poser, coucher; lay a table, mettre une table.

lead, to, amener, conduire, mener, tenir par la bride.

leaf, feuille (*f.*).

league, lieue (*f.*).

lean, to, s'incliner.

learn, to, apprendre.

learning, savoir (*m.*).

least, at, au moins, du moins.

leave, to, abandonner, laisser, quitter; leave go, laisser; leave off, cesser; s'empêcher de.

left, gauche.

leg, jambe (*f.*).

length, at, enfin.

less, moins.

lest, de peur (crainte) que.

let, to, laisser.

Lethe, Léthé (*m.*).

letter, lettre (*f.*).

level (*adj.*), plat.

Lewis, Louis (*m.*).

liberty, liberté (*f.*).

library, bibliothèque (*f.*).

lick, to, lécher.

lie, to, reposer; lie down, se coucher; to lie quite still, rester bien tranquille.

life, vie (f.).

lift, to, lever; lift down, descendre.

light, lumière (f.).

light (adj.), léger; to be light, faire clair.

light, to, allumer, éclairer; light up, (s')éclairer.

lightly, légèrement.

like (adj.), pareil; (prep.), comme, en; dressed like, habillé en; to be like, ressembler à.

like, to, aimer, vouloir.

lily, lis (m.); lily of the valley, muguet (m.).

line, ligne (f.); (of descendants), lignée (f.); (of poetry), vers (m.).

lineally, en droite ligne.

lion, lion (m.).

lip, lèvre (f.).

listen, to, écouter.

little (adj.), petit; (adv.), peu.

live, to, demeurer, habiter, vivre.

lo, voilà! hélas!

load, to, charger.

loaf, miche (f.).

lobster, *homard (m.).

lock-up, prison (f.), 'violon' (m.).

lodging, logis (m.).

loft, grenier (m.).

log, log of wood, bûche (f.).

London, Londres (m.).

lonely, solitaire.

long (adj.), long; (adv.), longtemps, depuis longtemps; all night long, toute la nuit durant; to be a long time, tarder; make longer, allonger.

long to, to, avoir envie, vouloir bien.

longing, grand désir (m.).

look, œil, regard (m.).

look, to, avoir l'air, paraître;

regarder; look at, regarder; look across at, regarder vers; look back at, se retourner pour regarder; look down, baisser la tête; look like, avoir l'air, ressembler; look round, détourner les yeux; look up, lever les yeux; it would look pretty, cela ferait joli; what does she look like? quel air (quelle mine) a-t-elle?

looks, aspect (m.).

lop off, to, trancher.

lord, seigneur (m.); my Lord, monseigneur; (referring to a judge), Monsieur le Président.

lordship, seigneurie (f.).

lose, to, perdre; be lost, disparaître.

loss, perte (f.).

loud, fort, haut.

loudly, tout haut.

Louisa, Louise (f.).

love, amour (m.); (as a term of affection), chéri.

love, to, aimer, aimer beaucoup.

lovely, beau, charmant.

luck, fortune, chance (f.).

Lucy, Lucie (f.).

lying, couché.

mad, fou.

madam, madame (f.).

magic (adj.), magique.

magician, magicien (m.).

magistrate, magistrat (m.).

magnificent, magnifique.

magnificently, magnifiquement.

maid, bonne, jeune fille; (of Saint Joan), pucelle (f.).

maiden, jeune fille (f.).

maintain, to, soutenir.

majesty, majesté (f.).

major, commandant (m.).

make, to, faire, rendre; make out, découvrir.

malady, mal (m.), maladie (f.).

male, mâle.

mamma, maman (f.).

man, homme (m.).

manifest, to, manifester.

manner, façon, manière, mode (*f.*); in such a manner that, de façon que.

mantle, manteau (*m.*).

manuscript, manuscrit (*m.*).

many, beaucoup, nombreux.

map, carte (*f.*).

March, mars (*m.*).

march, marche (*f.*); to begin the march, se mettre en marche.

march, to, s'avancer à pied.

mark (= aim, goal), but (*m.*).

marquis, marquis (*m.*).

marry, to, (se) marier, épouser; *see p. 15, § 7.*

marshal, maréchal (*m.*).

Mary, Marie (*f.*).

mass, masse (*f.*).

mast, mât (*m.*).

master, maître (*m.*).

master-work, chef-d'œuvre (*m.*).

match, allumette (*f.*).

matter, affaire (*f.*); What is the matter? Qu'avez-vous? Qu'est-ce qu'il y a?

May, mai (*m.*).

may, might, pouvoir.

mayor, maire (*m.*).

me, me, moi.

meadow, prairie (*f.*).

meal, repas (*m.*); meal-time, l'heure du (des) repas.

mean, to, avoir l'intention; mean ill, penser à mal.

means, by no, pour rien au monde.

meanwhile, cependant.

meat, viande (*f.*).

meet, to, rencontrer.

meeting, rencontre (*f.*).

meeting-place, rendez-vous (*m.*).

Megacles, Mégaclès (*m.*).

melt away, to, fondre, se disperser.

memory, souvenir (*m.*).

men-at-arms, gens d'armes.

menial, laquais (*m.*).

mention, to, faire mention de, parler.

mercy, merci (*f.*).

mermaid, néréide (*f.*).

merrily, allégrement, joyeusement.

merry, gai.

message, message (*m.*).

messenger, messager, porteur (*m.*).

Michael, Michel (*m.*).

middle, milieu (*m.*); in the middle, au milieu.

midnight, minuit (*m.*).

midst, milieu (*m.*); in the midst, au milieu.

mighty, imposant, puissant.

mild, doux.

mile, mille (*m.*).

military, militaire.

milk, lait (*m.*).

millionaire, millionnaire (*m.*).

mind, esprit (*m.*); to make up one's mind, (se) décider.

mind, to, se soucier.

mine, le mien; *see p. 49, § 35.*

minister, ministre (*m.*).

Minotaur, Minotaure (*m.*).

minute, instant (*m.*), minute (*f.*).

miraculous, miraculeux.

misfortune, malheur (*m.*), infortune (*f.*).

missing, to be, manquer.

mission, mission (*f.*).

mistake, erreur (*f.*).

mistaken, to be, se tromper.

mistress, maîtresse (*f.*).

moan, to, geindre, gémir.

mock, to, se railler de, se moquer de.

moderate, moyen.

modest, modeste.

modesty, modestie (*f.*).

moment, moment (*m.*), minute (*f.*); to speak for a moment, accorder un instant d'entretien.

monarch, monarque (*m.*).

money, argent (*m.*).

monk, moine (*m.*).

monkey, singe (*m.*).

monster, monstre (*m.*).

month, mois (*m.*).

monument, monument (*m.*).

moon, lune (*f.*)

moonlight, clair (*m.*) de la lune.

moorland (*n.*), lande(*f.*); (*adj.*), sur la lande.

more, davantage, plus; something more, davantage, quelque chose de plus.

morning, matin (*m.*), matinée (*f.*); next morning, le lendemain matin.

morning (*adj.*), matinal.

morsel, morceau (*m.*).

Moscow, Moscou (*m.*).

moss, mousse (*f.*).

most, la plupart, le plus.

mostly, pour la plupart; presque partout.

mother, mère, maman (*f.*).

mound, tertre (*m.*).

mount, to, monter; (*a horse*), monter en selle.

mountain, montagne (*f.*).

mournful, triste, dolent.

mournfully, tristement.

mouth, bouche, gueule (*f.*).

move, to, (s')agiter, bouger, (se) remuer, transporter.

movement, mouvement (*m.*).

Mr, Monsieur.

Mrs, Madame.

much, beaucoup (de), très.

muse, to, rêver.

music, musique (*f.*).

musician, musicien(ne).

must, falloir; devoir.

mutter, marmotter.

my, mon, ma, mes.

myself, me; moi-même.

name, nom (*m.*); in the name, au nom.

named, to be, s'appeler.

Napoleon, Napoléon (*m.*).

narrative, récit (*m.*).

narrow, étroit.

nationality, nationalité (*f.*).

native (*n.*), indigène; (*adj.*), natal.

naturalist, naturaliste (*m.*).

nature, nature (*f.*).

naughty, méchant, sot; to be

naughty, être méchant, faire des sottises.

near (*adj.*), prochain; (*prep.*), près de, auprès de; nearer, de plus près.

nearly, presque; nearly to do, faillir faire.

necessary, nécessaire.

neck, cou (*m.*).

need, besoin (*m.*).

needle, aiguille (*f.*).

neglect, to, négliger.

negotiate, to, négocier.

neigh, *hennissement (*m.*).

neighbour, voisin (*m.*), voisine (*f.*).

neighbourhood, voisinage (*m.*).

neither...nor, ne...ni...ni.

nephew, neveu (*m.*).

nest, nid (*m.*).

nestling, blotti.

net, filet (*m.*).

never, ne...jamais, ne...pas, ne ...point; never more, ne... plus jamais.

new, nouveau, neuf.

news, nouvelle (*f.*).

next (*adj.*), suivant; (*adv.*), puis; the next moment, le moment d'après.

nice, gentil, beau, bon.

niece, nièce (*f.*).

nigh, près de.

night, soir (*m.*), nuit (*f.*), see p. 15, § 7; last night, hier soir; the night before, la veille au soir.

nightfall, tombée (*f.*) de la nuit.

night-lamp, veilleuse (*f.*).

nine, neuf.

no, non; pas de; no one, aucun, nul, personne; no one beside, personne d'autre.

noble, gentilhomme (*m.*).

noble (*adj.*), majestueux, noble.

nobody, personne.

noiseless, silencieux, sans bruit.

none, aucun.

Norman, normand.

north, nord (*m.*); the North Sea, la Mer du Nord.

not, ne...pas.

nothing, ne...rien.
notice, to, apercevoir, s'apercevoir de, remarquer.
notion, idée, supposition (f.).
notwithstanding, en dépit de.
novelist, romancier (m.).
now, maintenant, or; now... now, tantôt...tantôt.
number, numéro (m.), nombre (m.); see p. 15, § 7.
numerous, nombreux.
nursery, nursery (f.).
nymph, nymphe (f.).

O, ô.
oak, oak-tree, chêne (m.).
obey, to, obéir.
oblige, to, obliger.
obliged, see grateful.
observe, to, observer, remarquer, voir.
occasion, occasion (f.).
occasionally, de temps à autre.
occur to, to, venir à la tête de.
ocean, océan (m.).
odious, odieux.
of, de.
off (nautical), au large de.
offend, to, blesser.
offer, to, offrir.
often, souvent.
oho! ohé!
old, âgé; ancien, vieux; old man, vieillard (m.); old woman, vieille (f.); how old was he? quel âge avait-il?
Olympic Games, Jeux (m.) Olympiques.
once, une fois, jadis; at once, aussitôt, du premier coup, immédiatement, tout de suite; all at once, tout à coup; once more, une fois encore.
one, un, un certain, on; one who, celui qui.
oneself, se, soi, soi-même.
only (adv.), ne...que, seulement, encore, pas plus tard que; (adj.) seul; only one, seul.
onward, to walk, (s')avancer.
open, ouvert.

open, to, (s')ouvrir.
opinion, avis (m.).
opportunity, occasion (f.).
opposite, opposé, autre.
or, ou, ou bien.
order, ordre (m.); in order to, afin de, pour; in order that, afin que, pour que.
order, to, commander, ordonner.
ordinary, ordinaire.
organize, to, organiser.
Orleans, Orléans.
other, autre; see § 46.
our, notre, nos.
out, dehors; out of, par, *hors de; to choose out of, choisir entre.
outstretched, étendu.
outstrip, to, surpasser.
over, au-dessus (de), par-dessus, sur.
overhanging, surplombant, en surplomb.
overhear, to, entendre par hasard, surprendre, écouter.
overlook, to, négliger; dominer.
overshoot, to, dépasser.
overtake, to, rattraper.
overwhelming, accablant.
own, propre; see p. 49, § 35, 3.
own, to, avouer.
ox, bœuf (m.).

pa, petit père (m.).
Pactolus, Pactole (m.).
page (boy), page (m.).
paint, to, peindre.
pair, paire (f.).
palace, palais (m.).
pale, pâle.
pannier, panier (m.).
pant, to, haleter.
papa, papa (m.).
pardon, pardon (m.); to beg pardon, demander pardon.
Paris, Paris (m.).
part, morceau (m.), partie (f.), région (f.); to play (bear) a part, jouer un rôle; take someone's part, prendre parti pour quelqu'un, prendre son parti.

particular, particulier, tel.

particularly, particulièrement, surtout.

party, parti (*m.*), troupe (*f.*).

pass, to, (se) passer.

passage, couloir (*m.*).

passenger (railway), voyageur (*m.*).

passion, passion (*f.*).

past (*adj.*), passé; (*adv.*), devant.

pat, to, caresser.

path, sentier (*m.*).

patience, patience (*f.*).

patiently, patiemment.

patriarch, patriarche (*m.*).

patriot, patriote (*m.f.*).

pause, moment (*m.*) de silence; dead pause, silence subit.

pause, to, s'arrêter.

pay, paie (*f.*).

pay, to, payer.

peace, paix (*f.*).

peaceful, paisible, tranquille.

peacefully, paisiblement.

pear, poire (*f.*).

pear-tree, poirier (*m.*).

peasant, paysan (*m.*).

peculiar, particulier.

pedestal, piédestal (*m.*).

peg (of coat-rack), patère (*f.*).

pen, plume (*f.*).

people, gens (*pl.*); (=nation), peuple (*m.*).

perceive, to, apercevoir.

peremptory, péremptoire.

perhaps, peut-être, peut-être que.

perilous, périlleux.

period, espace (*m.*), moment (*m.*), période (*f.*).

permit, to, permettre.

person, personne (*f.*).

persuade, to, persuader.

pervading, envahissant.

petal, pétale (*m.*).

Philip, Philippe (*m.*).

phrase, phrase (*f.*).

piano, piano (*m.*).

pick up, to, ramasser.

picture, tableau (*m.*), image (*f.*).

piece, morceau (*m.*), pièce (*f.*).

pierce, to, percer.

pile up, to, empiler.

pipe, pipe (*f.*).

pit, fosse (*f.*).

pitfall, fosse (*f.*).

pity, pitié (*f.*); to have pity on, avoir pitié de; take pity on, prendre en pitié.

pity, to, plaindre.

pityingly, apitoyé.

place, endroit, lieu (*m.*); to take place, avoir lieu; to take the place, occuper la place.

place, to, mettre, placer, poster.

placid, calme, paisible, tranquille.

plaid, plaid (*m.*).

plain, plaihe (*f.*).

plain (*adv.*), lisiblement.

plainly, simplement.

plan, plan, dessein (*m.*).

plant, to, planter; fonder.

plantation, (petit) bois (*m.*).

plate, assiette (*f.*).

platform, quai (*m.*).

play, to, jouer, s'ébattre.

plaything, jouet (*m.*).

plead, to, plaider.

pleasant, agréable, beau, doux, riant.

pleasantly, agréablement.

please, to, plaire.

pleased (with), content (de).

pleasing, agréable.

pleasure, plaisir (*m.*).

plentiful, abondant.

plenty, abondance (*f.*); to have plenty of time, avoir tout le temps.

plenty (*adj.*), assez, beaucoup.

plough, to, labourer.

pluck, to, cueillir.

plunge, to, plonger.

Pluto, Pluton (*m.*).

pocket, poche (*f.*).

pocket, to, empocher.

poem, poème (*m.*).

poet, poète (*m.*).

poetry, poésie (*f.*).

point, to, montrer; point out, faire remarquer; point to, désigner.

pomegranate, grenade (*f.*).
pond, étang (*m.*), mare (*f.*).
pony, poney (*m.*), petit cheval.
poor, pauvre.
poplar, peuplier (*m.*).
poppy, coquelicot (*m.*).
port, port (*m.*).
portal, portail (*m.*), grande porte (*f.*).
porter, porteur, facteur (*m.*).
portfolio, portefeuille (*m.*).
portion, partie (*f.*); sort (*m.*).
portmanteau, portemanteau (*m.*).
portrait, portrait (*m.*).
possess, to, posséder.
possible, possible.
pot, pot (*m.*).
pound, livre (*f.*) sterling.
pour out, verser; (*p.* 186), sortir.
poverty, pauvreté (*f.*).
power, pouvoir (*m.*); powers, talents (*m.*).
powerful, puissant.
powerless, impuissant.
practise, to, s'exercer.
praise, to, louer.
pray, to, prier; pray! je vous en prie!
prayer, prière (*f.*), vœu (*m.*).
precious, précieux.
prefer, to, avoir une préférence, préférer, aimer mieux.
prelate, prélat (*m.*).
prepare, to, préparer.
prepared, préparé, prêt.
presence, présence (*f.*).
present, cadeau (*m.*).
present, to be, assister.
presently, aussitôt, bientôt.
preserve, to, préserver.
press, to, serrer, coller.
presume, to, avoir la présomption.
pretend, to, faire semblant de.
pretty, beau, gentil, joli.
prick, to, piquer.
pride, fierté (*f.*), orgueil (*m.*).
priest, prêtre (*m.*).
prince, prince (*m.*).
prisoner, prisonnier (*m.*).
privately, secrètement.

probably, probablement.
proceed to, to, se mettre à.
Procrustes, Procruste (*m.*).
produce, to, produire, sortir, montrer.
professor, professeur (*m.*).
profit (by), to, profiter (de).
profitable, qui en vaut (vaille) la peine, profitable.
progress, to, cheminer.
promise, promesse (*f.*); to keep a promise, tenir une promesse.
promise, to, promettre.
pronounce, to, prononcer.
proof, preuve (*f.*).
prophecy, prophétie (*f.*).
Proserpina, Proserpine (*f.*).
protector, protecteur (*m.*).
protest, to, protester.
proudly, fièrement.
prove, to, prouver.
proverbial, proverbial.
provide, to, fournir, munir.
provider, pourvoyeur (*m.*).
provision, provision (*f.*).
prudence, prudence (*f.*).
puff, bouffée (*f.*).
pull, to, tirer; pull down, décrocher, descendre; pull out, sortir; pull up (*a flower, etc.*), arracher.
punishment, punition (*f.*).
purple, pourpre, violet.
purpose, intention (*f.*).
pursue, to, poursuivre.
pursuit, in, sur les pas.
push, to, pousser.
put, to, mettre, déposer; put down, baisser, déposer; put on, enfiler, mettre; put out, faire descendre, débarquer; put up, mettre.
puzzle, to, embrouiller l'esprit, intriguer.

quality, qualité (*f.*).
quantity, masse, quantité (*f.*).
quarrel, querelle (*f.*); to pick a quarrel with, chercher querelle à.
quarter, quart, quartier (*m.*).
quartz, quartz (*m.*).

queen, reine (*f.*).
query, question (*f.*).
quest of, in, à la recherche de.
question, question (*f.*); **to ask a question**, poser (faire) une question.
question, to, (s')interroger, questionner.
quick, vif.
quickly, rapidement, vite, vivement.
quiet, sage, tranquille; **to be quiet**, se taire.
quietly, tranquillement.
quit, to, quitter, sortir de, se dégager de.
quite, bien, tout, tout à fait.
quiver, to, trembler, se mettre à trembler.

raise, to, élever, soulever; **raise up**, soulever.
rank, rang (*m.*).
ransom, rançon (*f.*).
ransom, to, rançonner.
rash, imprudent, téméraire.
rate, at any, du moins.
rather, plutôt, assez.
rattling, bruit (*m.*).
ravine, ravin (*m.*).
ray, rayon (*m.*).
reach, to, arriver, atteindre, gagner.
read, to, lire, faire la lecture.
ready, disposé, prêt; **to get ready**, (se) préparer.
realize, to, comprendre, se rendre compte.
really, vraiment.
realm, royaume (*m.*).
reappear, to, reparaître.
rear, to, élever.
reason, cause, raison (*f.*).
reassure, to, rassurer.
recall, to, rappeler.
receive, to, accueillir, recevoir.
recently, récemment.
recess, lieu (*m.*).
reclaim, réclamer.
recognize, to, reconnaître.
recollect, to, se rappeler.
recover, to, se remettre, re-

trouver; **recover oneself**, se ressaisir.
red, rouge.
reformation, réforme (*f.*).
refresh, to, rafraîchir.
refuge; **to take refuge**, se réfugier, chercher refuge.
refuse, to, refuser; **still refused to reply**, s'obstinait à ne pas répondre.
regiment, régiment (*m.*).
regular, régulier.
reign, règne (*m.*).
relate, to, raconter.
release, to, dégager, libérer.
religion, religion (*f.*).
remain, to, rester, demeurer.
remains, restes (*m.pl.*).
remark, propos (*m.*), remarque (*f.*).
remark, to, faire remarquer.
remarkable, remarquable.
remember, to, se souvenir de, se rappeler.
remind, to, rappeler.
remorse, remords (*m.*).
render, to, rendre.
rendezvous, rendez-vous (*m.*).
renegade, renégat (*m.*).
renounce, to, renoncer à, abandonner.
renown, renom (*m.*).
rent, loyer (*m.*).
repair, to, réparer.
repeat, to, répéter, reprendre.
repent, to, se repentir.
reply, réponse (*f.*); **to make reply**, donner la réponse.
reply, to, répondre.
report, rapport (*m.*).
repose, to, dormir.
request, to, demander, prier.
resemble, to, ressembler à.
resentment, ressentiment (*m.*).
resist, to, résister (à).
resolution, résolution (*f.*).
resolve, to, se promettre, résoudre.
respect, respect (*m.*); **in that respect**, à cet égard.
respect, to, respecter.
respectfully, respectueusement.

rest, autres (*pl.*), reste (*m.*); repos (*m.*).
rest, to, appuyer, dormir, (se) reposer.
restless, agité.
restore, to, rendre.
restrain, to, retenir.
result, résultat (*m.*).
retire, to, se retirer, se soustraire.
retort, to, repartir.
retreat, retraite (*f.*).
return, retour (*m.*).
return, to, rentrer, répliquer, retourner, revenir.
reveal, to, révéler.
revelation, révélation (*f.*).
revenge, revanche (*f.*).
reverence, révérence (*f.*); **to make a reverence**, tirer une révérence.
review, to, passer en revue.
revisit, to, revoir.
revolution, révolution (*f.*).
reward, récompense (*f.*).
reward, to, récompenser.
Rheims, Reims (*m.*).
rich, riche.
ride, to, chevaucher, monter.
rifle, fusil (*m.*).
right, droit; **right gladly**, de bon cœur.
ring, anneau (*m.*), bague (*f.*).
ring, to, sonner, retentir; (*of a peal of bells*), carillonner.
ringing, bruit (*m.*), retentissement (*m.*).
ripe, mûr.
rise, to, s'élever, se lever.
risk, risque (*m.*).
rite, rite (*m.*).
rival, rival.
river, rivière (*f.*).
road, chemin (*m.*), route (*f.*).
roadside, bord (*m.*) de la route.
roam, to, errer, rôder, s'éloigner.
roar, to, rugir.
roast, to, rôtir.
rob, to, dépouiller, voler.
robber, voleur (*m.*).
rock, roche (*f.*), rocher (*m.*).

rogue, coquin (*m.*).
roll (*of drums*), roulement (*m.*).
roll, roll down, to, rouler.
Roman, romain.
romance, roman (*m.*).
roof, toit (*m.*).
rook, corneille (*f.*).
room, chambre, pièce, salle; place (*f.*); **rooms**, appartement (*m.*); **no room!** pas de place!
Rosamond, Rosamonde (*f.*).
rose, rose (*f.*).
rosy, rose, vermeil.
round, rond; (*prep.*) autour de.
route, chemin (*m.*).
row, rang (*m.*); **front row**, premier rang.
rub, to, frotter.
rude, grossier, sauvage.
rudely, grossièrement.
ruffle, to, rider.
rug, couverture (*f.*).
rule, to, gouverner.
rumbling, grondement (*m.*).
run, to, courir, s'enfuir; **run away**, se sauver.
rush, jonc (*m.*).
rush, to, se précipiter.
rushing (*adj.*), impétueux.
rustic, paysan (*m.*).

sabre, sabre (*m.*).
sad, triste.
saddle, selle (*f.*).
sadly, tristement.
safely, en sûreté, sans danger, sain et sauf.
sail, voile (*f.*); (*of a windmill*), aile (*f.*).
sail, to, mettre à la voile, s'embarquer, voguer; **sail away**, mettre à la voile.
saint, saint (*m.*).
salmon, saumon (*m.*).
same, même.
sand, sable (*m.*).
sandal, sandale (*f.*).
satin, satin (*m.*).
satisfied, content, satisfait.
satisfy, to, satisfaire.
savage, cruel, sauvage.

save (*prep.*), sauf.

save, to, épargner, sauver, laisser la vie à.

say, to, dire; be said to, passer pour.

scamper off, to, s'échapper, se sauver.

scarcely, à peine.

scared, effaré.

scene, paysage (*m.*), spectacle (*m.*), vue (*f.*).

school, école (*f.*).

Scottish, écossais.

scour, to (*the country*), parcourir.

scream, cri, cri perçant (*m.*).

sea, mer (*f.*); at sea, out at sea, en mer.

search, to, chercher; (= to search the premises), faire une perquisition.

sea-shore, grève, plage (*f.*).

second, deuxième, second.

secret, secret (*m.*).

section, section (*f.*).

security, sécurité, tranquillité (*f.*).

sedan, chaise (*f.*) à porteurs.

see, to, apercevoir, voir.

seed, grain (*m.*); semence (*f.*).

seek, to, chercher.

seem, to, sembler.

seize, to, s'emparer de, prendre, saisir.

seldom, rarement.

sell, to, vendre.

send, to, envoyer; send away, renvoyer; send for, envoyer chercher; send into, faire entrer.

sense, sens, sentiment (*m.*).

sensitive, sensible.

sentence of death, arrêt (*m.*) de mort.

September, septembre (*m.*).

serious, sérieux.

servant, domestique (*m.f.*), serviteur (*m.*).

serve, to, servir.

service, service (*m.*); to do a service, rendre service.

sesame, sésame (*m.*).

set forth, to, se mettre en route; set off, s'élancer, partir; set about, se mettre à.

settle, to, (s')établir; settle a difficulty, aplanir (régler) une difficulté.

seven, sept.

seventeenth, dix-septième.

several, plusieurs.

sew, to, coudre.

shade, shadow, ombre (*f.*).

shady, ombreux, ombragé.

shake, to, agiter, brandir; trembler; shake hands, serrer la main; shake one's head, *hocher la tête; shake off, se débarrasser.

shame, *honte (*f.*).

share, part (*f.*).

sharply, durement, sèchement.

she, elle.

shed, abri, *hangar (*m.*).

sheep, mouton (*m.*).

shelf, rayon (*m.*), planche (*f.*).

shelter, abri (*m.*).

shepherd, berger (*m.*).

shilling, shilling (*m.*).

shine, to, briller, rayonner.

ship, bateau, navire (*m.*).

shoe, soulier (*m.*).

shoot, to, fusiller, tirer.

shooter, chasseur (*m.*).

shop, boutique (*f.*), magasin (*m.*).

shore, grève (*f.*), plage (*f.*), rivage (*m.*).

short, bref, court.

short-lived, de courte durée.

shoulder, épaule (*f.*).

shout, cri (*m.*).

shout, to, crier, *hurler.

show, to, faire preuve de, montrer, faire voir; show someone in, faire entrer quelqu'un.

shrill, perçant.

shrub, arbuste (*m.*).

shut, to, (se) fermer; shut up, enfermer.

shutter, volet (*m.*).

sick, malade.

side, côté, flanc (*m.*); **by the side of,** à côté de; **by her side,** à côté d'elle, à ses côtés.

siege, siège (*m.*); **to raise the siege,** faire lever le siège.

sight, vue (*f.*).

sign, signe (*m.*).

silence, silence (*m.*).

silent, silencieux.

silently, silencieusement.

silk, soie (*f.*).

silver, argent (*m.*).

simple, simple.

simplicity, simplicité (*f.*).

since (*prep.*), depuis; **since then,** depuis lors; (*conj.*), comme, depuis que, puisque, vu que.

sing, to, chanter.

singer, chanteur (*m.*).

singing, chant (*m.*).

single, seul.

single out, to, distinguer.

sink, to (*into slumber*), tomber.

sip, to, déguster.

sir, monsieur (*m.*); (*to a boy*), mon garçon.

sire (*to a king*), sire (*m.*); auteur (*m.*) de ses jours.

sister, sœur (*f.*).

sit down, to, s'asseoir; **be sitting,** être assis.

six, six.

sixth, sixième.

sixty, soixante.

size, grosseur, taille (*f.*).

skill, adresse (*f.*), talent (*m.*).

skin, peau (*f.*).

sky, ciel (*m.*).

slave, esclave (*m.f.*).

sleep, sommeil (*m.*); **sleep came upon me,** le sommeil me gagna: **to put to sleep,** endormir.

sleep, to, dormir; (= **fall asleep**), s'endormir.

sleepy, assoupi.

slight, léger, petit.

slip, to, glisser.

slowly, lentement.

slumber, sommeil (*m.*).

small, petit.

smell, odeur (*f.*).

smell, to, sentir.

smile, sourire (*m.*).

smile, to, sourire.

smilingly, en souriant.

smoke, fumée (*f.*).

smoke, to, fumer.

smooth, plat, lisse, uni.

snare, piège (*m.*).

snatch, to, arracher.

sneeze, to, éternuer.

sniff, to, sniff at, flairer.

snow, neige (*f.*); **snow-white,** blanc de neige.

snowdrop, perce-neige (*f.*).

so, ainsi, alors, aussi, si, tellement, donc, c'est pourquoi; **so as,** de façon; **so many** (**much**), autant, tant; **so that,** de manière que, si bien que.

sober man, to be a, boire peu.

softly, doucement, légèrement.

soil, sol (*m.*).

soldier, soldat (*m.*).

solemn, solennel.

solemnity, solennité (*f.*).

solid, solide.

solitary, solitaire.

sombre, sombre.

some (*adj.*), du, de la, des, quelque(s); (*pron.*), en; quelques-uns.

someone, quelqu'un.

something, quelque chose (*m.*); **something else,** autre chose.

sometimes, quelquefois, parfois.

somewhat, légèrement, quelque peu, assez.

son, fils (*m.*).

song, chant (*m.*).

son-in-law, gendre (*m.*).

soon, bientôt; **as soon as,** dès que; **as soon as possible,** le plus tôt possible.

Sophy, Sophie (*f.*).

sorceress, sorcière (*f.*).

sorrow, tristesse (*f.*).

sorry, to be, avoir du chagrin, regretter.

sort, façon (*f.*); **all sorts of,** *turn by* les plus divers.

sound, bruit, son (*m.*); (*of a bell*) its sound had gone out, sa voix avait résonné.

soup-bowl, écuelle (*f.*).

sour, aigre.

south, sud (*m.*).

Spaniard, Espagnol.

Spanish, espagnol.

spare, to, épargner.

spark, étincelle (*f.*).

sparkle, to, étinceler.

Spartan, Spartiate (*m.f.*).

speak, to, parler.

spear, épieu (*m.*); lance (*f.*).

speck, point (*m.*), parcelle (*f.*).

spectator, spectateur (*m.*).

speech, discours (*m.*).

speedily, bientôt.

spend, to, dépenser, passer.

spin, to, filer.

spire, flèche (*f.*).

spirit, esprit (*m.*).

spit, broche (*f.*).

spite of, in, en dépit de, malgré.

splendid, magnifique, somptueux, splendide.

splendour, éclat (*m.*).

spoil, to, gâter.

sport, in, en se jouant.

spot, coin, endroit, site (*m.*); **on the spot**, sur place.

spot, to, tacheter.

spread, to, s'étendre; **spread out, (s')**ouvrir.

sprightly, joyeux.

spring, to, bondir, sauter; **spring at**, bondir sur; (*of water*), sortir, sourdre.

square, carré (*m.*).

stable, écurie (*f.*).

staff, bâton (*m.*).

stage-coach, diligence (*f.*).

staircase, escalier (*m.*).

stamp upon, to, fouler aux pieds.

stand, to, *see* § 49; se dresser, s'élever, rester, se tenir, se trouver; **stand still**, s'immobiliser, s'arrêter court; **stand on one's head**, se mettre la tête en bas.

standing, debout.

star, étoile (*f.*).

start, to; **start off**, partir; **start up**, se dresser.

start, with a, en sursaut.

starve, to, (se laisser) mourir de faim.

state, état (*m.*), condition (*f.*).

stately, somptueux.

station, gare (*f.*).

station-master, chef (*m.*) de gare.

stature, taille (*f.*); **low stature**, petite taille.

stay, to, demeurer, rester; **to stay long**, être long à.

stead, place (*f.*).

steady, ferme.

steal, to, voler; (= **to insinuate oneself**), se faufiler; **steal upon**, envahir peu à peu.

steep, abrupt; à pic.

step, pas (*m.*).

stern, sévère.

stick, morceau (*m.*) de bois, brindille (*f.*).

still (*adj.*), silencieux, tranquille; (*adv.*), cependant, encore; **still refused to reply**, s'obstinait à ne pas répondre.

stir, to, bouger, émouvoir, réveiller.

stir and din, brouhaha (*m.*).

stocking, bas (*m.*).

stone, caillou (*m.*), pierre (*f.*); **flat stone** (= **slab**), dalle (*f.*).

stool, tabouret, escabeau (*m.*).

stoop, to, se baisser.

stop, to, (s')arrêter, cesser; **stop for**, attendre.

story, anecdote (*f.*), histoire (*f.*), récit (*m.*).

straight (*adv.*), tout de suite.

straightway, aussitôt.

strait, passage (*m.*).

strange, étrange, inconnu; **strange to say**, chose étrange.

strange-looking, bizarre.

stranger, étranger (*m.*).

stray, to, s'écarter.

stream, courant, ruisseau (*m.*).

stream, to, ruisseler.

street, rue, chaussée (*f.*).
strength, force (*f.*).
strew, to, éparpiller, joncher.
stride, to, marcher à grands pas.
strike, to, frapper, sonner, lâcher des coups de poing; **strike up**, entonner.
strong, fort, vigoureux.
struggle, lutte (*f.*).
student, étudiant (*m.*).
study, bureau (*m.*), étude (*f.*).
stuff, étoffe (*f.*).
subconscious, subconscient.
subject, sujet (*m.*).
submit, to, céder, se soumettre.
substance, substance (*f.*).
subterfuge, prétexte, subterfuge (*m.*).
suburb, faubourg (*m.*).
succeed, to, réussir.
success, succès (*m.*).
successor, successeur (*m.*).
such, pareil, tel; **such as**, tel que.
sudden, soudain; **all on a sudden**, tout à coup.
suddenly, soudain, soudainement, subitement, tout à (d'un) coup.
suffer, to, souffrir.
suffering, souffrance; (= *ordeal*), épreuve (*f.*).
sufficient, suffisant; **to be sufficient**, suffire.
suffused, baigné.
suitor, prétendant (*m.*).
summer, été (*m.*).
summon, to, appeler, faire venir, sommer.
sumptuous, somptueux.
sun, soleil (*m.*).
sunburnt, *hâlé.
Sunday, dimanche (*m.*).
sundial, *see* dial.
sunset, coucher (*m.*) du soleil.
sunshine, soleil (*m.*).
supper, souper (*m.*); **suppertime**, heure (*f.*) du souper; **to have supper**, souper.
supplicate, to, supplier.
suppose, to, croire, se dire, estimer, supposer.

sure, sûr.
surely, bien, pour sûr, assurément.
surface, surface (*f.*).
surpass, to, surpasser.
surprise, surprise (*f.*).
surprise, to, faire une surprise, surprendre, étonner.
surrender, to, se rendre.
survive, to, vivre.
suspect, to, soupçonner.
suspicious of, to be, se méfier de.
swallow, hirondelle (*f.*).
swallow, to, avaler.
swear, to, sacrer; dire de gros mots, lâcher des jurons.
sweep, to, balayer.
sweet (*adj.*), doux.
sweet, sweetmeat, bonbon (*m.*).
swim, to, nager.
swoon, in a, évanoui.
sword, épée (*f.*); **drawn sword**, épée nue.
syllable, syllabe (*f.*).

table, table (*f.*).
tail, queue (*f.*).
take, to, accepter, conduire, s'emparer de, entreprendre, prendre, transporter; **take back**, reprendre; **take down**, décrocher; **take hold of**, empoigner; **take off**, décharger, enlever, ôter; **take out**, retirer, sortir.
tale, histoire (*f.*).
talent, talent (*m.*).
talk, to, causer, parler.
tall, grand; **tall story**, histoire invraisemblable.
tame, apprivoisé.
task, tâche (*f.*).
taste, goût (*m.*).
taste, to, goûter.
tax to the utmost, to, mettre à une rude épreuve.
tea, tea-party, thé (*m.*).
teach, to, apprendre, instruire.
tear, larme (*f.*).
tear, to (*down, off, out*), arracher.

tell, to, charger, commander, dire, raconter; **tell about,** raconter.

temper, to lose one's, se fâcher tout rouge, se mettre en colère.

tempt, to, tenter.

temptation, tentation (*f.*).

ten, dix.

tend, to, garder.

tendency, tendance (*f.*).

terminus, terminus (*m.*), arrivée (*f.*).

terrace, terrasse (*f.*).

terrible, terrible.

territory, territoire (*m.*).

test, to, éprouver.

than, que.

thank, to, remercier; **thank God,** grâce à Dieu; **thank you,** merci.

that (*adj.*), ce...-là; (*pron.*), ce; cela; *rel.* qui (*objective* que); (*conj.*), que; pour que, afin que; **those who,** ceux qui.

the, le la, les.

theatre, théâtre (*m.*).

thee, te, toi.

their, leur, leurs.

them, les; eux, elles; **to them,** leur.

theme, thème (*m.*).

themselves, se.

then, alors, puis; (=**therefore**), donc.

there, là, là-bas; **there is** (**are**), voilà, il y a; § 49, p. 91.

therefore, donc.

thereupon, alors, là-dessus, sur ce.

Theseus, Thésée (*m.*).

they, ils, elles; eux, elles; on.

thick, dru, épais, feuillu.

thicket, fourré, *hallier, maquis, taillis (*m.*).

thief, voleur (*m.*).

thine (=**thy**), ton, ta, tes.

thing, chose (*f.*).

think, to, croire, penser; **think of,** penser à, se soucier de; **think on,** penser à; **think over,** réfléchir sur, se rap-

peler; **to think it best,** penser qu'il vaut (valait) mieux.

third, troisième.

thirst, soif.

thirsty, to be, avoir soif.

thirteen, treize.

this (*adj.*), ce...-ci; (*pron.*), ce; celui-ci; ceci, cela.

thou, tu; toi.

though, bien que, quoique+ Subjunctive.

thought, pensée (*f.*).

thoughtful, pensif.

thoughtfully, pensivement.

thousand, millier (*m.*); (*adj.*), mille.

thread, fil (*m.*).

threaten, to, menacer.

three, trois.

threshold, seuil (*m.*).

thrice, trois fois.

throat, gorge (*f.*).

through (*prep.*), durant, par; (*adv.*), **through** (*the river*), *use* à l'autre bord *or* traverser.

throw, to, jeter; **throw open,** ouvrir tout grand.

thrust, to, plonger, enfoncer.

thumb, pouce (*m.*).

thunder, tonnerre (*m.*).

thus, ainsi.

tide, marée (*f.*).

tie (= **neck-tie**), cravate (*f.*).

tie, to, attacher.

tiger, tigre (*m.*).

till (*prep.*), jusqu'à; (*conj.*), jusqu'à ce que.

time, époque (*f.*), fois (*f.*), heure (*f.*), temps (*m.*); **in time,** à temps; **keeping time to,** au rythme de.

timid, timide.

timidly, timidement.

tinge, to, teinter.

tiny, petit.

tip, pourboire (*m.*).

tire, to, fatiguer, lasser.

title, titre (*m.*).

to, à, chez, jusqu'à, pour; **to come to,** arriver auprès de.

tobacco, tabac (*m.*).

to-day, aujourd'hui.

together, (tous) ensemble; l'un contre l'autre.

tolling, to set a-, mettre en branle.

to-morrow, demain; **by to-morrow morning**, d'ici demain matin.

tone, voix (*f.*), ton (*m.*).

to-night, cette nuit.

too, aussi; trop; **too many, much**, trop.

tooth, dent (*f.*).

top, *haut, sommet (*m.*); **at the top**, en haut.

torch, flambeau (*m.*), torche (*f.*).

toss, to, jeter.

touch, to, toucher.

towards, à, envers, vers; *see p. 86, § 48.*

tower, tour (*f.*).

town, ville (*f.*); **to the town**, en ville.

trace, trace (*f.*); **to obtain a trace**, découvrir une trace.

trade, good, de bonnes affaires.

trading, trafic (*m.*).

tradition, tradition (*f.*).

train, train (*m.*).

traitor, traître (*m.*).

tranquil, tranquille.

transfigure (*p. 208*), illuminer.

trap, piège (*m.*); trappe (*f.*).

travel, to, voyager.

traveller, voyageur (*m.*).

travelling, les voyages (*m.*).

tread, to, marcher; **tread down**, fouler aux pieds.

treason, trahison (*f.*).

treasure, trésor (*m.*).

treaty, traité (*m.*).

tree, arbre (*m.*).

tremble, to, trembler.

trial, procès (*m.*).

tribute, tribut (*m.*).

triumph, triomphe (*m.*).

triumphal, triomphal.

troop, troupe (*f.*).

trot, to, trotter.

trouble, détresse (*f.*), peine (*f.*), souci (*m.*).

trouble, to, (se) déranger.

true, vrai.

truncheon, bâton (*m.*); **leader's truncheon**, bâton de commandant.

trust, to, (= *hope*) espérer; **trust again**, rendre sa confiance.

truth, vérité (*f.*); **to speak the truth**, dire la vérité.

try, to, s'efforcer, essayer, tenter, mettre à l'épreuve.

tub, cuve (*f.*).

tulip, tulipe (*f.*).

tune, air (*m.*).

turf, gazon (*m.*), mottes (*f.pl.*) de terre; **piece of turf**, carré de gazon.

turn, to, tourbillonner, tourner, se tourner; **turn back**, retourner, rentrer.

turns, by, tour à tour.

turnspit, tournebroche (*m.*).

tusk, défense (*f.*).

twelve, douze; (*o'clock*), midi, minuit (*m.*).

twenty, vingt.

twice, deux fois.

twiddle, to, tourner; **to twiddle his horns**, tourner ses antennes.

twilight, crépuscule (*m.*).

twist, to, entortiller.

two, deux.

typical, typique, même.

tyrant, tyran (*m.*).

um! hum!

umbrella, parapluie (*m.*).

unable, to be unable, être incapable de, ne pas pouvoir.

unarmed, sans armes.

uncle, oncle (*m.*).

uncover, to, découvrir.

under, au pied de, sous.

understand, comprendre, reconnaître.

undertone, voix basse.

uneasily, avec embarras.

uneasy, agité, inquiet.

unfasten, to, détacher.

unfortunate, malheureux; (*of an incident*), malencontreux.

unfurl, to, déployer.

unhappy, infortuné, malheureux.
unpleasant, pénible.
until (*prep.*), jusqu'à; (*conj.*), jusqu'à ce que.
unusual, indu.
up above there, là-haut.
upon, sur.
upright, sitting, assis sur son séant.
upstairs, to go, monter l'escalier.
upwards (*of age, number of years*, *etc.*), et même plus.
urge, to, pousser.
us, nous.
use, utilité (*f.*); **to be of use**, servir; **make the best use of one's time**, occuper son temps de son mieux.
use, to, faire usage; **use for the good of**, mettre au service de.
used, habitué.
useful, utile.
usher in, introduire.
usual, habituel.
usually, généralement.
utmost, le plus grand.
utter, to, prononcer.

vain, vain.
valley, vallée (*f.*), vallon (*m.*).
valuable, de grand prix.
various, divers.
vase, vase (*m.*).
vast, énorme.
vault, cave, voûte (*f.*).
Vendée, Vendée (*f.*).
venerable, vénérable.
venture, to, risquer, se risquer à.
verdure, verdure (*f.*).
very (*adj.*), même; (*adv.*), bien, très; **very much**, bien, beaucoup.
vessel, vaisseau (*m.*).
vex, to, vexer.
vexation, in, vexé.
vibration, vibration (*f.*).
victorious, victorieux.
victory, victoire (*f.*).
victuals, victuaille (*f.*), victuailles (*f.pl.*).

vie, to, rivaliser.
view, vue (*f.*).
villa, villa (*f.*).
village, village (*m.*).
vine, vigne (*f.*).
violently, violemment.
vision, vision (*f.*).
visit, visite (*f.*); **to pay a visit**, rendre visite.
visit, to, visiter, faire une visite, rendre visite.
vocabulary, vocabulaire, répertoire (*m.*).
voice, voix (*f.*).
voyage, voyage (*m.*).

wag, to, remuer.
wager, gageure (*f.*).
wail, plainte (*f.*).
waistcoat, gilet (*m.*).
wait, to, attendre, rester.
wake, to, (s')éveiller, (se) réveiller.
walk, marche (*f.*), promenade (*f.*), sentier (*m.*); **to go for a walk**, partir se promener.
walk, to, marcher, aller à pied, se promener, faire des promenades.
walker, marcheur (*m.*).
wall, mur (*m.*).
wand, baguette (*f.*).
wander, to, errer; **wander away**, s'éloigner.
want, to, demander, vouloir; avoir besoin.
war, guerre (*f.*).
wardrobe, armoire (*f.*).
warfare, guerre (*f.*).
warm, chaud.
warmly, chaleureusement.
warrior, guerrier (*m.*).
wash, to, laver; se laver.
washerwoman, lavandière (*f.*).
waste, to, gaspiller, perdre; **waste in sleep**, gaspiller à dormir.
waste of seas, le vaste océan.
watch, to, regarder, surveiller; **watch for**, guetter.
watcher, guetteur (*m.*).

water, eau (*f.*); **running water,** eaux vives.

water-lily, nénuphar (*m.*).

wave, flot (*m.*), vague (*f.*).

wave, to, (s')agiter, flotter au vent.

way, chemin (*m.*), côté (*m.*), façon (*f.*), route (*f.*); **way out,** issue (*f.*); **a great way,** loin; **to give way,** céder; **go one's way,** aller (passer) son chemin; **make way,** s'écarter; **take one's way,** se diriger.

we, nous.

weakness, faiblesse (*f.*); (=partiality), faible (*m.*).

wealth, richesse (*f.*).

wear, to, porter.

weariness, ennui (*m.*).

weary, fatigué, lassé.

weather, temps (*m.*); **wet weather,** pluie (*f.*); temps humide.

weathercock, girouette (*f.*).

week, semaine (*f.*).

weep, to, pleurer.

weight, poids (*m.*).

weighty, grave.

welcome, to, souhaiter la bienvenue.

well, puits (*m.*).

well, bien; **to be well,** se porter bien, être remis, ne pas avoir de mal; **be well again,** être guéri; **be very well,** se sentir très bien; **well!** eh bien!

what (*adj.*), quel; (*pron.*), que; ce qui (que); quoi; **what is it?** qu'y a-t-il?

whatever, quoi que.

wheel, roue (*f.*).

when, lorsque, quand, alors que.

whence, d'où.

where, où.

wherefore, pourquoi.

wherever, partout où.

whether, si.

which (*pron.*), qui (que); ce qui (que); (*adj.*), quel; **of which,** dont.

while, whilst, pendant que, tandis que; **the while,** pen-

dant ce temps-là; **after a while,** bientôt.

whirlpool, tourbillon (*m.*).

whiskers, favoris (*m.pl.*).

whisper, to, chuchoter, murmurer.

white, blanc; (*of personal appearance*), tout blême.

white-washed, blanchi à la chaux.

whither, dans quel endroit.

who, qui.

whoever, celui, quel qu'il soit.

whole, entier, tout; **upon the whole,** à tout prendre.

whom, que, qui.

whose, dont.

why, pourquoi; **why or wherefore,** pourquoi.

wicked, impie, méchant, vilain.

wide, large; **wide open,** grand ouvert.

wife, femme, épouse (*f.*).

wild, sauvage.

wildly, *turn by* tout ahuri.

will, testament (*m.*); volonté (*f.*).

will, to, vouloir.

William, Guillaume (*m.*).

willingly, volontiers.

wind, vent (*m.*).

windings (*of a river*), cours sinueux (*m.*).

windmill, moulin à vent (*m.*).

window, croisée, fenêtre; (*of a railway carriage*), glace, portière (*f.*).

wine, vin (*m.*).

wink, to, cligner des yeux.

winter, hiver (*m.*).

wipe away, to, essuyer.

wise, savant, sage.

wish, souhait (*m.*).

wish, to, avoir envie, désirer, vouloir; **to wish very much,** avoir grande envie, avoir bien envie; **to wish so much,** avoir tant envie, vouloir tant.

wit, esprit (*m.*).

with, avec, de.

withe, osier (*m.*); **of withes,** en osier.

wither, to, (se) flétrir.
withered, fané.
within, à l'intérieur (de), dans un délai de.
without, sans.
woe is me! malheur à moi!
woman, femme (*f.*).
wonder, étonnement (*m.*); merveille (*f.*).
wonder, to, se demander; (=be surprised), s'étonner.
wonderful, merveilleux.
wondering (*adj.*), émerveillé.
wood, bois (*m.*).
woodman, bûcheron (*m.*).
wool, laine (*f.*).
word, mot (*m.*), parole (*f.*); **chance word** (*p.* 209), mot retrouvé par hasard.
work, tâche (*f.*), travail (*m.*).
work, to, broder, travailler.
working-man, workman, ouvrier (*m.*).
world, monde (*m.*); **in the world,** au (du) monde, qui soit.
worn out, épuisé.
worship, to, adorer.
worth, to be, valoir.
worthy, brave, digne.
wrap up, to, envelopper.

wreath, couronne (*f.*).
wreck, débris (*m.pl.*).
wrestle, to, lutter.
wretched, misérable.
write, to, écrire.
writer, auteur (*m.*).
wrong, to do, faire mal; **wrong thing,** mauvaise action.

yard, cour (*f.*); mètre (*m.*).
yawn, to, bâiller.
yea, oui.
year, an (*m.*), année (*f.*).
yearning (*noun*), tendresse (*f.*).
yellow, jaune.
yes, oui, si.
yesterday, hier.
yet, cependant, encore, jusque-là, pourtant.
yield no..., to, refuser.
yonder (*adj.*), ce...-là; (*adv.*), plus loin.
you, tu, te, toi; vous.
young, jeune.
your, votre, vos; ton, ta, tes.
yours, le vôtre.
yourself, vous, vous-même.
youth, jeune homme (*m.*); (*pl.*) jeunes gens.

Zoo, jardin zoologique (*m.*).

INDEX OF PASSAGES FOR TRANSLATION

For EU product safety concerns, contact us at Calle de José Abascal, 56–1°, 28003 Madrid, Spain or eugpsr@cambridge.org.

www.ingramcontent.com/pod-product-compliance
Ingram Content Group UK Ltd.
Pitfield, Milton Keynes, MK11 3LW, UK
UKHW012328130625
459647UK00009B/147